Max Brand

Twayne's United States Authors Series

Joseph Flora, Editor
University of North Carolina

TUSAS 641

Frederick Faust in 1941.
Photograph from family archives.

Max Brand

William A. Bloodworth, Jr.

Augusta College

Twayne Publishers ∎ New York

Maxwell Macmillan Canada ∎ Toronto

Maxwell Macmillan International ∎ New York Oxford Singapore Sydney

Max Brand
William A. Bloodworth, Jr.

Copyright 1993 by Twayne Publishers

Twayne Publishers
Macmillan Publishing Company
866 Third Avenue
New York, New York 10022

Maxwell Macmillan Canada, Inc.
1200 Eglinton Avenue East
Suite 200
Don Mills, Ontario M3C 3N1

Library of Congress Cataloging-in-Publication Data

Bloodworth, William A.
    Max Brand / William A. Bloodworth, Jr.
        p.   cm. – (Twayne's United States authors series; TUSAS 641)
    Includes bibliographical references and index.
    ISBN 0-8057-7646-X (alk. paper)
    1. Brand, Max, 1892-1944 – Criticism and interpretation. 2. Western stories – History and criticism. I. Title. II. Series.
PS3511.A87Z57   1993
813'.52 – dc20   93-29767
                                                            CIP

10 9 8 7 6 5 4 3 2 1

Printed in the United States of America.

To Julia

Contents

Preface

The subject of this book is one of the most widely read United States authors, a writer who published more than 25 million words between 1917 and 1944. Most of these words were originally written as magazine fiction, especially for so-called pulp magazines, though many of the Max Brand stories in those magazines were later published as hardcover and paperback novels. Moreover, a substantial portion of the writing took the form of westerns, the most popular kind of story in American history. Despite these facts, or perhaps because of them, Max Brand has struggled to attain literary respectability. It has always been easy to disregard his fiction as unworthy of serious attention. *Time* magazine, for example, referred to it in 1952 as "only a phenomenal flow of unreality, as impressive as an endless herd of buffalo stamping upside down across the stage in a mirage."

I take a different view in this book. Max Brand, the pen name of Frederick Schiller Faust, deserves attention for a number of reasons, among them the fact that Faust wrote more than westerns and may have cared less about westerns than other kinds of stories. Another reason for studying Max Brand is to gain insight into the attitudes and styles of American popular culture. E. L. Doctorow once wrote that "a novel is a printed circuit through which flows the force of the reader's own life." The genius of Frederick Faust, which he himself had difficulty appreciating, was his ability to create such circuits for millions of readers; to examine the circuits is to examine the readers as well. Finally, Faust was a skilled writer of stories, a natural teller of tales; many of his texts serve as reminders that the word *text* comes from a Latin root meaning "to weave."

It is Faust's ability to tell stories that accounts for the steady, unbroken stream of his books since 1919, continuing even five decades after his death. Bill Nolan, novelist and Faust bibliographer, likes to remind me that a "new" Faust book – a magazine story never published in book format – has appeared, on average, every four months for the past 74 years. What other writer can match this incredible record?

My goal in this book is to introduce readers to Faust more than it is to interpret or evaluate his work. I have sought, first, to create a useful intellectual picture of Max Brand's work, showing its diversity, from poetry to medical drama, understanding that most assumptions about Max Brand derive narrowly and exclusively from his western stories. Second, I have looked closely at many individual works, pointing out salient details of character, plot, and theme. This study offers both panoramic and closeup shots of its subject – trying all the while to keep the perspective in focus.

I have sought also to introduce readers to the texture and dimensions of Frederick Faust's life. While I did not set out to write a biography, I have included detailed biographical information, much of it derived from primary sources, including interviews with persons who knew Faust as early as 1910. I quote frequently from Faust's personal correspondence. It is important, I think, to understand the individual human origins of Max Brand's larger-than-life range, themes, and quantities. There is also the point, obvious to me, that the facts of Faust's life parallel his stories in terms of interest and style.

Many things this book does not do. It does not claim that Faust's poetry was very good. It does not, for reasons of space and focus, deal with the many unpublished manuscripts, including long verse works, remaining after Faust's death. For the same reasons it does not provide extensive discussion of his short stories, though many of those published after 1934 in slick and highbrow magazines are quite good. Most notably, this book does not comment on many individual Max Brand westerns that, I am sure, particular readers find important. The Silvertip series in the 1930s, for instance, receives scant attention. For such omissions I can blame only my own selective judgment – and perhaps ask for sympathy from my readers. Max Brand is a very large territory.

In covering this territory I have received much help, especially from two Californians who long have been working on Max Brand themselves. Robert Easton, Faust's son-in-law and the author of a Faust biography, has given me material, advice, encouragement, and warm friendship for more than 10 years. Without Bob Easton this book would never have been started, much less finished. The other person to whom I am deeply indebted is William F. Nolan, whose own career as a writer was inspired by Faust. Bill has encouraged, cajoled, shamed, and inspired me to finish this book.

It has also been my privilege to know Jane Faust Easton, Frederick Faust's daughter, and to benefit from her impressions of her father, her sensitivity to others, and her wisdom.

Many other persons with whom I have spoken or corresponded gave me important information or impressions about Frederick Faust, often opening up their own lives for view in the process. I am especially grateful for the assistance of Dr. John Cooper, Dorothy Rieber Joralemon, Ilse Downey Adams, Jack Cressey, Gilbert Sefton Faust, Katherine Faust French, Marion Bradford, Carol Brandt, Howard Bloomfield, Margaret Calder Hayes, and, especially, Judith Faust.

The staff of the Bancroft Library at the University of California at Berkeley gave me courteous and professional service on several occasions; I owe special thanks to the Bancroft's late director, James D. Hart. The Beinecke Library at Yale and the New York Public Library were helpful in locating Faust material in their collections.

Anyone with a spouse and children who tries to write a book knows the value of a family's love and forbearance. The deepest appreciation of all goes to three other Bloodworths: Julia, Nicole, and Paul.

Chronology

1892	Frederick Schiller Faust is born in Seattle, the third child of Louisa Uriell and Gilbert Leander Faust.
1895-1897	The Fausts move to California.
1900	Frederick's mother dies, and he is put in the care of relatives in California's San Joaquin Valley near Stockton.
1905	His father dies in Milwaukee.
1911	Faust graduates from Modesto High School and enters the University of California.
1911-1915	Publishes dozens of poems and other works in the university literary magazine. Criticizes the university president in print. Is denied his degree in 1915.
1915	Travels to Hawaii and then to Vancouver, where he joins the Canadian Army.
1916	Deserts the Canadian Army and goes to New York City.
1917	Meets Robert H. Davis and begins writing stories for *All-Story Weekly* and other magazines published by the Munsey Company. Marries Dorothy Schillig in California.
1918	Daughter Jane born in New York City. Enlists in the U.S. Army and is stationed in Virginia until the Armistice.
1919	First book, *The Untamed*, a western, published. Son, John, born in New York City.
1919-1921	Writes more westerns. Begins to produce stories for Street and Smith's *Western Story Magazine*.
1921	Suffers a severe heart attack at age 29.

1922	Publishes *The Village Street*, a poetry collection.
1925	Moves with his family to Europe. Continues to write extensively for *Western Story*.
1926	Takes up residence in Florence.
1928	A second daughter, Judith, born.
1930	*Destry Rides Again* published.
1931	*Dionysus in Hades* (poem) published.
1932	Pulp magazine market for westerns begins to soften.
1934	Two Faust stories published in *Harper's Magazine*.
1934-1936	Faust publishes many historical adventures and crime stories as well as some stories in slick magazines.
1936	First Dr. Kildare story, "Internes Can't Take Money," published in *Cosmopolitan*.
1937	The film *Internes Can't Take Money*, starring Joel McCrea and Barbara Stanwyck, is released by Paramount.
1938	Faust moves to Hollywood and begins working for MGM.
1938-1941	MGM produces seven Dr. Kildare films from Faust stories. *Destry Rides Again*, starring James Stewart and Marlene Dietrich, released by Universal in 1939.
1941-1944	Faust writes for Columbia Studios, Warner Brothers, RKO, Universal, and Fox.
1944	Serving as a war correspondent for *Harper's*, is killed on 12 May on the front lines in Italy.

Chapter One

Max Brand and Frederick Faust

He had at least picked up that dangerous equipment of fiction which enables
a man to dodge reality and live in his dreams.
                                                    – Max Brand, *Free-Range Lanning* (1921)

Max Brand, famous author of western novels in particular, was not a
person. He was only one of many pseudonyms – at least 18 – used
by Frederick Schiller Faust for hundreds of stories.[1] But the popularity of Max Brand has long been a source of identity problems. For
instance, when notices of Faust's death as a war correspondent in
1944 appeared in newspapers, a photograph that had been labeled
"Frederick Faust" in one paper would appear in another paper on
the same day and in the same city as a picture of Max Brand. He was,
claimed an obituary notice, "One of the mystery men of the fiction
world." While Max Brand is now less of a mystery than he was in
1944, his identity as a fictitious author and his role as public representative of Frederick Faust's career in fiction remain important to
understand.

Max Brand

Faust had no interest in becoming a literary celebrity. In fact, he privately claimed to be ashamed of the fiction he wrote for public
consumption, choosing even to keep such work a secret from his
own children for many years. As far as Max Brand was concerned, he
was quite content to let readers believe whatever magazine editors
wanted to say about that or any other of his pseudonymous authors.
In 1928 *Western Story Magazine* published a short biography of Max
Brand claiming that he was a working cowboy in the great American
West who had earlier spent time in New York City trying to become a
journalist. Nothing could have been much farther from the truth of

1

Frederick Schiller Faust, who was at that time living in Florence, Italy. Not until 1938 when Faust moved to Hollywood – where Max Brand achieved new notoriety as the author of the Dr. Kildare stories in print and on screen – were readers given much reason to believe that one of their favorite writers was any less rough-hewn than his western characters.

The popularity of Max Brand not only provided a screen for Faust but it also obscured the diversity of his fiction. Although the Max Brand byline was used for many kinds of writing, even for occasional poems, it was associated most of all with westerns. Faust chose other names, although not exclusively so, for other fiction genres. He also published westerns under many pen names besides Max Brand. After Faust's death, especially during the great surge of interest in westerns after World War II, the marketing of Max Brand downplayed even further the other pen names and the other genres. The publication of more than 60 Max Brand westerns after the war, including many that had been published earlier under other bylines, reinstated with a vengeance the earlier image of Max Brand as a two-fisted western writer. The colorful paperback illustrations were sufficient in themselves to establish such an impression.

In reality Max Brand – taken as it should be as the chief and best means of identifying the popular fiction written by Frederick Faust – is a complicated literary matter including not only westerns but also urban romances, detective stories, spy thrillers, historical adventures, stylish short stories, medical dramas, and other categories of mass-market fiction. The work of Max Brand involves more than 500 stories, predominately of novel length, published between 1917 and 1944 as well as later reissues of earlier books and the publication of new books based on magazine fiction published during Faust's life. William F. Nolan, the chief bibliographer for Max Brand, has pointed out that during one three-year period in the 1930s, Faust published more than five million words, or the equivalent of 75 novels.[2] More significant than numbers is the accumulated cultural impact of Max Brand on millions of readers – as well as on viewers of movies based on Max Brand material, including *Destry Rides Again*. Max Brand is, in Nolan's apt phrase, "a vast tapestry of adventure."[3]

Frederick Faust

No attention to the public literary phenomenon of Max Brand can escape – nor should it escape – the even more complex life of Frederick Schiller Faust. Not only was Faust's life the basic human context of Max Brand, but it also has achieved almost legendary status. Although Frederick Faust is not as widely known as Max Brand, the story of "Fabulous Faust" is a minor American classic. The story begins with Faust born poor and orphaned young, fighting for physical survival as he grew up, struggling thereafter to be a poet but ultimately wedded to the money that his pulp magazine writing earned, becoming a person forever generous to friends, always in debt, frequently drunk, but always writing. He was Scott Fitzgerald and Jay Gatsby combined in one grand American dream of the good life. "I dream of money, endless amounts of money," he told his agent once, but to his wife he claimed that "decency, faith, and courage are the only actualities."[4] He was a people's writer but he lived much of his life in isolated splendor. He wrote stories of action and violence but loved classical beauty. He wrote westerns while living in Italy. He loved his wife but had affairs. He had a serious heart problem that never slowed him down. He left a trail of stories about himself in Hollywood. He died a hero's death in World War II.

The story could have been written by Fitzgerald, Dreiser, Wolfe, or Ayn Rand – perhaps even by Max Brand. But no one ever captured Faust in prose better than did Martha Bacon, a family friend, in a 1955 *Atlantic* article, especially in her description of his daily life in Italy:

> He lives like a medieval prince in his Florentine villa. His swimming pool and tennis court are the envy of the petty aristocracy for miles around. He runs a pack of Newfoundlands and keeps the stars in sight with a telescope on his terrace. He has a weak heart which threatens momentarily to kill him; and against the advice of a battery of doctors he puts the heart in its place by drinking deep, smoking like Vesuvius, playing tennis like a champion, driving an Isotta Fraschini a hundred kilometers an hour through the Rhône valley, and keeping a work schedule that would murder a stevedore. He argues that the heart is a muscle and should be exercised. . . . And the novels are stacked like cordwood in the offices of Brandt & Brandt. He writes them faster than they can be printed. Faust is a one-man factory.[5]

Beneath these activities and this intensity of living, if we trust Faust's own words, was "the inner story . . . of an aspiration gone wrong."[6] But many persons who knew Faust were more impressed with the aspiration than with anything gone wrong. "Moral, idealistic, a poet and a dreamer. Of tremendous energy and tremendous emotion," a fellow Hollywood screenwriter found him to be.[7]

It was Faust's misfortune, and perhaps his many readers' good luck, that he was influenced by Malory, Chaucer, Dante, Shakespeare, and other classic Western European writers at a time immediately before the rise of literary modernism. It was his fate, moreover, to position himself at an early age in a situation where he could depend completely on magazine writing for his livelihood. These two conditions, classic literary influence and a practical ability to earn money by writing commercial fiction, determined much of what he became as a person and a writer. Together with his failure to see action in World War I, these conditions shielded him from participation in the major literary trends of his times. Unlike Hemingway, Faulkner, Fitzgerald, and other writers born in the 1890s, Faust did not become nor ever feel compelled to become a "modern" American writer. What he yearned most to do – write "verse" in the manner of the classics – had an antique quality to it. What he mostly did – write stories for mass entertainment – was free of twentieth-century pessimism and ambiguity.

Like the protagonist of *Free-Range Lanning*, a Max Brand western, Faust tended to live in his dreams and dodge some aspects of reality. That he was never satisfied with his efforts as a writer, poetry as well as prose, is a central fact of his life.

Writings about Max Brand

The very first printed attention to Faust came in a 1938 *Publishers Weekly* article written by Edward H. Dodd, his book publisher, and entitled "Twenty-Five Million Words." This was the only publication of any substance and accuracy to be published about Faust during his lifetime – and it concentrated on the amazing quantity of his work. Not until after Faust's death on the front lines in Italy did other writers begin to comment on his life and writings. Those who knew him felt that there was something both heroic and tragic, even

Faustian, in his character. Leonard Bacon, then a recent Pulitzer Prize winner for poetry and Faust's instructor when he had been a student at Berkeley, published a moving tribute in the *Saturday Review of Literature* two weeks after Faust's death. An expanded piece by Bacon appeared later in 1944 in the University of California alumni magazine: it was entitled "The Fabulous Faust."[8]

As facts about Faust became public after his death, he also attracted fans and collectors. These were readers who for the most part admired his Max Brand stories and then became fascinated with Faust almost as a cult figure. Darrell C. Richardson, a Baptist preacher and Faust fan, published *The Fabulous Faust Fan-Zine* (1948-51), which provided the means of printing and preserving reminiscences written by many of Faust's friends and fellow writers. In 1952 Richardson's *Max Brand: The Man and His Work*, primarily consisting of items published earlier in the fanzine, was published by a small press in Los Angeles. The book attracted a surprising degree of attention, including a review in *Time*. It was the first publication since 1944 to draw any kind of national attention to Faust, and nothing followed it in that regard until Martha Bacon, Leonard's daughter, published her *Atlantic* article in 1955. Entitled "Destry and Dionysus," it pointed out the paradox of Faust's extreme passion for poetry, especially his long *Dionysus in Hades* (1931).

In 1970 Robert Easton, Faust's son-in-law and a respected writer himself, published *Max Brand: The Big "Westerner."* A full-scale biography from the University of Oklahoma Press, this book brought Faust to the attention, finally, of historians and literary scholars. Russel G. Nye's comprehensive history, *The Unembarrassed Muse: The Popular Arts in America* (1970), which discusses Max Brand in a section devoted to the western, appeared the same year. In his studies of popular culture *The Six-Gun Mystique* (1971) and *Adventure, Mystery, Romance* (1976), John G. Cawelti also mentions Max Brand westerns.

In the late 1970s Faust began to receive some detailed, individual attention from literary scholars. Edgar Chapman published an excellent long article in 1978, "The Image of the Indian in Max Brand's Pulp Western Novels," in *Heritage of Kansas*, a regional journal published then by Emporia State University, and Jack Nachbar in the same year provided a critical introduction to a Gregg Press reprint of *The Untamed*. My own "Max Brand's West," seeking to identify distinctive features of Max Brand and to set him apart from the traditional popular western tradition represented by Zane Grey and others, appeared in *Western American Literature* in 1981. In his *Max Brand: Western Giant* (1986) William F. Nolan edited a number of essays about Faust and provided a comprehensive bibliography. Nolan, who had been writing about Faust since the first issue of Richardson's *Fan-Zine*, thus provided later scholars with a complete understanding of the writer's voluminous and easily confusing oeuvre.

Recent work on Faust has tended to see Max Brand as part of larger themes or concerns. In *Selling the Wild West: Popular Western Fiction, 1860 to 1960* (1987) Christine Bold devotes a chapter to Max Brand's westerns, discussing individual novels as illustrations of Faust's conflicts with the demands of the pulp magazine market. Cynthia S. Hamilton's *Western and Hard-Boiled Detective Fiction in America* (1989) offers a psychological approach to Max Brand westerns, drawing heavily on both biographical and textual evidence, as part of a larger study of popular fiction. Joseph Turow offers a particularly interesting commentary on Max Brand's Dr. Kildare stories in his *Playing Doctor: Television, Storytelling, and Medical Power* (1989).

With the exception of Easton's biography and the descriptive bibliographical work of Nolan, studies of Max Brand have generally neglected the range and diversity of Faust's work. Bold's chapter, for instance, refers to only 18 Faust novels, all westerns, and Hamilton bases her claims on 11 of the same. Attention to Max Brand has almost always meant selective attention, for an understandable reason. There is simply too much Max Brand to do the whole.

The chapters of this book that follow also pay selective attention to Max Brand, but they do so in a conscious effort to display the diversity and the development of Faust's career as a writer. They tell the story, together, of Max Brand and Frederick Faust – and to some extent of popular American fiction between the two world wars.

Chapter Two

California

But at my shoulder is the strong command
Of thirsty passions that control my choice –
The laughter and the tyranny of youth!
                              – Frederick Faust, "College Sonnets" (1914)

Frederick Faust was born into an unusual German-American-Irish itinerancy. His father, Gilbert Leander Faust, the child of a German immigrant, grew up in Buffalo, New York, and spent most of his life moving west. He was a Union soldier in the Civil War, a lawyer in Illinois, a farmer in Iowa, and, by the late 1880s, a land speculator in California. In Iowa he had met a tall Irish woman, Louisa Uriell, who became his third wife and the mother of two sons, the second of which was Frederick Schiller Faust. Schiller, as he was called, had half-siblings named Karl Irving and Gilbert Goethe Faust, and his older brother was Thomas Carlyle Faust. His father was not shy with his literary pretensions.[1]

By May 1892, when Schiller was born, the Faust household had moved to Seattle, Washington, where Gilbert tried once again to establish himself as a lawyer and businessman. After a few years of relative prosperity, however, his efforts failed, and the family returned south – this time to the Stockton area of the San Joaquin Valley, where many of his wife's relatives had settled. For Gilbert Leander Faust, the move was an admission of defeat and the beginning of poverty that left his youngest son with bitter memories. "I started in great poverty . . . crushed with shame because of dodged bills at local stores," Schiller later wrote.[2] Irish in-laws cushioned the poverty, but the damage was substantial. For the son the greatest blow was the death of his mother in the year 1900. Shortly thereafter, Gilbert made arrangements for his deceased wife's relatives to take care of the two boys, and he headed for Milwaukee to live around German friends. A few years later, when Schiller was 13, news came that his father had died.

The circumstances of his early years had pushed Schiller Faust close to his mother. "My mother was a very large woman," he wrote in a 1915 letter, "about six feet tall and built statuesquely. She had steady gray eyes that went wonderfully dark when she was angry, and she was frequently angry. She was pure Irish, you see. . . . But the things I remember best about her were a very deep, soft voice and a wonderfully caressing hand." She passed on to him her interest in reading. "She read perpetually and included everything from philosophy to light fiction in her reading." This influence, combined with the shame he felt as a result of his father's failure, had an exaggerated effect on the future writer: "When I was seven I commenced to read. First thing was Malory's Morte D'Arthur. And from that time on I simply wore myself out over books. You see, I never played with other kids and never was with them except to fight my way into position when I moved to a new school. I veritably lived the printed lives of others."[3]

Faust's memories of his father were different. Even late in his life he recalled his father's "German false sentimentality" and the "shame" of his father's pronouncements and ideals – artifice that he could see through even as a child.[4] But the primary fact about Faust's relationship with his parents was the lack of it, combined with his often unhappy life with his mother's relatives after her death.

Modesto

Frederick Schiller Faust spent much of his time for several years on an uncle's wheat ranch in Collegeville, California, a few miles outside Stockton. This experience came to an end in 1907, however, when Schiller moved 15 miles south to attend high school in Modesto. The drawing power of Modesto lay in the high school principal, Thomas Downey, who was a cousin, by marriage, of Schiller's mother. Downey was also an academic legend in the Valley, providing a rigorous, classical curriculum for Modesto High School students. Schiller lived with the Downey family for part of his four high school years; it was a family surrounded by books and dominated by the learned but stern tone of Thomas Downey.

Outside the Downey house was Modesto itself, a town whose population included a rough, transient group of teamsters engaged in the grain-shipping business, a well-known brothel, plenty of saloons, and even a brewery. It was a good place for the education that Schiller increasingly discovered outside books under the influence of two mentors. One was his older brother, Thomas Carlyle Faust, and the other was John Cooper, later to become Modesto's most beloved and respected physician. In high school, however, John Cooper was open to rough-and-tumble activity, including fistfights that pitted him, Tom Faust, and Schiller against local toughs. As a writer for the high school literary magazine, Cooper also wrote about racial injustice in the form of an ill-treated black track star. Cooper remained Faust's close friend for the rest of his life.[5]

In Modesto Schiller Faust developed in the two contradictory directions that he would continue later. On the one hand he was the bookish youth who wrote high-toned poetry in the high school literary magazine and who engaged Thomas Downey in serious intellectual discussions. In this mode he impressed others as a boy who spent all of his time, nights included, reading – and who published a high school poem, "The Three Arts," claiming that poetry was the only truly lasting and worthwhile art form.[6] On the other hand Schiller Faust was the tall, skinny street fighter who sought experience of a sort that clearly separated himself from traditional expectations of behavior and from most of his high school peers. The dichotomy of behavior and interests in Faust's high school years would make itself known, of course, in the later division of identity between Frederick Faust and Max Brand.

In both directions the adolescent Schiller kept much to himself and to his limited association with John Cooper and Tom Faust. He eventually began to pull away from Downey, even moving his residence to other homes for periods of time and returning during the summers to work long, hot hours in the hayfields around Collegeville. In 1911, after graduation from Modesto High School, he was eager to leave the town. Aided by a $50 loan from Downey, he entered the University of California. He left behind him three items published in the high school literary magazine during his senior year: a story of chivalry told by a dying Welsh knight, a poetic monologue delivered by the emperor of an unnamed country in the distant past, and an Arthurian poem narrated by Isolde as she prepares to drink the potion that leads to her tragic affair with Tristram.

Berkeley

In 1911 the University of California was enjoying a "golden era of undergraduate instruction" under the guidance of President Benjamin Ide Wheeler.[7] Its curricula were generally modeled on Yale's, and the university took great pride in its various forms of "spirit," including that which a history professor, Henry Morse Stephens, typically referred to as "a Spirit of toleration and romance and gay courage."[8] The president promoted an educational philosophy, the "abundant life," that stressed breadth of learning rather than narrow specialization, and he claimed that a university educated best by experience and inspiration rather than by the specific facts offered in classrooms. California was a university of 6,000 students where a young person so inclined could find shelter from the turmoil of the world in the genteel orientation of most faculty members and of the Berkeley community itself. The essential gentility of Berkeley's residents was wonderfully expressed later in the memoirs of one of Faust's classmates, the daughter of a faculty member: "It was as if a gentle mildness was sifting down through their entire beings, like a thin rain through leafless trees."[9]

As a Berkeley student, Schiller Faust initially fit well into this afterglow of the Victorian era, even earning from his classmates a fondly bestowed nickname, "Heinie," which he and others retained for the rest of his life. Also, he was attracted to several faculty members in the English department, especially to a young assistant professor not long out of Yale. This was Leonard Bacon, who took a particular interest in Heinie Faust and remained a literary mentor and confidant for life. On his part, Faust wrote a great deal of poetry, essays, drama, fiction, and even humor during his years at Berkeley. In the *Occident*, an undergraduate literary magazine that many at the time considered on a par with the *Yale Literary Magazine*, he published 56 poems. The September 1914 *Occident* paid Faust a particularly high honor in publishing his "College Sonnets," a collection of 21 poems.

Faust also made friends with a remarkable group of fellow students. These included Sidney Coe Howard, later a Pulitzer Prize–winning playwright and author of the screenplay for *Gone with the Wind*, Kenneth Perkins (also later a screenwriter), and George Winthrop ("Dixie") Fish, later a prominent New York City urologist and the source of inspiration for Dr. Kildare. For Faust himself, the tall, awkward youth from the San Joaquin Valley, college life was an extraordinary entrance into a new kind of society where literature and camaraderie came together. Liquor helped him make his entrance. In a letter written to his daughter almost three decades later, Faust remembered how alcohol seemed to help, especially as he sought to associate with members of the English Club: "Suddenly I begin to drink with them, all the dark walls fall down, I am in the midst of glorious, shining, noble humanity. . . . People listen to me rave. They scratch their chins. They're not used to hearing about men, women, historical events, what is poetry, what is prose, what is the true beauty, wherein lies honor, glory, and what is the essential mystery of man, the God in him."[10]

There was another side to Faust's experience at Berkeley. If his drinking with the English Club led to his leadership in matters of beauty, honor, and glory, his drinking with others led to San Francisco and the saloons of the Barbary Coast, where, according to John Cooper, he and Heinie went "just to fight with the sailors in the bars."[11] Faust also sought relationships with what he and others called "regular guys," who often gathered at the Hofbrau Rathskeller in Oakland to honor the glories of male experience by reading from beer-stained volumes of Kipling's *Barrack-Room Ballads*. Throughout his years at Berkeley, Heinie Faust moved among both the genteel student literati and the raucous "regular guys." His college writings exemplify the differences in the company he kept. He wrote not only for the *Occident*, with its high literary standards, but also for the campus humor magazine, the *Pelican*, which he edited during his senior year, and for the *Daily Californian*, which published a humor column that he wrote from behind a pen name.

Faust struggled to support himself at Berkeley, having gone there without any financial resources. His first two years, during which he worked full-time at various low-paying jobs off campus, were especially difficult. In his junior year he earned a small scholarship and was paid for his work as associate editor of the *Occident*. As a senior he was also paid for his work on the *Pelican* and the *Daily Californian*. College taught him that writing could be a source of income.

His Berkeley experiences were powerful in many ways. Faust discovered in himself a flair for social interaction, especially when assisted by beer or wine, as well as an ability to produce poetry and prose that drew the admiration of faculty as well as classmates. He made friends, especially among other California men, with whom he would discuss literary matters for virtually the rest of his life. In his junior and senior years he became truly a big man on campus – towering above other students both physically and intellectually and remaining constantly on view for faculty and administrators. He won the university's most prestigious poetry prize in 1914. When he was a senior he fell in love with a first-year student named Dorothy Schillig, who would eventually become his wife.

College Poet

According to a classmate, Heinie Faust was "far and away the most prolific of the young writers at the university" (Schoolcraft, FP). The bulk of his writing was poetry. Although he liked sonnets and dramatic monologues, he often settled on narratives drawn from historical or classical sources. Romantic themes, especially those drawn from Arthurian and neo-Arthurian material, interested him greatly. But he was not truly a romantic poet, at least not of the Wordsworthian variety, and in his verse (he preferred the term *verse* to *poetry*) he did not place any particular stress on the sensibility of the poet. Instead, he emphasized the characters and situations of stories in which the most familiar theme was the importance of living life to its fullest.

For instance, in a 1912 poem entitled "Guenevere," published during Faust's sophomore year, his Guenevere proudly claims that she would not behave differently if she had the chance to turn back the clock. "Though they tore me on the rack," she says, "I would answer unafraid" because "We were placed on the earth to live, / Not to move in solemn spell."[12] Faust's forte as an undergraduate poet was to re-create a literary or historical voice from the past, particularly one championing life and love over morality or religion. Although in an *Occident* essay on Oscar Wilde he praised "the thirst of the mind for the lofty thoughts," his own literary thoughts remained for the most part on the side of passion and action rather than reflection.[13]

By his junior year Faust had turned to the Tristram and Isolde story once again. The reasons for his interest in this particular medieval legend may be seen in the 1907 edition of *The Cambridge History of English Literature*, which Faust himself may have consulted in the university library: "Coloured by scarcely any trace of Christian sentiment, and only faintly touched, as compared with the story of Lancelot, by the artificial conventions of chivalry, the legend of Tristram bears every mark of a remote pagan, and Celtic, origin. Neither in classical, nor in Teutonic, saga is there anything really comparable with the elemental and overmastering passion which makes the story . . . second to none of the great love-tales of the world."[14] Beginning to chafe under conventional expectations of behavior, Faust was drawn to the raw emotions of the legend. For instance, in one of his poems a Saracen knight tells a Christian hermit of the death of Tristram and Isolde and defends their passion against the "written laws in blood" of the Christian god, saying "there are mandates of the mortal heart / More binding than his."[15]

It may be that Faust failed to write but one piece of fiction as an undergraduate because he could not easily adapt his themes to the expectations of that genre. In an essay on Thomas Hardy he expressed his own distaste for literary realism, obviously preferring the pulpitlike role of poetry at Berkeley. He assumed such a role in a particularly obvious way in the fall of his senior year with the publication of 21 "College Sonnets" in the *Occident*. Before this time Faust as a poet had tended to speak through the voices of narrators and characters. Now he spoke in his own – and a sometimes strident – voice, with little effort at understatement. His strongest theme in the sonnets was the value of action over contemplation and life over learning. He attacked "critics of nature, cautious, searching men, . . . worshipers of reason" and announced his assent to "the strong command / Of thirsty passions that control my choice."[16] His sonnets were not poems aimed at pleasing President Wheeler, whose notion of an "abundant life" was somewhat different from Faust's.

Campus Critic

Faust's poems were protected by a reasonable degree of poetic license, however, and probably gave the university little reason to punish their author. But they came in the company of Faust's sometimes egregious behavior and, more important, his use of the *Pelican* as a platform for social criticism. The magazine was a well-established vehicle for light verse, wit, and humor when Faust became its editor for the 1914-15 academic year. He soon gave to *Pelican* editorials a new flavor, described later in the university yearbook as "a more serious cast."[17]

Much of what he wrote as editor was simply an expression of shared opinion. For instance, taking some cues from Theodore Roosevelt, he criticized the absence of "manly spirit" on campus at a time when the world was moving toward war. He also attacked intellectualism, saying that "the regular guys are waking up and proving that they have as much right to exist as any of the intellectual giants," a statement not likely to have been challenged by the majority of Berkeley students.[18] In a mid-year editorial opposing religious moralism, however, Faust stationed himself at the frontiers of campus opinion. "The moralizers, the familiar Christers, are among us! Help!" he wrote. He defended the right of the magazine's humor to be, as he put it, "immoral." Referring to Voltaire, Swift, and Rabelais as models, he stated that "humor from the beginning of time has been intimately associated with the immoral."[19]

He also criticized the university in a direct manner, claiming that many professors, who merely lectured to students, were burdened with calcified brains. Students were glad to attend the university, he said, because "it's a mighty tiresome job to have to think" – implying that thinking was not required in most Berkeley classrooms.[20]

If anything specific in Faust's writing turned the university against him, however, it was several statements that he made about President Wheeler. Faust claimed, in particular, that Wheeler had grown too old for his job and was too sympathetic to Germany. Faust, a proponent of American entrance into the Great War on the side of the Allies, fabricated the following "Pelican Interview" for the January 1915 issue of the magazine: "PRESIDENT BENJAMIN IDE WHEELER, author of 'Provincial California,' 'The Kaiser and I,' etc., said: 'It was good to be away [in Germany]. The university is doing as well as can be expected. I had a letter from Wilhelm yesterday. He said the same about Germany. For the rest see Mr. Torrey [Wheeler's secretary]. I am getting old.' "[21] Such criticism, with a touch of viciousness to it, may have influenced the events that overtook Faust four months later.

May 1915

In early May of 1915 Heinie Faust was at the zenith of his college career. The *Daily Californian* printed an elaborate paean to him in revealing at the end of the semester that "Little Bobbie," the pen name for a Mr. Dooley-like columnist in the newspaper, was actually Heinie Faust. "Over in Wales," an editorial stated, "the wise men believe today that when the time arises and the tribes need him, King Arthur will be coming back. It seems that if you really amount to enough they can't get on without you. That's the philosophy of the second coming. Well, if the campus were to elect their one real senior, there's no doubt who has earned himself the honor. So poet and editor . . . and 'regular,' here's a second coming to Little Bobbie."[22] The editorial had been written most likely by Harvey Roney, the editor of the paper, who restated his point 30 years later: "As Senior Week approached, Faust was looked upon as the most illustrious man to be graduated."[23]

One of the features of Senior Week was the Senior Extravaganza, written by the two most famous undergraduate literary stars: Heinie Faust and Sid Howard, editors, respectively, of the *Pelican* and the *Occident*. Entitled *Fiat Lux* (let there be light), the Extravaganza was a farcical spoof on contemporary trends in which the Greek god Hermes, searching for a woman equal to man, ends up as a Berkeley senior on Commencement Day 1915 amid cubists, eugenicists, and Mexican dancers.

In reality, the graduation ceremonies on 12 May, held outdoors in the Hearst Greek Theatre, were of the usual solemn cast. President Wheeler delivered the commencement address. The only surprising feature of the event was the absence of Frederick Faust from the ranks of his class. The "most illustrious man to be graduated" had been denied his degree.

The ostensible reason for the university's action was Faust's poor class attendance during his final semester. He had chosen to avoid classes almost entirely, electing instead to sit for departmental examinations, which he easily passed. While some members of the department had no quarrel with this procedure, other faculty members objected, and the matter was taken up by the campuswide Faculty Council. Many persons on campus at the time believed that the complaints against Faust had less to do with class attendance than with his *Pelican* writings, especially his attacks on President Wheeler.

After lengthy arguments, a majority of the Faculty Council voted "that Mr. Faust be not recommended for his degree" (Roney, 2). The recommendation went to President Wheeler two days before commencement, and he requested a meeting with Faust. Apparently, Wheeler was willing to override the recommendation of the Faculty Council if Faust would make "necessary concessions." Whatever the desired concessions might have been, the rebellious Faust was not interested in making them. In fact, he had to be dragged out of a local bar by his friends and escorted to the meeting with Wheeler (Roney, 2). A few months later, Faust wrote a letter to Thomas Downey explaining his behavior before Wheeler: "It was my own stubbornness and my own insane bluntness and pride in an interview with President Wheeler which ruined my chance after the diploma was already signed."[24]

Although Faust must have felt disappointed as he watched his classmates receive their diplomas on 12 May, he was protected at the time by his arrogance. In fact, he probably took a perverse pride in his behavior when he heard President Wheeler's speech that day. The commencement address specifically condemned "the non-moral doctrine of action," precisely the doctrine that Faust had promoted both in poetry and in editorials.[25] Although he had not received his degree, Faust had certainly gotten the attention of the university.

In the following years, the terms of Faust's departure from Berkeley would bother him on occasion. College had been a powerful experience, giving him many friends and a high degree of intellectual respect. He maintained most of his Berkeley friendships for the rest of his life. The later accomplishments of some friends – especially Dixie Fish in medicine and Sidney Howard in literature – were sources of inspiration and sometimes jealousy. When the class of 1915 convened for its twenty-fifth reunion in 1940, Faust not only attended but also wrote an essay for the reunion booklet. Yet when the university offered to grant him his degree that year, in effect apologizing for its earlier action, he refused to accept it. The bitterness never went away completely, even though Faust knew that his own impulsive behavior during his interview with Wheeler had sealed his academic fate. As he told Harvey Roney, "I suppose I deserved . . . all that I got." "Though what I got still stings," he added.[26]

Chapter Three

Becoming Max Brand

"Bah! How can she love him? He is nothing but a mind. She is meant for the real passion of a real man."
— Billy Newlands in Max Brand, *Fate's Honeymoon* (1917)

In 1915 Frederick Faust was a college student tyrannized by youth, filled with poetic enthusiasm, and shaped by his unusual personal circumstances of poverty, orphanhood, and reading. He saw himself as a writer fully capable of vigorous poetry on ancient themes expressed in traditional prosody. His inspirations came from Malory, Chaucer, Shakespeare, Dante, and other classic writers. His literary disdain drew its strength from contemporary letters. He had little interest in fiction, producing only one short story among the more than 50 poems and plays that he published while he was a student at the University of California.

Given his experiences and interests, no one in 1915 could have predicted that by 1917 he would be a successful New York City writer of popular stories in great numbers published for the sake of mass entertainment. Faust's emergence as a popular writer, as Max Brand, a writer so different from his personal literary preferences as to require another identity, was the central feature of his life between May 1915 and early 1917. These two years provided Faust with remarkable experiences in the world beyond Berkeley and gave him a literary career, as Max Brand, that he had never anticipated or desired.

From Hawaii to New York

Had Faust been sitting in an upper row of the Hearst Greek Theatre during the commencement ceremony, he could have raised his eyes and seen the blue waters of the Pacific through the Golden Gate. It is still an impressive view, even though a bridge now spans the Gate. On that day in 1915, Faust would have had a special interest in the view. In fact, he would have been looking to India – and thinking about it. The denial of his degree did not dampen his enthusiasm for plans that he had made several months before. Then, visiting at the home of a philosophy professor, he had been introduced to a leader of the nationalist movement in India, who convinced him to join others in the struggle against British rule. In late August of 1915 Faust and his college friend Dixie Fish headed west across the Pacific, bound for the Punjab region of India. Faust himself was eager for adventure, filled with poetic enthusiasm for a world that seemed to be boiling with change.[1]

Dixie Fish and Heinie Faust never made it to India. Reaching Hawaii by tramp steamer, they received word from their Indian contact that the situation in the Punjab was now violent to the point where he could not guarantee them safe passage to the subcontinent. Faced with this turn of events, Faust took a job as a reporter with the Honolulu *Star-Bulletin* and started thinking about the war in Europe. If he could not make his way to a glorious revolution in India, he would find more glory on the battlefields in Europe. All along he wrote long letters back to his fiancée in California, Dorothy Schillig, giving her literary advice ("Never read Zola if you love me or yourself") and assuring her of his affection as he made plans to become a soldier.[2]

Writing to a friend back at Berkeley, Faust said, "I see that the only part of the world where there is anything doing today is dear old Europe and everyone who hopes to enter heaven ought to be over on the Western front collecting chilblains and 42 centimetre shells. In the meantime I whang away at the Corona in order to get bloodthirsty."[3] His whanging away was directed primarily at a long poem that he had begun in California; it was about Tristram and Isolde. He truly wanted to be a poet, and within a few months would have thousands of lines completed for the Tristram effort and more than 30 other poems ready for submission to magazines.

Faust and Fish left Hawaii in late October, again by tramp steamer, and headed for Vancouver, where, after a stormy voyage across the eastern Pacific, they enlisted in a medical unit of the Canadian Army. To make sure that he could pass the army's medical examination, Faust went first to a private physician, who told him that he had some kind of "functional disorder of the heart."[4] This was the first he heard of a problem that would remain with him the rest of his life. The army failed to detect the problem, however, and Heinie Faust soon became a hospital orderly in the medical unit.

Changing bed pans was not what Heinie and Dixie hoped to do in the military. Dixie soon used money from his family to buy his way out of the army and then joined up with a volunteer ambulance corps in New York City. Faust, envious of Fish's new opportunity to reach Europe, tried to desert. But he was caught in Victoria and, after spending 10 days in an army jail, was given a chance to purchase his discharge from the medical unit at a reasonable price if he would seek enlistment in another Canadian Army battalion. This was mid-December of 1915. He was now alone and very broke.

On 2 March 1916 he joined the 97th Overseas Battalion, soon to become infamous as the central battalion of an ill-conceived unit known as the American Legion. The Legion was an illegal effort intended to attract 60,000 American citizens into the Canadian military forces and thus into the war in Europe at a time when the United States was pledging neutrality and the Canadian government had promised not to recruit south of the border.[5] Faust joined the 97th in Vancouver and then traveled with more than 1,000 other recruits to Toronto, where the battalion was headquartered. Most of the other recruits joined for the same reasons he did: they were hungry and cold. Some, however, were seasoned mercenaries with experience in the Mexican Revolution and elsewhere. It was a very rough crowd.

After three months in Toronto and countless barroom brawls, the battalion headed east. Faust hoped, of course, that he would soon be fighting in Europe. Like many other young American men at the time, he often talked of war as a grand athletic contest. "One thing I want to do is jazz a couple of the Deutschers," he wrote to a friend. "I've talked with a bunch of returned soldiers, and they say there's no sport in the world like a bayonet charge."[6] But he got no closer to the war than Nova Scotia, where the unruly 97th bogged down in red tape and its own absence of leadership. Meanwhile, Faust listened to stories, wrote lines of verse about Tristram and Isolde, and thought – now – about a literary career in New York City as soon as he could "accumulate a couple of wounds" in the war.[7]

By the middle of the summer the 97th was still in Nova Scotia. The British had refused to accept any overseas units with ties to the still-neutral United States. The extended delay was too much for Faust, and he again went AWOL, heading this time for New York City with little more than old clothes on his back and hundreds of manuscript pages of poetry.

From Poetry to the Pulps

Faust had not given up getting to the front. In fact, one of his reasons for striking out for New York was to seek an assignment as an ambulance driver for the Allies. By July 1916 Dixie Fish had made his way to France and was writing letters to Heinie requesting cigarettes and giving him details of the war. Sid Howard, Faust's collaborator on the Senior Extravaganza at Berkeley, was on his way "over there" and would soon be flying French combat planes. Ambulance service now seemed to Faust the best way to get to the war, as it would be for Ernest Hemingway, John Dos Passos, Malcolm Cowley, and E. E. Cummings.

But he had no luck. His German name was part of the problem; another was his ragged appearance. Nearly destitute, he made an impression quite unlike that of most college men whom the various ambulance corps seemed to recruit. "I am pretty well decided now that I shall not try to get over to the front," he finally admitted, "unless someone actually approaches me on the street and sticks a ticket in my hand."[8]

Instead he concentrated on his dreams of poetry and love. John Schoolcraft, a graduate student at nearby Yale, saw him frequently during this time at his residence in the Bowery YMCA. "We went up to the roof," Schoolcraft later wrote, "where we could see the glow of the great city and feel, rather than glimpse, the shapes of the great buildings on the horizon." Faust "poured out his ambitions: to write great verse, to make money out of his writings, to marry and rear a family." The thoughts of marriage and family involved Dorothy Schillig, 3,000 miles west in California. At the time Faust wore second- or third-hand clothing, none of which fit, and worked part time in the warehouse of a New York department store. For a while he lived in the home of a Jewish rabbi on the Lower East Side (Schoolcraft).[9]

His efforts at verse throughout the fall of 1916 resulted, finally, in two publications. One poem appeared in a small weekly poetry magazine that paid its contributors nothing. The other poem, however, was published by William Rose Benét in the February 1917 *Century*. For Faust this was an exciting recognition of his talent. The poem paid him $50 and gave him an entrance into Benét's circle of New York literati, including the Yale professor and critic Henry Seidel Canby and Benét's younger brother, Stephen Vincent, still at Yale. This circle was also Leonard Bacon's, a fact that expanded the membership rights of Bacon's ex-student. These newfound literary friends did not guarantee the publication of Faust's poetry, however; not until 1933, when he published a poem in *Harper's*, did he again see his verse appear in a magazine of the *Century*'s stature.

But there were other possibilities at hand. By the time that "The Secret," an autobiographical lyric about the death of his father, appeared in the February 1917 *Century*, Faust was discovering a far more lucrative use of his literary talent. This discovery would forever change his life. It happened when the mother of a college friend visited him in New York and recommended that he contact a particular editor highly placed in the publishing empire of Frank A. Munsey. The editor's name was Robert Hobart Davis.

Davis, originally from Nebraska, with Twain-like experience in Nevada and San Francisco, had been working for Munsey for more than 10 years. His own literary interests were wide, and he had worked closely at times with writers ranging from O. Henry to Joseph Conrad. In his work for Munsey he had published Edgar Rice Burroughs, Upton Sinclair, and Mary Roberts Rinehart, among others. He had been responsible particularly for the discovery of much new writing talent for several so-called "pulp" magazines that Munsey published. These included *Railroad Man's Magazine*, *Argosy*, *Woman*, the *Cavalier*, and *All-Story Weekly*. Munsey's chief competitor was Street & Smith, which published *Ainslee's*, *Popular Magazine*, and other periodicals that were readily available along with the Munsey magazines at the newsstands.

The pulps were low-cost magazines printed on newsprint (hence the term *pulp*) and less reliant on advertising revenue than the more prestigious magazines of the day. To stay alive, they had to appeal directly and effectively to their readers' interests. They tended to be exploratory and even experimental in content, hoping always to hit a vein of public interest that would propel sales ahead of competing magazines. The pulps were never avant-garde in style or content but were driven by market forces to discover exactly what it was that readers wanted in the way of literary entertainment. Using dramatic covers with bold statements about their contents, they printed stories told in styles capable of grabbing readers' attention. As one editor put it, the pulps had to "deliver the goods." "No attitudes or affectations" were countenanced, and the writing had to be exciting prose "sans baloney of any sort."[10] Melodrama, of course, was OK.

Davis needed material without "attitudes or affectations" for *All-Story Weekly*, a successful Munsey magazine for which he assumed direct editorial responsibility. As its title indicated, it was a weekly that included nothing but fiction. Always interested in finding new writers, Davis agreed to Faust's request for an interview sometime very late in 1916. Faust appeared at the Munsey office and proved in short order that he could write the kind of stories the magazine needed. Easton's biography of Faust tells about the first encounter of the young writer and the seasoned editor. Faust apparently took from Davis a one-sentence plot outline, went to an empty office in the Munsey building, and emerged a few hours later with a publishable story of almost 8,000 words. According to Easton's account, Davis asked Faust where he learned to write such fiction, and the brash young man said, "Third door on the right – down the hall" (quoted in Easton, 46).

Whatever the reality of that first encounter, Bob Davis opened a door to Faust's unusual narrative powers. While Faust continued to write verse, constantly maintaining that poetry was all he really cared about, he began in early 1917 to produce stories regularly for Davis. He wrote excitedly to Davis in those early months, claiming at one point that a story idea would impress even "the most casual and time weary literary critic who ever reviewed a book"; on another occasion, explaining his idea of a story involving a brain transplant from a dwarf to a giant, he told Davis, "If you once allow this beginning, there are . . . infinite ways in which we can make a thrilling plot."[11] The pronoun "we" indicates that Faust's pulp fiction was to some extent collaborative, relying on Davis's advice and encouragement. But Faust provided the words: a 2,000-word plot summary in an evening, a completed story of 4,000 or 5,000 words the next afternoon.

In his stories for Davis, Faust was particularly drawn to melodramatic action. Melodrama had dominated his reading and his verse, and he sought it in his own life. In later years, trying to write for "slick" magazines rather than the pulps, he was never entirely comfortable. Realistic fiction, sans melodrama, did not appeal to him. The stage was narrower, the action less sweeping, the emotions less intense. The pulps, however, were an ideal market for his particular talents.

Moreover, they paid well. Faust started at the basic Munsey rate of a penny a word but quickly moved up the scale.

Enter Max Brand

Even though some of the basic features of Faust's early pulp stories would continue in later works, his fiction underwent considerable development during his first year as a pulp writer. He began writing stories of conventional sentiment, publishing them under his real name, but soon moved toward "yarns" (a word he liked to use) that were at times much darker in character and, given the pace at which he produced them, surprisingly unconventional in characterization and plot. Within a year he had also moved away from "Frederick Faust" as author. In 1917 Max Brand came to life both as a pen name and as a particular style of magazine fiction.

Faust's first commercial story was published in the 31 March issue of *All-Story Weekly*. Entitled "Convalescence," its 4,000 words combined expected sentiment with a touch of urban reality. In the story a wounded gangster enters a hospital where he comes under the care of a nurse who once had been a part of the underworld herself. The gangster falls in love with her and through her is led out of the hospital and away from a life of crime.

Several similar stories came out of Faust's typewriter in early 1917. He had a tendency to apply overdoses of sentimentality and melodrama, but Bob Davis usually was capable of restraining his excesses. "Damn you, Faust," he wrote in a note complaining about one story idea. "Come in and talk with me about a rational story and get back to work on the earth. Can the bronze hair, the violet eyes and the hectic flush."[12]

At some point Davis must have suggested that he also can the German name. His third piece in *All-Story Weekly*, a novelette entitled "Mr. Cinderella" in the 23 June issue, bore the byline of Max Brand. It was the story of a war veteran who wins a woman away from the man she was scheduled to marry, telling her in the final lines of the novelette, "It was the great god chance who picked us out of the muddy river of life and gave us to the unknown adventure of unknown seas. Shall we resist him?"[13]

A degree of chance also may have been involved in discovering the pseudonym. Faust decided to use a pen name for several reasons, not only to avoid the Germanic "Frederick Faust" at a time when the United States had just declared war on Germany but also to reserve his real name for poetry. According to Robert Easton, the name Max Brand was chosen by Faust and some of his friends during a party in New York City in early 1917. It was a good choice: only two syllables and suggestive of something exotic, perhaps western, perhaps even Jewish. Bob Davis took so well to the name that he began addressing Faust in his letters as "Dear Max," a compliment to the great value of the pen name in marketing Faust's fiction.

The pseudonym undoubtedly had internal consequences as well. Easton says it formalized a basic division in Faust between poetry and prose. At the very least, by bestowing a separate identity on his prose efforts, the use of Max Brand authorized (literally *author*-ized) Faust's proclivities toward fiction and freed them from inner restrictions of taste or guilt.

Almost as a result of the Max Brand name, it seems, Faust's pulp fiction began to move away from the themes of regeneration, romance, and marriage in which his first few stories trafficked in obvious ways. The real Max Brand would emerge later in stories of violent action and hard-souled protagonists, but a shift was under way in his writing almost as soon as he began using his newly invented name. Especially in his first novel-length serial, which began in a July 1917 issue of *All-Story*.

The title was *Fate's Honeymoon*. Although not truly a western, it was set in the mining region of California. Faust built his novel around the pulp theme of his first story: the regeneration of an apparently bad man. The story begins in San Francisco when an accused embezzler named Billy Newlands decides to fake a marriage to the daughter of a recently deceased friend for the sole purpose of gaining her inheritance. After a phoney wedding that the young woman, Beatrice, assumes is legitimate, Newlands takes her off on a train through the Sierras for the honeymoon. Newlands drinks heavily on the train and soon attempts to consummate the false marriage. Before he can do so, the train is wrecked and he is separated from Beatrice.

Beatrice meanwhile has pulled from the wreck another man, named Crawford, the owner of a nearby mine, and in the months that follow she nurses him back to health at his residence. Others begin to presume that she is his wife. Crawford's expressions of affection toward her only cause her to think of Newlands, however. Her earlier response to the irresponsible Newlands had been genuine, and in the presence of Crawford's protestations of love, she recalls how Newlands's hands "had touched her very soul through her body. Remembering it now she knew that was love, perhaps the physical part of love only, but something so intense and vital that it made her tremble now."[14]

Faust thus offered to his magazine readers the bait of "true love" dangled before them on a string of melodramatic action. The action lay in Billy Newlands's behavior after the train wreck; glad to be alive, he seeks work as a miner in Crawford's mine, helps put down a violent strike, and ultimately finds himself back in the arms of Beatrice. This time the affection of both is genuine, and Newlands has redeemed himself from crime and alcohol. Instead of marrying the good-hearted but romantically unexciting Crawford, Beatrice in the end is united with her true and only love.

Movies, Money, and Marriage

One of the most dramatic episodes of Faust's own life in 1917 followed the plot of his first novel-length fiction. In *Fate's Honeymoon* he wrote about the conquest of true love over circumstances that would have resulted in the marriage of the heroine to a man for whom she felt little passion. Faust faced the same set of circumstances in early 1917.

He had been separated from Dorothy Schillig for more than a year and a half when he wrote *Fate's Honeymoon*. Yet he continued to believe that she should and would be his wife, even though he did not refrain from seeing – and sleeping with – other women in New York.[15] He wrote his usual long letters protesting his affection and drawing scenarios of a future together. By the spring of 1917, however, Dorothy had grown convinced that life with him was increasingly out of the question and, in fact, had accepted the proposal of a young lawyer in her California hometown of Yuba City. The situation was complicated for Faust by the attitudes of Dorothy's parents, who felt that he would never be much of a success at anything and had thrown their weight behind the hometown lawyer.

The news of Dorothy's engagement and Bob Davis's possible sale of *Fate's Honeymoon* to Thomas Ince in Hollywood spurred Faust to action. He renewed his pleas for her hand and in early May boarded a train for California. En route he learned via telegram from Davis that the Hollywood deal was set. "Picture contract closed," the message read, "Two thousand on account" (quoted in Easton, 53). Buoyed by this success, Faust made a triumphant entrance into California, impressed old friends in Berkeley, convinced Dorothy's father that his Hollywood contract was a sure sign of future financial security, and (from Faust's point of view) saved Dorothy Schillig from a dull life as the wife of a small-town lawyer. On 29 May 1917, Faust's twenty-fifth birthday, he and Dorothy were married at her parents' house in Yuba City.

Faust's own fate's honeymoon cannot be underestimated as an influence on his career. Success in the pulps had been the essential factor in regaining Dorothy's affection. His marriage was proof positive that the production of words for Bob Davis could produce tangible benefits in his own life. The monetary success of *Fate's Honeymoon* established a pattern of expectations that Faust would never escape thereafter. Though he would continue to claim that his deepest urges were in the direction of poetry, he had proved to others and to himself that fiction was the means to a desired end. His pulp work soon became the stake on which all else depended. As years went by, Faust would turn constantly to his typewriter for support of his family and of an increasingly lavish style of living. He would even fool himself into thinking that he could earn enough money from the pulps to support the time he needed to write poetry.

The events of May 1917 were also the beginnings of a long and complicated marriage. Whether Dorothy ultimately benefitted from it as much as her husband is doubtful, though she would have claimed that she did. For Faust, Dorothy represented his California roots and a connection with ordinary family life that he had always lacked. To him Dorothy brought stability and care, and she spent the next 27 years of her life trying to support the Faustian drives of his personality. It was not an easy job for her. His unusual literary career was hers too.

That literary career was always with them. Even as they married and embarked on their honeymoon, a long train trip back to New York City with a stopover of several days in New Orleans, Faust spent several hours each day at the typewriter. He had told Bob Davis of his plans a few days earlier. There had been "too much excitement and too much booze" in his life before; now he was going "to cut all that out" (as had his hero in *Fate's Honeymoon*) and give Dorothy "the squarest deal in the world." He also mentioned a new serial – the second Max Brand novel – on which he had begun to work in earnest. Its title was *The Sword Lover*. "I think you will rather like the story."[16]

The Sword Lover

The story Faust mentioned to Davis was not what Davis preferred. Faust actually had started it with another Munsey editor in mind. Robert Simpson, the editor of *Argosy* in 1917, reported to Davis but made his own decisions on stories. Simpson preferred historical adventure, preferably with an exotic bent. Colorful, dramatic illustrations on the magazine's cover enhanced this *Argosy* hallmark. Men on the way home from work, teenagers looking for diversions, travelers on trains: these and many others paid 10 cents a copy or $4 a year for vicarious participation in the adventures promised by the cover illustrations. The 10 November 1917 cover illustrated a serial beginning in that issue; the author was Max Brand. This was not an author that *Argosy* regulars then knew. Nor, as the installments appeared each week for seven weeks, ending shortly before Christmas, did it turn out to be a very ordinary story, especially for Faust.

With *The Sword Lover*, Frederick Faust's career as a writer broke free of the traces of genteel melodrama that had been guiding it through his first few months as one of the new workhorses in Bob Davis's literary stable. In this novel, for the first time, his fiction incorporated the near-excesses of action and violence that would characterize much – and often the best – of his fiction for the next 25 years. *The Sword Lover* was, in fact, the birth of Max Brand.

The Sword Lover is a difficult novel to discuss for a reason common to Faust's work: it is not readily available to readers. Ten years after its initial serial publication in *Argosy* under the Max Brand byline it was published as a hardcover under the byline John Frederick by the Henry Waterson Company, a little-known New York City publisher. It has not been republished since then and certainly does not meet the usual criteria of a literary "text" in circulation among readers. Yet if we are to understand Max Brand it is important that we understand how this novel came about, the general nature of its plot and characterization, and the tone and material that its writing appears to have awakened in Faust.

Faust's ability to write such a novel as *The Sword Lover* derived partly from the type of magazine for which he wrote it. It was his first magazine work that was not directly motivated by the editorial needs of Bob Davis. Davis had been pointing Faust toward the pages of *All-Story Weekly*, which published a variety of story types, including (by fall of 1917) Faust stories about big-city crime, urban romance, romantic melodrama (in *Fate's Honeymoon*), and war. But *Argosy* was Munsey's entry in the competition for readers of adventure stories. Faust's contribution was a novel whose eighteenth-century protagonist is peculiarly obsessed with ritualistic violence. The ritual is that of sword fighting, leading in the story's closing pages to a hellish scene of fire, blood, and passion.

The protagonist, Colin Ornald, born in Virginia, has become by the beginning of the story a famed swordsman in London. His relationship with his sword extends beyond mere skill. He is quite literally in love with the weapon. In fact, its name is Nicolette, and early in the story one of Ornald's friends says, "Of this I am sure, that he will never love a woman till he has lost his sword, for she is companion, friend, and wife to him."[17] A long, slender weapon of death is an odd vehicle for female symbolism, transferring a psychological peculiarity to the character of Colin Ornald. As with many of Faust's later heroes, there is something distinctly strange about Ornald, some sense of obeying the call of forces and urges that do not affect ordinary people.

Ornald's love of his sword is not absolutely indiscriminate, however. Like later Max Brand gunmen, he abides by a code of violence. Nicolette finds her proper use only in certain circumstances: "Death at the point of the sword on fields of honor and of battle," Ornald states (121). Nevertheless, when the story opens, Nicolette's lover is already a killer.

The story presents a contradiction common to Max Brand novels. On the one hand it moves toward a moment of redemption, beginning with a character who is outside both the law and conventional moral boundaries. By the end of the novel, Colin Ornald has redeemed himself in the eyes of legal authorities and has captured the heart of a woman, the latter event serving as a traditional sign of moral redemption and confirming, for readers, their story-long sympathy for the protagonist.

On the other hand, the novel moves via its plot toward increasing violence. While carrying out a legal, romantic, and moral redemption of the hero, the story thus serves to transform the reader into a moral voyeur with an opportunity to observe with sympathy a sequence of ordinarily questionable behavior. In other words, *The Sword Lover* encourages a knowing deception; the relationship between the story and the reader seems to be an implicit compromise between the need to maintain public values and a need to encounter, vicariously, human behavior that contradicts those values. Thus the reader keeps the cake and eats it too: enjoying violence while cheering on a hero who, at the end of the story, represents the triumph of public values.

The plot of the novel begins with Ornald having to flee England after accosting King George III and his henchmen. He returns to his native Virginia where his dying mother lives. There, 100 miles up the James River, he finds not his mother but a band of highwaymen whose leader is a masked man named Jack Reed. Neither Reed's victims nor the members of his gang have ever seen his face. Ornald meets the masked Reed and his men as they are attempting to rob a stagecoach and steal a necklace from an attractive and wealthy young woman on board. Ornald is able to subdue Reed momentarily and take the necklace from him, but because he himself is being pursued by one of King George's agents, who has tracked him to Virginia, he cannot return the necklace. Instead, he seeks safety by disguising himself as Jack Reed and assuming the leadership of Reed's gang.

The novel then moves into a territory of multiple deceptions. Faust had already created a character whose goodness is denied by English authorities and to some extent by his own behavior as a swordsman. Now, in Virginia, his true character is further concealed by his disguise as an outlaw. So disguised, Ornald visits his blind and dying mother. Because she has noble illusions about him, he pretends to be rich and respectable, adding another layer to the deceptions in the story. Next, having learned that the stolen necklace belongs to Charity Hampton, the daughter of a local squire, he goes in masquerade as Jack Reed to her house, where he learns the contempt she feels for Reed. Meanwhile, the real Jack Reed appears under an alias as a new member of his own gang, which Ornald, posing as Reed, is now leading.

The disguised identities in the story produce some scenes of unusual power. At one point Ornald (as Jack Reed) must roughly subdue Charity in a scene, suggestive of rape, where it is difficult to distinguish between Charity's intense hatred of the real Jack Reed and her affection for Ornald himself. Even the language is charged with combinations of violence and love. At one point in this scene, Ornald explicitly compares Charity to his sword: "I . . . always shall love you just as I love Nicolette . . . for your own cold self, your indomitable heart, and your wild temper." When the scene is interrupted by someone who asks where Charity is, Ornald replies, "At the very door of hell – and love!" (171).

The novel continues with the same combination: hell and love, bad and good, violence and redemption. Ornald, disguised as the outlaws' leader, is challenged by a revolt within their ranks led by the real Jack Reed, also operating under an assumed name. To retain leadership, Ornald must order the gang to attack the house of Squire Hampton even though he is by now in love with the squire's daughter. The result is bloody conflict. Ornald's own conflict makes him both an attacker of the Hamptons and their defender. For Charity Hampton, the scene puts her behind a musket and a knife, and the raging battle releases in her some strange potential for violence. At one point, Ornald "saw only her lighted eyes, heard only her voice crying out encouragement and fierce joy of battle to her defenders, like the spirit of some terrible valkyr come back to earth" (193).

Charity Hampton, first appearing as a helpless, genteel woman, turns out to be a killer, though she kills under conditions that grant her a degree of moral immunity. Yet the scene is a rare one for a romantic heroine:

> The outlaw, in his eagerness to reach her, leaned far forward, running up the steps and was almost unbalanced. At the very moment he was in reach of her, therefore, he stumbled. The moment of hesitation was all that Charity needed. Colin saw her run down one step and thrust the palm of her left hand out with all her force. The strength of the blow and its unexpectedness combined to force back the outlaw's head. At the same moment she drove her knife deep into his throat. He stood wavering a moment, making a hideous choking sound, and then toppled back down the steps. (200)

Faust not only lets his readers know that Charity had to kill the outlaw to save her own life, but he also reveals the gory details of the action: Charity's instinctive movement forward when the outlaw falters, her powerful blow which forces the man's head backward and reveals his throat as the target for her knife, the driving of the knife "deep" into that throat, and the "hideous" sound of his dying.

At the climax of the novel, as the outlaws retreat under fierce attack into a cave used by Jack Reed's gang as a hideout, a symbolic hell erupts. Squire Hampton's forces throw burning trees into the cave, turning it into an inferno. Charity Hampton is then attacked by the real Jack Reed, and the story gives the reader a combination of fire, bloodshed, and attempted rape. Reed even suggests that the girl might be shared by all members of the gang. "If the plunder is divided," he says, "perhaps the girl should also be" (221). When Ornald appears trapped, Read says, "Make no doubt, Ornald. While you are burning in hell I shall be merry with her, and after she has wearied me, perhaps there may be strength in her to amuse these four good fellows here" (265).

Ornald must kill Reed, of course, but the ending of the story is a far more complicated matter than simply eliminating the villain. Both Colin Ornald and Charity Hampton change. Ornald breaks Nicolette, his sword, as he kills Reed, an act symbolizing his transformation from a mere swordfighter, literally in love with the weapon, to a man capable of loving a woman. Charity, on the other hand, who had been fiercely resisting her own romantic urges, putting up a screen of anger between herself and Ornald, finally surrenders to love. Much of her anger had been directed at Ornald because she assumed he was not Ornald but was, instead, the Jack Reed he pretended to be. In the end, his passion for her cuts through her anger, and she announces to the crowd that has gathered around the wounded Ornald, "I tell you I had rather be his broken sword than the queen over you all!" (274).

The Sword Lover was a remarkable piece of magazine fiction. The melodramas that Faust had written earlier for Bob Davis are pallid in comparison. Although the story contains a traditional girl-falls-in-love-with-mysterious-stranger plot line, as well as the schmaltz of a hero dedicated to his dying mother, the degree of explicit violence and implied sex has no precedent in Faust's earlier work. *The Sword Lover* combined the "elemental and overmastering passion" in Tristram and Isolde, the chase-and-pursuit plot so common in popular fiction, and an unchecked fascination with violence and death. Reading the story is a voyage into both the strange depths of Faust's imagination and a dark area of American popular culture where the only illumination is the gleam of the hero's character and the promise of a happy ending.

The Sword Lover was for Faust a matter of breaking through to themes and a style of adventure fiction that would sustain much of his later fiction. Colin Ornald is the first Max Brand hero who is a killer. The novel's combination of murderous action and gentler ideas of heroism would often be repeated. Later heroines would follow Charity Hampton's lead and join the hero as a killer. It is tempting to say that *The Sword Lover*, written as the Great War was raging in Europe, was Faust's substitute for a life of action. The novel reflects his imaginative receptivity to violence, an ironic contrast to his often expressed love for measured poetry and literary study.

Above all else, *The Sword Lover* was the emergence of Max Brand, a true authorial alter ego, no mere pen name, the medium for the complex narrative power within Faust. It was a power that he sometimes despised, a source of both income and shame, but he used it frequently after 1917. The moniker announced a new force in popular fiction, soon allied with the established appeal of the western story.

Chapter Four

The Untamed

"I've got to finish him. That's the only way I can forget the taste of my own blood."

– Dan Barry in Max Brand, *The Untamed* (1918)

When Faust finished *The Sword Lover* in the summer of 1917, he hoped that it, like his first serial, would be of interest to Hollywood or even to a book publisher. While his hopes were disappointed, he must have taken satisfaction in his first appearance in a magazine that he had once read as a source of "infinite adventure." As he explained in 1918 to Bob Davis, "The magazine carried the connotation of its name – The Argosy, the magazine which carried riches for the imagination."[1] The serial showed Faust that he could expand his fiction into imaginative areas that he found congenial; it was a spur to more pulp writing.

After his romantic raid into California to recapture Dorothy, he returned with her to New York and settled in to make his mark as a professional writer. He still yearned to publish poetry and continued his work on the Tristram and Isolde narrative, sending parts of the poem to Henry Seidel Canby for an opinion, which turned out to be discouraging. He also wrote frequently to his Berkeley classmates, especially Dixie Fish and Sidney Howard, both of whom were in Europe. Much of the conversation in letters had to do with Faust's literary hopes, but he said almost nothing about his writing for Munsey. Yet he continued to turn out the stories and to propose new ideas to Bob Davis. His marriage and, soon, Dorothy's pregnancy gave new impetus to his magazine work. He needed the money.

Making it was not much of a problem. In the 18 months that followed his wedding, Faust produced at least five book-length serials, seven novelettes, and five short stories, all of which were published in Munsey magazines before the end of 1918. This amounted to

600,000 published words. Even at Munsey's lowest rate, the dollars were flowing in. Dorothy Rieber visited the Fausts in January of 1918. "Heinie has begun to sell his stories," she noted. Four months later, Rieber observed that the Fausts had moved twice in the interim. "Each time Heinie and Dorothy move, their apartment grows more elegant. Heinie is making skads of money."[2] For Faust himself, the money was never enough to keep up with his spending habits, but for a while the doors were wide open to the Munsey accounting department. Bob Davis, of course, was the doorman.

By early 1918 Faust was hard at work on the story that would become the first Max Brand book. Its title was *The Untamed*, appearing first as an *All-Story* serial starting in December and then as a book in March 1919. By August 1920 the novel had been made into a movie starring Tom Mix. The success of *The Untamed* made Max Brand a household name and compelled Faust to continue writing westerns. Like *The Sword Lover*, *The Untamed* was a matter of Faust once again discovering his unique voice as a storyteller.

Getting to *The Untamed*

As he finished writing *The Sword Lover* in the summer of 1917, Faust turned his talents to a variety of story types for Davis. One subject was the war. A humorous tale about one man's difficulty with an army enlistment center appeared in an August issue of *All-Story*. An issue in September included a novelette, "The Sole Survivor," told from the perspective of a merciless German soldier who left behind a manuscript after his death on the front lines.

Three weeks later the magazine published another Max Brand novelette, "One Glass of Wine," rich this time in the social and literary details of early eighteenth-century London but drawing its action from dueling and swordfighting. As Faust had done in *The Sword Lover*, he gave his heroine the right to kill: at the end of the story a woman loved by two men must kill the villainous one to prevent his death at the hands of the other. It was a good piece of historical fiction, among Faust's best in that line. Six months later *All-Story* published another historical novelette by Max Brand, entitled "Rendezvous with Death," set amid seventeenth-century conflict between Puritans and Cavaliers.

Faust's longest work for Bob Davis at the time, however, was a contemporary story with a woman as the main character. *Who Am I?* began as an *All-Story* serial in February 1918. Although it was never republished later, it offered a unique treatment of orphanhood in an urban environment corrupted by gambling and crime. The protagonist is a young woman, Ruth Burns, raised in the absence of parents, who inherits a gambling house from a father she has never met. The plot of the serial is complicated by mistaken identities and hidden motives; the story ends sentimentally in marriage, but it points in the direction of Faust's later detective stories.

Two other serials appeared much later in 1918. *The Double Crown* was a novel based on contemporary history, co-written with his college friend John Schoolcraft. It was Faust's second *Argosy* publication, appearing as a serial starting in October, almost a year after *The Sword Lover*. The serial had two bylines, John Frederick and Peter Ward, with Ward representing Schoolcraft. Faust would use the John Frederick name many times in the future. This time it appeared above a story set in a mythical Slavic country torn by revolutionary violence resembling the turmoil in Russia. The "double crown" of the title refers to a young queen's choice between a crown of love represented by her attraction to a revolutionary hero and the crown of power represented by her country's monarchy. In the end she chooses love and a republic.

One week after *The Double Crown* began its appearance in *Argosy*, a Max Brand serial made its debut in *Railroad Man's Magazine*, the third Munsey magazine to carry Faust's fiction. The title was *Harrigan* and the story was loosely based on Faust's own experience aboard the tramp steamer that took him and Dixie Fish from Hawaii to Vancouver three years earlier. But it was a clumsy story and a sign that his narrative powers were not particularly effective when he tried to apply them directly to his own experiences, as he seldom did.[3]

Amid such a variety of fiction – wartime stories, historical adventures, tales of urban crime, narratives based on contemporary geopolitics, and a saga at sea – Faust also found time to experiment with the western. In *The Sword Lover* he had used the early Virginia frontier as a setting. Perhaps the story could have been set entirely in England or on the Continent, but it is difficult to imagine Colin Ornald's adventures in an urban setting. Faust needed the frontier, as he also had in *Fate's Honeymoon*. Yet neither story exploited the contemporary interest in the West that had begun with Owen Wister's *The Virginian* in 1902, was sustained by such writers as B. M. Bower and Clarence Mulford, and had been flamed into raging popularity by Zane Grey. In the five years prior to Faust's emergence as a pulp writer, American readers had been treated to Grey's *Riders of the Purple Sage* (1912), *Desert Gold* (1913), *The Light of Western Stars* (1914), *Lone Star Ranger* (1914), and *The Rainbow Trail* (1915). While Faust was writing his swordfighting adventure, Grey's largest effort yet, *The U.P. Trail*, was appearing as a magazine serial; in 1918 it would be the best-selling book in the country. For any serious writer of popular fiction at the time, westerns looked like a gold strike.

Of course, Faust was himself a westerner, in letter if not in spirit. Moreover, he was writing for an editor who had spent much of his life in the West. Having determined by mid-1917 that he should make his mark in Bob Davis's corner of the literary world, regardless of its distance from William Rose Benét or Leonard Bacon, Faust could hardly have avoided some attempts at the western story.

Before the first installment of *The Untamed* in December 1918, Davis published four Max Brand stories that involved some trappings of the contemporary western. If Faust composed these in the order of publication, which is likely, they show his increasing effort, at the time, to write westerns in the mode of Zane Grey. The first story, published in October 1917, was a sentimental novelette in which an ex-cowboy from Texas returns to Tennessee and resolves a feud by keeping his family identity a secret. The second try at a western came 10 months later in another novelette, "Above the Law," drawing on stock characters and, again, mistaken identities. But the story was set entirely in the West and included, as did many of Zane Grey's stories, the transformation of an apparent outlaw into a hero deserving of a woman's love. The hero, named Black Jim, who happens to keep copies of Shakespeare, Poe, Byron, and Malory in his cabin, seems at first "like a powerful and sinisterly beautiful beast of prey."[4] But by the end of the story he chooses marriage, children, and civilization rather than an outlaw's life.

In the last two western stories published before *The Untamed* Faust moved particularly close to Zane Grey's popular evocation of western landscape. In one of these stories, an eastern woman visiting

Nevada looks out her hotel room window to see "the wild outlines
of the mountains. They stepped back in four great ranges, the last
imperious with purple. She smiled as she stared, for her heart wan-
dered as freely as her eyes."[5] The passage could have come from
Riders of the Purple Sage. In the other story, a novelette entitled
"No Partners," another eastern woman falls in love with a western
roamer – Slim Malone – who claims that he wants no partners in life.
But the powerful western male sexuality that he represents is like a
magnet to the woman, Jacqueline Hill: "She watched him with a sort
of hungered tenderness, her breast raised by great breaths. And she
noted that one of his hands had fallen upon the handle of his
revolver as he talked and was fondling it while the other hand held
hers."[6] In the final paragraphs of the story, Slim and Jacqueline ride
off together into a radiant western landscape:

> They rode up the side of the hill at a gallop and drew rein together at the top.
> Over the far horizon of the east the reds and the pinks were swiftly dying out
> to a white light. There was a waiting hush through all the world. Then, with a
> flare like the opening of a furnace door, the red sun pushed up above the
> rolling hills.
> Framed darkly against it they set their horses side by side, with the wind
> urging at them. At the same moment they spurred their horses and rode
> directly toward the rising sun, and disappeared behind the hilltop on the long
> hike for Arizona – partners. (63)

This is an intriguing passage because it suggests the direction in
which Faust could have continued to take his western stories. He
obviously had the ability to work with established western elements
and could, if called on to do so, outwrite Zane Grey in the arena of
purple prose, including even the phallic implications of a six-shooter.
As *The Untamed* was soon to show, however, Max Brand blazed a
new trail. The dominant fact of Faust's westerns after "No Partners"
was, in fact, a refusal to write like Zane Grey.

The Western

Western stories of various kinds had been published in the United
States for many years, especially as "dime novels" after the Civil War.
In 1902, however, with the appearance of Owen Wister's *The Vir-
ginian*, the western story suddenly matured. Dime novels had

appealed to adolescent tastes as a form of nineteenth-century "cheap thrills," with an emphasis on improbable adventure. In *The Virginian* and its followers, the western novel incorporated significant themes, romance and nationalism among them, and helped sustain within American popular culture a powerful national mythology. More than anything else, Wister's novel was serious about the West, seeing it less as a place of adventure than as a testing ground for the national character.

The Virginian introduced the western hero not as a mountain man or military adventurer but a common man – a cowboy – who embodies uncommon strengths of skill and, most important, of character. This kind of hero operates within and as representative of the values associated with the frontier – values implicitly defined as better and less corrupted than those of "civilized" society. In Wister's formulation, the hero also enters into a love affair that, when consummated in marriage, adds a sense of human generativity and progress to the story.

What Owen Wister began in 1902, in high style, was continued by more prolific writers, especially Zane Grey. Grey took Wister's elements and embedded them in a florid style that, far more than Wister's, stressed the presence and influence of the western landscape. In both writers, and in the works of others before World War I (including Andy Adams, Frank Spearman, William McLeod Raine, B. M. Bower, and Clarence Mulford), history and place were essential. Traditional westerns then and later suggested that the frontier experience was usable history, expressing human values that needed reaffirmation. Zane Grey, in particular, wrote novels asserting the power of the West, even the western landscape itself, to redeem and regenerate men and women. Like Wister, Grey felt a strong personal attachment to the West's places and history. His stories were mythic celebrations of the West, its landscape, and its values as he perceived them to be.

Frederick Faust, however, had no special affection for the West. He had escaped it in 1915 and had no intention of returning. He felt little nostalgia for his own early experiences in rural California, and his personal literary interests were almost entirely European. Yet he published four western stories in 1918, seven in 1919, nine in 1920, and 22 in 1921. Eventually he published almost 400 western magazine stories, more westerns than any other American writer before or after him.

The Untamed was the true starting point for this achievement. Later Faust would be accused of being a "formula" writer. If so, the formula he followed in his westerns was of his own devising. Often it even failed to idealize the frontier, and its mythology was frequently imported from Europe.

The Max Brand Western

Bob Davis knew that the novel was going to be a hit as soon as he saw the completed manuscript. Faust wrote it over what was for him an unusually long period of time, starting in early January of 1918 and not finishing it until June. But the work paid off.

The Untamed is an important Faust work. While it was not Faust's first western, it clearly identified Max Brand in the public mind as a western writer. The novel was also a matter of self-discovery and of literary innovation. No one – certainly not Faust – had written such a western before. It remains not so much a classic of the genre but a strange, off-center exploitation of it. *The Untamed* is to the classic western novel what a film like the mysterious *High Plains Drifter* is to *Stagecoach*.

At the center of the story is the character of Dan Barry, a peculiar hero of unknown origins whose nature bears more resemblance to classical mythology than to the history of the American West. In fact, Faust identifies him specifically as a "Pan of the Desert," a moniker serving as the title of the novel's first chapter. He shows up in the life of rancher Joe Cumberland when the latter finds him as a child following a flock of wild geese in the sky. Faust emphasizes the mysterious origins of the boy in the opening pages of the novel. Joe Cumberland says that the child made him "think of fairy stories – and things like that!" "It seemed," the rancher admits, "like he was sort of a gift of God."[7]

It is a strange and distinctly unhuman gift, however. It turns out that as the child grows older he develops an odd affinity for wild animals. As he enters manhood his constant companions are his wolflike dog, Black Bart, and a black stallion, Satan, neither of which can be controlled by anyone other than Barry or persons Barry specifically identifies as his friends. Also, Barry's faunlike quality expresses itself from the beginning of the story in a strange, almost unearthly whistling: "Over the shoulder of a hill came a whistling which might have been attributed to the wind, had not this day been deathly calm. It was fit music for such a scene, for it seemed neither of heaven nor earth, but the soul of the great god Pan come back to earth to charm those nameless rocks with his wild, sweet piping" (1). In fact, he becomes known quickly as "Whistling Dan," and his character seems allied with a variety of figures in European legendry and mythology. Some Germanic legends of Faust, for instance, include a black dog as the character's companion.

However Dan Barry might be interpreted through allusions, he is clearly a character who moves quickly from a state of natural innocence to animalistic violence. The code of behavior in the typical American western demands that the hero marshall the will and skill to control evil through the use of personal force. Summoning such force is no problem for Whistling Dan. In fact, when he is roused to anger, even as a child, his eyes turn yellow and he is gripped by an "untamed" animal wildness. It is this untamed nature, violence in the guise of innocence or, like *Billy Budd*, violence and innocence inextricably combined, that drives the plot.

Faust had hinted at a similar trait in Black Jim, the protagonist of his earlier novelette, "Above the Law," in comparing him to "a powerful and sinisterly beautiful beast of prey which hunts where it will through the forest, and when it is pressed in its haunts by man turns and strikes him down."[8] The animal metaphor also appears in the opening description of the Virginian in Owen Wister's novel. In both *The Virginian* and "Above the Law," however, the animalistic qualities of the cowboy hero are transformed by the civilizing influence of a woman into the power to do good. In the classic western, the hero also gains a degree of self-knowledge as he moves from initial innocence to his role as savior of society. None of this happens in *The Untamed*. Instead of a reluctant use of force to protect civilized interests, the pattern of *The Virginian* and countless other westerns, *The Untamed* depicts uncontrollable power that is almost accidentally unleashed by an agent of disorder. The moral "trick" in most westerns is the justification of violence when it is used for good purposes under conditions of necessity and restraint. *The Untamed* refuses to play such a trick.

The novel begins with an almost random act. An outlaw, Jim Silent, comes to town and taunts Dan Barry. Whistling Dan, it turns out, has unusual abilities. Although he is small of frame and delicate in appearance, he is particularly skilled with a six-gun. Silent challenges Barry to a shooting contest, which Barry easily wins. In frustration, Silent hits Barry in the face and causes him to taste his own blood. At this point, the atavistic yellow glow appears in Barry's eyes and he sets out on a trail of revenge. The story, in effect, is the story of Barry's efforts to repay the outlaw and remove the taste of blood from his lips.

The story as Faust wrote it is not without many of the traditional elements of the western. The hero has, as do western heroes in general, superb skill at such matters as horseback riding and gunplay. Dan Barry seems to have superhuman ability, in fact. Even though he does not even possess a gun in the early parts of the novel, he later has no trouble shooting coins out the sky when they are thrown up to test his shooting skill with a pistol. He is also a man of deceptive power. His slight frame, musical voice, and delicate wrists belie the strength he shows at the novel's climax when he chokes Jim Silent to death.

The novel incorporates some elements of romance through the character of Kate Cumberland, the daughter of the rancher who finds Dan following the geese and ultimately adopts him. In a Zane Grey novel this situation would lead, predictably, to love and the woman's tempering of the hero's wildness. That this does not happen in *The Untamed* indicates the extent to which Faust moved the western outside its usual territory. He turned the western away from its usual details of landscape and avoided almost entirely the sense of history and continuity that Grey's novels repeatedly evoke. Faust's first western lacks even place names and dates; it is set in some mythological realm unconnected to geography, time, or ordinary human nature.

Even the romantic elements in the story seem misplaced. In *The Virginian* Wister raised the western to the status of adult fiction largely by taking seriously the love affair between a cowboy and an Eastern-bred schoolmarm. It is that love affair, in fact, which ultimately leads the cowboy hero from a life alone in the West to life as a leading citizen in civilized society. Quite the opposite happens to Dan Barry.

In *The Untamed* Kate Cumberland obviously loves Dan Barry, and Barry responds to her emotional interest in him – but only up to a point. Even when he is engaged irrationally in his wild quest for revenge against Jim Silent, Kate offers him her affection. But in the end it is only the gruesome killing of Silent that can quiet the rage in Barry. The heroine is helpless in this matter. Therefore, when readers have every right to expect that he will now settle down with the woman who loves him, the hero, still untamed, hears the call of wild geese. At the very end of the story there is something still instinctive and animalistic in him, something that draws him away from human relationships and toward wildness. He follows not Kate but the geese. Instead of taking up the benefits of romance, home, and civilization, he resumes his strange whistling, which is "sad with the beauty of the night" and "joyous with the exultation of the wind" as he walks almost trancelike away from his action and from Kate (186).

The essential feature of *The Untamed* is character in conflict with the expectations of plot. Faust's story involves any number of close scrapes, near misses, and miraculous recoveries as Dan Barry pursues and is pursued by the outlaw gang. The affections and concerns of Kate Cumberland are woven smoothly into the plot. But the plot itself, including the woman's role, fails to produce any effect on the character of the hero; there is no revelation through love, nothing even on the order of *Fate's Honeymoon* and *The Sword Lover*, both of which move ultimately away from wildness and toward the sort of social redemption that the main characters experience through their relationships with women. Both the character and the logic of the plot in *The Untamed* remain essentially untamed. The same would be true in many – but not all – of Faust's best works. He was fully capable of stories that reinforced cultural expectations and validated conventional social structures. In *The Untamed*, however, Faust showed narrative instincts of a different kind.

Chapter Five

"Your Forte Is the West"

Now the moon, which had been buried in a drift of clouds, broke through them, and seemed in an instant to slide a vast distance towards the earth, a crooked half moon with its edges eaten by the mist. Under this light she could see him more clearly, and she became aware of the things she dreaded, the faint smile which barely touched at the corners of his mouth; and in his eyes a swirl of yellow light, half guessed at, half real. All of her strength poured out of her. She felt her knees buckle, felt the fingers about the light revolver butt relax, felt every nerve grow slack. She was helpless, and it was not fear of the man, but of something which stalked behind him, inhuman, irresistible; not the wolf-dog, but something more than Satan, and Bart, and Whistling Dan, something of which they were only a part.

– Max Brand, *The Seventh Man* (1921)

The Untamed turned out to be a crucial work for Faust. He knew even as he was writing it, but especially after it was published, that the story was possibly the beginning of real success. Before it appeared he had been providing a steady stream of fiction for Munsey magazines, but he had not been paid more than the standard rate for his work, and Max Brand, as a Munsey "author," had not developed a particular following among readers. *The Untamed* changed all of this. And much of the credit was due to Faust's editor, Bob Davis, who not only spurred him to write the novel but who also encouraged him to stick to westerns, including sequels to *The Untamed*.

Bob Davis and Whistling Dan

Faust wrote to Davis about the story in February of 1918, indicating that Davis had been involved in shaping ideas for the serial. He was worried about the title, which to that point had been simply "Whistling Dan." "I don't like Whistling Dan as a title, Chief," Faust wrote. Apparently, Davis and Faust had already discussed the story extensively. "This is the story of an atavism, a terrible fighter. I think when he learns of his almost weird power through his first fight the blood lust should go to his head like wine. He should be in a perpetual struggle to hold himself back from violence." Faust thought that a better title might be either *The Lone Wolf*, "because Dan will feel himself shut off from the rest of mankind by his peculiar nature," or *Wine of Power*. But Faust admitted that neither title was exactly right.[1]

He wanted something right because the story had a particular interest for him, especially in the strange character of his protagonist. What Dan Barry does is less important than what Dan Barry is, and even when Faust had only started the story, he sensed that he was tapping into powerful, possibly mythic sources for his character.

By April Faust had finished the story. "Here's The Untamed," he told Davis in a note accompanying the manuscript. "If you find it O.K. will you shoot the needle into your finance department and have them send out a check?"[2] Faust also noted that he had not taken Davis's opinion on the final episode of the novel. Davis apparently had felt that a minor character needed more development. Faust explained that to do so would have "blurred" the main characters. He was probably right, but the note suggests how involved Bob Davis had been in his editorial role.

The story was a long time moving from completion in manuscript to its magazine and book appearances. Part of the problem had to do with the times. The war was on. In June 1918 Faust himself had finally managed to enlist in the army, hoping as always to be sent to Europe but ending up at an army engineers' camp in Virginia for the duration of the conflict. In addition to the war, the nation was battling an epidemic of influenza, which Faust contracted and survived. The Munsey staff around Bob Davis was hard hit, however. Also, the war made it hard for the Munsey Company to acquire the amount of paper it needed. Finally, though, on 13 October 1918, Davis sent Faust a copy of the cover for the magazine issue in which the first episode of *The Untamed* would appear:

I send you herewith a cover of "The Untamed." It's some good-looking job, Kid. This is going to be the turning point in your literary life. Don't smear yourself all up and down the map in the meantime. It's always darkest before dawn; and the damndest, finest dawn ever heard of is ready to bust in the

East. I could put this in very exquisite English, as you know, but I won't do it
because you don't like poetry from me.[3]

George Putnam published the book six months later in a hand-
some edition of 374 pages that sold for $1.50 and quickly went into a
second printing. The story was soon snapped up by Hollywood. Putnam had told Faust that Douglas Fairbanks, Jr., might buy rights to
the novel and play the title role himself. As it was, Faust had to settle
for Tom Mix. But it was still, in Davis's terminology, a pretty fine
dawn. In April of 1919, when the book was selling well, Faust told
Davis, "By the way The Untamed is not *my* book; it's *our* book."[4]

Davis was also helpful with the two novels that served as sequels
to *The Untamed*. These were published as *The Night Horseman*
(1920) and *The Seventh Man* (1921), carrying the story of Dan Barry
forward to his death. Not only did Davis advise Faust on his
manuscripts, but he insisted that he soak up some of the flavor of the
real West by taking a trip to El Paso, Texas, where he could visit a
working ranch. Yet any interest on Davis's part in the reality of the
West was tempered by his knowledge that Faust worked better out of
imagination than out of observed fact. At one point during his trip,
Faust told Davis that he was interested in writing about a particular
criminal trial in process. Davis's advice was to "fight shy of it." "It is
easier to dream fiction than to fake facts."[5] The advice was not lost
on Faust.

But Davis at times had to remind Faust of what he could do best.
In April of 1919, for instance, when *The Untamed* was moving
through several book printings and Davis was eager to see what his
young writer could do in the sequel, Faust sent him a story entitled
"Lady" that dealt, apparently, with a woman who grew up virtuous
in the presence of criminals. Davis did not like the story, nor did he
think Faust should be working on such material. "I don't like it," he
said. "Don't like the theme and don't like to see you writing stories
of that type." Moreover, he said,

There is nothing in it that will do your reputation a bit of good. I think the
situation of a child growing up in the society of four crooks and reaching
mature beauty without the coincident disaster, is pure tommyrot. It is dangerous for a girl to pass swiftly within striking distance of a criminal, but when
you give her eight or ten years in the darkness with four eminent flesh hogs
and expect to save her even in fiction, you are introducing a hell of a gal.[6]

Davis seems to have understood that Faust was not especially good at handling certain mature themes, including sexuality. His imagination, Davis knew, fed on elements of myth, and worked best in story settings that were somewhat removed from contemporary reality. If Faust's fiction had to meet tests of credulity, it would not always pass.

Davis sought, therefore, to protect Faust from his own inadequacies and to capitalize on his peculiar talents. "If you haven't discovered that your forte is the West," Davis wrote, "and that the public want your books about the West and that you have got the most magnificent flying start any Western writer ever had, the Lord knows I don't wish to persuade you from rushing pell-mell to perdition through plots of the 'LADY' type. It is like a great singer coming out and whistling for an encore or a violinist playing the jews [*sic*] harp in an east side barroom."[7]

Faust stopped working on "Lady." "I quite realize that there is a field for my Western junk as long as I have you to put the jazz in it," he told Davis, and he promised to take up the story of Dan Barry again.[8] He did not quite understand what it was about his first western book that made such an impression on readers. He told Davis, "I still fail to see why The Untamed has gone over, and it makes me feel that we can knock them dead with the sequel. For that reason I'm anxious to get back to New York and hit the collar again. No question about it, I work a hell of a pile better with you than away from you." He also wondered whether the public was sick of the "proper man" as a hero; it was all he knew that might explain the appeal of *The Untamed*.[9] He was, of course, right.

In the next 18 months he proceeded to turn out not one but two sequels to the story that had "gone over" so well. They, too, did well. Also, he wrote several other westerns for Munsey, generally avoiding the "proper man" as hero. He had discovered, with Bob Davis's assistance, a real forte. In later years he would not always write good westerns, and he would certainly not restrict himself to that genre. Also, he would claim, as necessary, that he cared not a whit for westerns. But the truth was otherwise.

In August of 1920 Faust saw his creation on the silver screen at The Capitol moviehouse in New York. The next day he wrote to Bob Davis about the film:

Jesus, what a blow-out!

I'll tell you what, they inserted a dexterous knife and cut out everything
that approached good stuff in the story. They had a tin whistle going behind
the stage every time Dan appeared and it was so damned ludicrous that the
audience began to laugh. They used few of the important scenes, and the
ones they did use they wrested from their real meaning. They made it a joke
picture, and to cap the climax they threw in the happy ending which of course
spoiled the whole yarn. The whole point of Dan's character and his coming to
life were obscured. The incidents rattled off so swiftly that it was almost
impossible to follow the meaning of the picture. The narrative was twisted,
changed, cut at will. And when Kate is in the cabin in the mountains they
frame it so that her virtue is threatened.

In a word, it's a cheesy piece of work. I went all set for a pretty good show,
even though the original story is nothing to get wild about. I saw, without
exaggeration, the worst picture I ever laid eyes on. Between you and me, I
think Tom Mix is O.K. but his directors are a joke.

And in conclusion, can't we have something to say about the way our stories are done? Can't we get in touch with the birds who write the scenarios?
Can't we write the scenarios ourselves? I'd rather put more time in and get
less out than see such fearful botches. You'll say more violent things than that
if you should ever be unlucky enough to have to see that abortion on the
screen. When am I going to see you?[10]

It is obvious that Faust cared about the story he had created and
thought it had points worth preserving. Whether his reaction to the
screen version of *The Untamed* influenced his attitude toward his
later work is hard to tell. Much of what he said later on, as well as
much of what he turned out on his typewriter, suggests that he wrote
mainly to get the stories out into magazines and money into his bank
account. But *The Untamed* and its sequels, guided by Bob Davis,
were more than merely lucrative.

The Night Horseman and *The Seventh Man*

The off-center quality of Faust's themes and characters continued in
The Night Horseman and *The Seventh Man*. Taken together with *The
Untamed*, the novels constitute a strange but powerful bit of popular
American literature.

Faust had trouble with the sequels. He had finished *The
Untamed* in April 1918 and by May was mentioning to Davis the idea
of a sequel entitled "The Wild Geese." In fact, on 15 May he sent
Davis several pages of a scenario for the beginning of the sequel. But

it lacked direction, and Davis had not been very encouraging about it. Faust had at least two reasons for staying on the trail of Dan Barry, however. First, he needed to capitalize on the success of *The Untamed* while it was still in the public eye; he admitted to his wife that their hopes for the future were pinned to the sequel. Second, even though he claimed not to know why *The Untamed* went over so well, he certainly was aware that he had somehow uncovered themes that satisfied large numbers of readers.

On 3 November 1918, however, he told Davis that his efforts on the idea of "The Wild Geese" were an absolute bust. Not until Davis chastised him for his "Lady" story in April of 1919 did Faust's efforts produce a salable manuscript, and even then it was months in coming. In the interim he wrote several other western stories, the best of which was *Luck*, published under the John Frederick byline as an *Argosy* serial beginning in August 1919. Reprinted as a book in 1920 under the title of *Riders of the Silences*, it presented for the first time the classic Max Brand superhero, a young man of both brawn and brain – a type often to show up later in the author's historical adventures and other genres. Pierre Ryder, the hero, is a trained fist fighter and a scholar who speaks perfect Latin. When a Canadian priest first sees him, he is stunned by the perfect physical beauty of the youth: "Like Father Victor, he was caught first by the bright hair. It was a dark red, and where the light struck it strongly there were places like fire. Down from this hair the light slipped like running water over a lithe body, slender at the hips, strong-chested, round and smooth of limb, with long muscles everywhere leaping and trembling at every move."[11]

Pierre Ryder was obviously a "perfect man" hero and not created out of the same formula that had produced *The Untamed*. But Faust continued to work on Dan Barry and by June of 1920 had completed a successful sequel to *The Untamed* and was beginning the third novel in the series. *The Night Horseman*, the titled settled on for the second novel, appeared in *Argosy All-Story Weekly* (the title reflecting a merger of two Munsey magazines) in mid-September of 1920, 22 months after *The Untamed* had begun its magazine run. More than a year later, in October 1921, the third novel, *The Seventh Man*, began appearing. Like *The Untamed*, each of the two sequels was published as a hardcover book by Putnam several months after the last weekly episode appeared in the magazine.

The three Dan Barry novels thus were written over three and a half years of Faust's career – a period that also saw the appearance of 14 other serials as well as many novelettes and short stories. Moreover, in 1923, two years after the publication of *The Seventh Man*, Faust returned to the setting and characters, sans Dan Barry himself, in *Dan Barry's Daughter*. While he was certainly not obsessed with his creation and first great success, he devoted a remarkable amount of attention to it, making *The Night Horseman* and *The Seventh Man* important items in the Max Brand legacy.

In the second novel Faust returned to the Kate Cumberland–Dan Barry relationship in a complicated plot involving the temporary "taming" of the hero. The novel opens with Kate's father, Joe Cumberland, near death and apparently needing the presence of Dan Barry to sustain his life. To lure Barry back both for Joe Cumberland's sake and to save him from his own wildness, his friend, Buck Daniels, strikes Barry on the face. The ploy works, and Barry comes raging back to the Cumberland ranch. He is often described as a wolf or a werewolf by those who fear his arrival. Kate, however, is able for a while to create in Barry some sense of human compassion. In the chapter "Victory" Barry puts his hand in hers and decides that he will not kill Buck Daniels. But when he faces Daniels and refuses to fight him, he seems lonesome, even saying, "I feel sort of lost and lonesome – like I'd thrown somethin' away that I valued most."[12]

In the end Dan Barry reverts to wildness. After two men refuse to fight him, thus frustrating his atavistic desires, he returns to the Cumberland ranch during a terrific nighttime storm and demands that Kate leave the ranch and come with him. In a scene more symbolic of rape than of love, the woman is once more drawn to Barry by his mysterious personal power. At the very close of the novel, she and Barry ride off into the night on Barry's powerful black horse with an even darker name: Satan. When they leave, Kate's father, Joe Cumberland, dies, and an observer wonders whether what has happened is "God's work or devil's work" (254).

The answer is by no means clear, nor does it become much clearer in the final novel about Dan Barry. In *The Seventh Man* Faust again created a plot that turns on furious action motivated by a lust for revenge. It begins with Dan Barry married to Kate Cumberland. Several years have elapsed since the tumultuous final scene of the previous novel. Barry and his wife appear to have settled down to a life of peaceful domesticity and the raising of a child in a mountain cabin. Early in the story Kate feels that Dan is safe from the uncontrollable rage that she had seen before in him: "there was no danger," she thinks, "of him ever slipping back into that terrible other self"; she would "never again have to dream of that whistling in the wind."[13]

Her expectations are shattered, however, when a sheriff's posse shoots a borrowed horse out from under Barry as he attempts to help a friend evade the lawmen. At the death of the horse, Barry is overcome by the internal wildness that his years of marriage with Kate had suppressed. He first shoots a member of the posse, thinking it right – in his untamed mood – to avenge a horse's life with a human life. Then, finding that he has been betrayed by the very friend whom he had earlier tried to help, he promises to take a total of seven lives to even the score.

The plot of *The Seventh Man* is largely the story of Barry's rage and revenge. He kills six men with ease, the sixth being the sheriff. The seventh man is the friend, Vic Gregg, who had betrayed him in the opening episodes. Getting to the seventh man is the primary task of the novel's plot.

But Faust introduces a secondary – yet more interesting – conflict in the story. This is the conflict between Dan and Kate Barry, husband and wife, two lovers fated now by Dan's rage to lose each other. As he hunts his seven victims, Barry lives in a cave alone with Satan and Black Bart, his dog. At one point Kate sends their daughter, Joan, with a message. Joan, aged four or five, shares her father's personality, especially his strange ability to communicate with wild animals. When she comes to Barry at his cave, she stays, taking a coyote pup as a pet and forcing her mother, now on the other side of a moral chasm from her husband, to fight for her return.

Ultimately this strange western turns not on some resolution between Dan Barry and those whom he pursues. Rather, it shifts with a deadly finality to the complicated struggle between Barry and his wife. By the conclusion of the story, Kate has managed to recapture her daughter from Barry's mountain cave. She and Joan then move to the home of her now-deceased father. Barry finally arrives at the Cumberland ranch, looking for Joan and whistling his strange music. Kate, whose love for Barry has never ceased despite his murderous rage against the killers of the horse, realizes now that her husband will remain forever untamed. Therefore, in a moment of terrible, mixed emotions – a combination of love and fear – she takes a small pistol that Barry had taught her to use, aims it at his heart, and shoots him. It is obvious that she is the only person capable of killing him.

The meaning of this event in the story is complicated. Above all, it points to the departure of Faust's western narratives from stories similar in setting and characters. By 1921 the western had become the carrier of a national mythology. The western hero was society's salvation, the answer to corruption and lawlessness. *The Virginian* had been archetypal in this regard. At the end of Wister's novel the hero sheds blood reluctantly, even killing a former friend, because it is something he must do in order to maintain social order. This kind of logic, with its implied apologia for violence, its participation in which Richard Slotkin refers to as "regeneration through violence,"[14] merges with a romantic plot that pulls together the western ways of the hero with the eastern background of the heroine. The classic western thus ends on a note of hope in which the coming together of hero and heroine is truly generative and progressive. This is the typical ending also of Zane Grey's westerns, stories that restate the "frontier thesis" first announced by historian Frederick Jackson Turner in 1893 – that life on the frontier has been the key determinant of American character and virtue.

Faust obviously felt little compulsion to idealize frontier experiences, and his Dan Barry novels do little to advance the value of western landscape and history. Moveover, the killing of Dan Barry by his wife at the end of the *Untamed* trilogy denies the power of love as a stabilizing force in society and – by extension – suggests that the western hero and all he represents is, after all, a matter of violence and death without regeneration. The contrast to Grey's novels in this regard is striking. In *Riders of the Purple Sage* the gunman Lassiter is ultimately united with and symbolically transformed by his relationship with the heroine. In *Nevada* a character burning with restlessness and shaped by the West finds stability and purpose when he falls in love with a 16-year-old beauty. In Max Brand, however, Kate Barry sends a bullet through the wild heart of her untamed spouse. Faust's first fully developed western hero is, in fact, not of the West;

he is "of something which stalked behind him, inhuman, irresistible" (236).

Westerns Off the Trail

The Dan Barry novels contain mythological overtones and hint at distant, dark origins of the powers that motivate the protagonist. They combine formulaic action with a deep ambiguity of motive and character. These were not the only kind of western novels Faust wrote during his early years of success as a pulp author. Three other westerns – all published, as the Dan Barry stories had been, in Munsey magazines – illustrate his versatility even within narrow limits of the western genre.

Trailin' (1919) followed *The Untamed* by almost a year in the pages of *All-Story Magazine*, but it went down a different path, spurred by a situation drawn from classical literature. In fact, in early 1919 while Faust was on his El Paso trip, he wrote to his wife from San Antonio to say how excited he was about his rediscovery of Sophocles. "But what an old glory that Sophocles is!" he said. "And what an infernal, vast stupendous, unspeakable idiot I've been to leave the Greek translations alone all these years. Why, I've been talking about these birds all the time, but I've never really waded into them. I wouldn't give up this Sophocles, even in a bum translation – for the whole lot." This followed a complaint about having to visit working ranches with J. Frank Dobie, whom he had met through Bob Davis's connections. "Lord, how I hate the prospect. It's worse than the army, in a way. I'd rather have my teeth pulled, one a day. Stinking cowpunchers – rides in all sorts of weather – all stuff that a hundred other men have done before me."[15]

Disliking the working West but loving Sophocles, Faust apparently drew from *Oedipus Rex* the idea of a western story in which a young man searching for his mother almost murders his father. In *Trailin'* he avoided any duplication of Sophocles' plot, but he did choose to depict a young easterner roaming the West to solve the mystery of his mother's identity and to avenge the death of the man he had assumed was his father. In the end, Anthony Bard, the protagonist, discovers that the object of his pursuit is actually his father. The novel thus ends much unlike the Dan Barry story, with Bard not only reunited with his father – and no longer an orphan – but also headed toward marriage with a young western woman named Sally Fortune.

The power of *Trailin'* as a pulp story lies less in its complicated plot, cheapened somewhat by withheld identities, than in the surprisingly intense emotions that flow from Anthony Bard in his romantic, even erotic response to Sally Fortune. Most of one chapter deals, for instance, with the mutual sexual attraction between the young man and the woman as they are forced to spend the night together in a cabin. In perfect neo-Victorian style, Faust was able to portray desire and yet pull his characters back from the brink of immorality. In the dark of the cabin, for instance, Anthony Bard feels Sally's sexual presence:

> Then, as if a shadow in which there is warmth had crossed him, he knew that she was leaning above him, close, closer; he could hear her breath. In a rush of tenderness, he forgot her beauty of eyes and round, strong throat, and supple body – he forgot, and was immersed, like an eagle winging into a radiant sunset cloud, in a sense only of her being, quite divorced from the flesh, the mysterious rare power which made her Sally Fortune, and would not change no matter what body might contain it.[16]

As his emotions move Bard from sexual desire to a sense only of Sally's "being," he decides to leave the cabin, preserving "the distinctive feature of the girl – a purity as thin and clear as the air of the uplands in which she drew breath" (186).

Even when he heeded Bob Davis's admonition to develop western themes, Faust could slant his prose toward his own literary bent and capture emotions that he generally assumed were the proper domain of poetry. As with his Dan Barry novels, the end result tended to be westerns whose distinctiveness lay in their subordination of western materials. Instead of the conventional western hero, Faust developed novels around the natural wildness of a Dan Barry or the complicated emotional life of an Anthony Bard.

Trailin' turned out to be one of the most widely circulated Max Brand westerns. Not only was it printed in hardback by Putnam a few months after its serial appearance in the Munsey magazine, and soon thereafter it was released as a film starring, once again, Tom Mix. In 1931 the film *A Holy Terror*, starring Humphrey Bogart, was based on the novel.

In July of 1920, six months after *Trailin'* appeared in *All-Story* and four months before the second Dan Barry novel appeared, Faust published another "off-trail" western. *Pride of Tyson* is a complicated, heavily plotted, and unabashedly sentimental story about the recent West. The basic circumstance of the novel involves the building of a large dam somewhere near the Mexican border. There are two protagonists – the engineer in charge of the construction project, Edward Garth, who represents reason and upward mobility, and Henry Tyson, a New York City tough who comes west, works with Mexican laborers on the dam, and then leads his co-workers in a rebellion against the dam because it will put the village church under the lake to be formed. Garth and Tyson are linked to two women: Tyson's sister Margaret, whom the engineer, Garth, loves, and a wildly passionate woman named Rona Carnahan, who is eventually paired with Henry Tyson.

Pride of Tyson is a tour de force of popular sentimental conventions, quite unlike either the Dan Barry stories or *Trailin'*. The novel ends spectacularly with the rebuilding of the village church in a new location followed by the rising of the water in the lake to cover the old church. As things work out, the aged church padre insists on staying with his original building. As the waters rise, and with a melodramatic flourish, the padre leaps from a collapsing bridge onto the old church grounds. He takes with him his violin so that the novel can close with a peculiar orchestration of sound, emotion, and landscape:

> Still the singing of the violin rose, small but clear. It was no solemn and tragic strain; it was a sound of rejoicing, dancing like the waves of the lake, and keen as the light on the waters. . . .
>
> The music soared to a pitch of triumph, rose to an incredible pitch, and then there was a bellow of falling walls, a splitting and rending; the lake rolled out and then swept back again, and from four sides the wave met in the center and leaped exultantly toward heaven.
>
> Far away, the bells of the new church of San Vicente began chiming. They looked by instinct toward the shining cross and then beyond the dam, where the water was spreading with incredible swiftness through the laterals.
>
> Now it passed beyond the slant, blue shadow of La Blanca. Now it slid out through a myriad of the smaller canals. The colors of the sunset fell upon that running water. First it was like keen fire, but now it was rich, molten gold that ran tangling through the darkening desert.[17]

As this passage shows, Faust was fully capable of matching the stylistic dramatics of a Frank Norris (as in *The Octopus*) or a Zane Grey.

If *Trailin'* and *Pride of Tyson* were not sufficient to convince Bob Davis that his young writer had extraordinary imaginative range, surely *The Garden of Eden* (1922) did the trick. Writing the novel in early 1921, at a time of great productivity for Faust, he turned to an assortment of Old Testament motifs for one of his strangest westerns.

In *The Garden of Eden* a race track tout visiting the West discovers a particular line of gray horses blessed with extraordinary speed; he traces the horses to a private domain, combining features of a monastery with those of a feudal kingdom, guarded by a contingent of black men. This is the Garden of Eden, a secluded, self-sufficient ranch ruled by David Eden. It is here where the special Eden Grey horses are bred. David Eden himself is part mystic, part poet, part dictator; he presumes to receive messages directly from God in a secret room within his castlelike headquarters. Symbolically, Eden represents tradition, the past, and a fear of change. Connor, the race track wheeler-dealer, is, of course, a man of chance who represents the outside world. As a ploy to convince David Eden to take his horses outside the Garden of Eden, race them, and make himself and Connor rich, Connor invites a woman, Ruth, into the Garden, hoping that Eden will fall in love with her.

Much of the story is devoted to the details of horses and horsemanship, always a favorite subject for Faust, and to the peculiar pastoral and feudal nature of David Eden's kingdom in the West. For instance, when Ruth sees yoked cattle plowing a field, the scene "carried the girl far back; it was like opening an ancient book of still more ancient tales; the musty smell completes the illusion. The cattle plodding slowly on, seeming to rest at every step, filled in the picture of which the primitive David Eden was the central figure."[18] To Connor, even the poetic language of Eden, man and place, is unreal; it was "wholly ludicrous to Connor. It was book-stuff" (152).

Unlike much of Faust's later western fiction, *The Garden of Eden* stresses psychological change at the expense of physical action. When Connor and Ruth enter Eden's secret room, Eden is enraged, and he banishes them from the Garden of Eden. But his identity is challenged by Connor, who tells him, "You've been alone so much that you've got to thinking that your own hunches came from God, and that'd spoil any man" (196). Thereafter, Eden's dominion crumbles; even his black servants abandon him. Finally, Eden himself leaves the Garden, recognizing that it and the life he maintained there was not truly life. Turning to Ruth's love in the final pages of the story, he describes his Garden sanctuary in dark terms. "It is black. It is full of death, and the world and our life is before us" (206).

When Bob Davis told Faust that his forte was the West, he probably meant that the West as a setting – and the expectations of the western story as guidelines – could provide the writer with some control, a means of focusing his rich and acquisitive imagination. Faust, for his part, was capable of expanding the range and definition of the western simply by writing westerns. He showed few inclinations of being a "formula" writer in his early Munsey westerns. In fact, he imbued them with personal themes, including orphanhood, and literary allusions. In *The Garden of Eden* he seems even to have constructed the novel to accord with his own divided interests. David Eden's fascination with the past and with poetic language is Faust the poet, the admirer of classical literature, the lover of the past. Connor, the gambler and modernist, eager to make money out of the Eden Grey horses, to take tradition out into the world of chance and commerce, is Max Brand.

But by the time that Faust wrote *The Garden of Eden*, he had been pulled far deeper into the commercial production of western stories than even Bob Davis had expected. If he had never written from a western formula, as he had not, he was, by 1922, in need of a formula. *Western Story Magazine* had entered his career.

Chapter Six

Western Story Magazine

He thought of the world as a place filled with many men, cunning, treacher-
ous, savage, cruel, remorseless, dangerous – and one woman, a green island
in the gray of ocean, a glimpse of heaven and happiness in the long winter of
his life.

– Max Brand, *The Smiling Desperado* (1924)

The success of the Dan Barry novels in the Munsey magazines, the
Putnam books, and Hollywood[1] pushed Faust into a role he had not
desired: that of a "western writer." As his lively correspondence with
Robert Davis so clearly shows, westerns had no real appeal for him.
Nor, he claimed, did the West itself, the place of "stinking cowboys."
Yet he was attracted to certain epic features of the frontier. Writing
to Davis from El Paso in 1919, he expressed an interest, for instance,
in writing about local political history, including some events connected to Pancho Villa. Davis's advice on this matter was clear: stay
away from it.[2]

Fiction it would be. And western fiction it mainly would be for
the next 15 years. The choice was not really Faust's alone, nor even
his and Davis's. Although Davis pushed Faust toward western themes
and material, his Munsey readers were not interested solely in western fiction. *All-Story* and *Argosy*, and then the combined *Argosy All-
Story Weekly*, published a variety of genres in each issue. But single-
genre magazines were growing in popularity, and publishers were
beginning to identify a number of distinct reader markets. As a result,
1919 saw the appearance of a magazine that would soon become
one of the most successful in the history of American publishing. Its
title was *Western Story Magazine*, and it was not published by
Munsey.

Western Story and Frank Blackwell

In 1920 Bob Davis found himself in the middle of Frank A. Munsey's effort to reorganize his publishing empire. Munsey had a reputation as a publisher who would either support a magazine lavishly (as he had *Argosy* since the 1880s) or else eliminate it; with his acquisition of five New York newspapers between 1916 and 1920, he had fewer resources to put into the many Munsey magazines. By 1922 he had pruned his magazines to three, one of which was the newly combined *Argosy All-Story*. Davis, meanwhile, had been buying manuscripts almost by the dozen from Faust. There was now nothing to do with them but wait until they could appear in the combined magazine. This meant, of course, that Faust had lost his primary market. With a growing family (Dorothy gave birth to their first child, a daughter, in 1918 and to a son in late 1919) and his interests spreading from raising bull terriers to collecting fine book editions, Faust could not stand to lose income. He was open game for other publishers.

Street & Smith, the largest company in the business and Munsey's chief rival, put its sights directly on him. Uncompromised by the ownership of newspapers, Street & Smith had been aggressively expanding its market share of magazine readers. In addition to such standbys as *Ainsley's* and *Popular Magazine*, Street & Smith had moved into the single-genre field in 1915 when it began publishing *Detective Story Magazine*. Starting as a biweekly, *Detective Story* became a weekly in 1917. The 30-year run that followed became "one of the most sensational and enduring careers any magazine in the country had ever enjoyed."[3]

The firm also published a magazine devoted to western fiction, an extension of an earlier dime novel publication entitled the *New Buffalo Bill Weekly*. Subscriptions and sales of *Buffalo Bill* had been falling until Street & Smith changed the title of the magazine to *Western Story Magazine* in 1919. At first the retitled magazine was planned to continue as a "boy's" publication, appearing every two weeks. Its cover announced "Big Clean Stories of Outdoor Life." By 1920 Street & Smith realized that its new magazine was attracting a large number of adult readers. In fact, in November 1920 the circulation reached 300,000 (Reynolds, 180). The editor decided that it was time for *Western Story Magazine* to become a weekly, doubling its need for stories.

The editor of the magazine was an acerbic fellow named Frank Blackwell, who would play a dominant role in Faust's career until the mid-1930s. Blackwell later wrote about the beginning of his relationship with Faust, saying that by 1920 "Bob Davis was over-bought. Munsey found it out, told Bob he'd have to shut off buying for as long as six months, and use up some of the stuff in the safe. Faust, always in need of money, no matter how much he made, came to me with a story. I bought it. He was mine, and mine only from there on."[4]

Blackwell needed Faust for *Western Story*. Each issue of his magazine published at least one complete novelette that ran 25 to 30 pages; two continuing serials, each weekly episode of which ran 10 to 15 pages; a short story or two; and assorted filler. Blackwell, who had learned of Faust through his association with Davis, was pleased to discover a writer of such prodigious talent in the creation of western tales. In fact, Street & Smith's decision to shift *Western Story* to weekly rather than semi-monthly publication was predicated on the availability of Frederick Faust.

The first of more than 300 Faust stories to appear in *Western Story* was published in the 25 November 1920 issue. "Jerry Peyton's Notched Inheritance," a five-part serial, appeared under a new byline – George Owen Baxter. During the next seven months, eight other serials and novelettes would appear under the Baxter name and also that of John Frederick, which Faust had used for several of his Munsey stories.

In July of 1921 the first Max Brand story, the novelette "Bullets with Sense," appeared. Up until then Faust had reserved the Brand pseudonym for stories that he was still placing with Bob Davis, but the sheer volume of fiction that Blackwell required soon pulled not only Max Brand, George Owen Baxter, and John Frederick into the pages of *Western Story* but also Peter Henry Morland, George Challis, David Manning, Martin Dexter, Evin Evans, Peter Dawson, Hugh Owen, and Nicholas Silver. Faust was obviously more than a single author; he was an entire team of writers. Soon many issues of *Western Story* carried two stories by Faust, and some carried three and eventually even four – all by apparently different authors.

As an editor, Frank Blackwell carried on a relationship with Faust that differed considerably from his experience with Bob Davis. Whereas Davis had served as a literary advisor and even at times as a surrogate father, Blackwell's interest was strictly business. He knew and cared less about literature than Davis, but he understood the magazine market better. As a result, he turned *Western Story* into one of the great success stories of American magazine history. Also, Street & Smith paid better than Munsey.

Faust often claimed to be virtually an indentured servant to Frank Blackwell, turning out prose he did not care to write. Faust let himself be trapped by something he did well, but he did it very well, showing a special proclivity for western "yarns." While he was chained to Blackwell by money, it was a form of slavery he did little to resist. Robert Easton, for instance, points out that in one 13-day period in October of 1920, shortly after the beginning of his relationship with Blackwell, Faust turned out 190,000 publishable words (Easton, 80). No degree of financial opportunity can explain adequately such creativity and persistence.

For Faust, the advent of *Western Story Magazine* meant that he would no longer have Bob Davis as his constant advisor. The ties were not broken entirely, and Davis continued for several years after 1920 to take an occasional manuscript for a Munsey magazine. Davis himself, however, soon moved into semi-retirement. As a result, Faust faced not only a different editorial personality but also a different business environment. In 1921 he said to John Schoolcraft, "It's a queer shop, that Street and Smith place. It's a caricature of a place. Looks like a prison and has a prison atmosphere inside. It is, literally, Grub Street. . . . But the money they pay is a noon-day fact if there ever was one."[5]

The majority of Faust's fiction between 1920 and 1934 was produced for Frank Blackwell. Blackwell bought a handful of detective stories for *Detective Story Magazine* between 1922 and 1935, but mainly he purchased westerns. Faust reached his highest point of productivity for Blackwell in 1932 when *Western Story* published 35 titles under five pseudonyms. After 1933, the market for pulp westerns declined dramatically, as did the number of Faust titles, dwindling to two in 1935 and none in 1936 and 1937. He published one last piece in *Western Story* in 1938. The grand total was 306 titles, all but seven being novelettes or book-length serials.[6]

The income from Street & Smith was indeed a "noon-day fact," especially in the 1920s. It allowed Faust and his growing family to live well. They moved to Italy, took up residence in a rented villa, hired domestic servants, and enjoyed a life rich in books, art, private schooling, and travel. All of this appealed greatly to Faust and gave him a chance to live his book-derived dreams of culture that put a necessary gloss on his memories of orphanhood and poverty. If Faust was a slave to anything, it was to such dreams, given life by Robert Davis, Frank Blackwell, *Western Story Magazine*, and the millions of American readers whose literary expectations were both shaped and satisfied by pulp magazines. In return, Faust's efforts helped increase the circulation of *Western Story* from 300,000 in 1920 to a half-million in 1921 (Reynolds, 180).

Western Story Westerns

To some extent, the new market had a detrimental effect on Faust's prose. Blackwell's need for fiction was an invitation to careless work and cynicism – two qualities that sometimes show up in the later stories. Given the conditions, the material in *Western Story* is surprisingly consistent in quality. Blackwell did not just purchase stories; he demanded that they be clearly plotted, unpretentious in style, and genuinely interesting to his readers. How someone could have produced so many different narratives in the same mode, however, remains the question that illuminates Faust's prodigious talent as a storyteller.

Given the sheer number of works that Faust published in *Western Story* and elsewhere, it is tempting to reduce his efforts to a single understanding. For instance, in a chapter on Faust in her *Western and Hard-Boiled Detective Fiction in America*, Cynthia S. Hamilton claims that the Max Brand western hero is a trickster, bluffing his way through the narrative, constantly fooling others who are more privileged by social class or opinion than he is, surviving oppression through "relentless watchfulness and . . . cunning."[7] Hamilton's argument on this matter is brilliant, and in her discussion of 11 Faust novels she shows how Faust's trickster heroes derive from his own early poverty and social rebelliousness. Without a doubt, this view of Faust is insightful and compelling; in particular, it vitiates those critics who have claimed that Faust's fiction has no particular significance. Yet Hamilton's view is not the whole story of his westerns. Produced in the quantities demanded by Frank Blackwell, they show more thematic range and variety than Hamilton admits.

In *Selling the Wild West*, a study of popular western fiction from 1860 to 1960, Christine Bold claims that Faust's pulp westerns changed over time as he became increasingly unhappy about the demands of the genre. The progress of his pulp westerns, according to Bold, was "from aloofness to irony to disdain."[8] Even though there are striking exceptions to this claim in some of the later work he turned out for Blackwell, it is generally true that Faust was more inventive at the beginning of his relationship with Street & Smith. His early prose for *Western Story* even suggests, at times, that he saw real opportunities for creativity as well as for income.

Faust wrote a variety of westerns for Blackwell, from the chase-and-retaliation story of *Destry Rides Again* to those that seem more in keeping with the original editorial decision to provide "Big Clean Stories of Outdoor Life" for boys. Virtually any collection of his *Western Story* work shows the imaginative range he enjoyed as the chief writer in Blackwell's stable. The themes and situations in four novels from his first eight years of association with the magazine – *Wild Freedom* (1922), *The Smiling Desperado* (1924), *Trouble Trail* (1926), and *Border Guns* (1928) – illustrate Faust's achievement in commercial western stories during the 1920s.

Wild Freedom

Wild Freedom appeared as a serial by George Owen Baxter in November 1922. Not published as a Max Brand book until 1983, it is, in part, a "lost boy" story similar in some details to *The Untamed* but ending conventionally and happily in romance. The strength of the story lies in its inventiveness and style, not in character or even theme.

In the novel Tommy Parks becomes an orphan at age 10 when his father is killed while they are trekking through the wilderness on the way to a new home. He is left, homeless, with only a few pieces of equipment, a Bible, and a copy of Malory's *Morte d'Arthur*. From this situation and these materials, Faust fashions a story in which

Tommy befriends a bear and grows into adolescence with animals as his constant companions. The books help, of course:

> There were vast, empty stretches when he was neither eating nor sleeping nor hunting nor cooking. But those periods he filled quite comfortably with reading the only two books which John Parks had put in his pack. Two books make up a small library, and these two could hardly have been better chosen for Tommy. . . . Malory he knew before in fragments. Now he devoured it whole. As for the Bible, he had felt it to be a great and dreary book fit for old women and Sunday, but, when the conversation-hunger drove him, he opened it perforce – and was suddenly lost in talks of old wars, wild vengeances, strange prophecies, inspired men . . . and many a long hour he spent tracing out the words, one by one, with the motion of a grimy little forefinger.[9]

Faust adds a new twist when Tommy wanders onto a settlement, observes the brutal treatment of a stallion, and then frees the horse, gaining the stallion as a second companion.

Halfway through the novel Faust introduces his wild boy – now in his early twenties and known to settlers as a mysterious "Indian" – to romance in the form of the 18-year-old daughter of a scientist who has set out to solve the mystery of the local Indian. The last half of the story is given to a series of chase-and-elude episodes, complete with false accusations of crime directed at Tommy Parks. Eventually he clears himself and gains not only respect but also the love of Gloria Themis, the scientist's daughter. The father had hoped to avert a union of the two by sending Tommy east, but he realizes in the closing lines of the story that his plan will not work: "He looked sadly at the girl's face. Great tears were running slowly down her cheeks. And Themis resigned himself to destiny" (239).

In *Wild Freedom* the story capitulates, as many but not all of Faust's *Western Story* pieces do, to love and sentimental expectations. Unlike Dan Barry, nothing in Tommy Park's personality or in his strange, lonely growing up, disqualifies him for full privileges in civilized society. Readers looking in 1922 for a pulp story with psychological depth would have had to put *Western Story* down and purchase a copy of the Putnam edition of *The Seventh Man*, where the wildness of Dan Barry – another lost boy – leads to the grave. Or they might have waited for some other Faust story to appear in the pages of their Street & Smith magazine.

The Smiling Desperado

While Tommy Parks has the depth only of his limited reading, the hero of *The Smiling Desperado*, another orphan, has the depth given to him by an unusual urge for vengeance. The novel appeared as a Max Brand serial in the 2 August 1924 *Western Story*. Originally titled "The Love of Danger," it was published as a book in 1953 under the title *The Smiling Desperado*. Like *Wild Freedom*, it begins with its hero, Danny Cadigan, at the age of 10. He is a boy of "dull, expressionless eyes," of emotionless behavior except when he has the opportunity to throw himself into a dangerous situation. His personality seems fixed by the deaths of his parents, especially his mother, in the next few years. The boy, now orphaned, takes a strange joy in danger and violence; even as a child "on each occasion, there had welled up in his blood and into his brain the same, tingling joy . . . but otherwise his life seemed a dull desert stretching to a dreary horizon of the commonplace."[10] Danny Cadigan is a relative, it seems, of Dan Barry.

He grows up to be a drifting cowpuncher until he is challenged by a gunman, Bill Lancaster, who knocks him unconscious with his gun butt. On awakening, Cadigan feels a "quiet delight" in the vengeance he now seeks: "When he tried to think back to what had happened, he was baffled, for it was like trying to contemplate two creatures. His old self was one. It had been sleepy, lazy, indifferent to the world. His new self was another" (28). His life is then shaped by his calm, calculated plans to master the art of the six-gun and kill Bill Lancaster, one of the deadliest of gunslingers.

Early chapters of the novel document Cadigan's peculiar fascination with danger, particularly his desire to place himself in a showdown with Lancaster. Once this aspect of his personality is established, and Cadigan – always coolly smiling – is on the trail of his dangerous adversary, Faust introduces the element of romance. As was virtually required by the expectations of readers, Cadigan as a hero must fall in love, quite literally at first sight in this case. The object of his infatuation is a young woman named Louise Morris. Faust's depiction of the event seems to link love with danger, both having a profound appeal to Cadigan:

All his life had been one long sleep, it might be said, broken by one lightning flash in his boyhood when he had discovered . . . that he loved danger for its own sake. Now there was another thunderstroke which stunned him and amazed him and opened his whole soul; it was on this day when he turned to Louise. But no one could have guessed it. Not a muscle in his face stirred; only a light glittered for an instant in his eyes and went out again, drawn deep into his heart where it was to glow and make a sad sunshine to the last day of his life. (90)

Louise Morris is for Cadigan "a glimpse of heaven and happiness in the long winter of his life" (121).

The last half of the novel is a complicated series of episodes in which Cadigan is falsely accused of crimes; his romance is threatened by Bill Lancaster; and he must kill a fully deserving blackmailer named Hugh Furness, a man of "ferretlike ferocity," "dangerous as a rattler," and "filled with horrible evil" (195). In the end he does not have to kill Bill Lancaster as planned, however, because Lancaster is discovered as the criminal he is and arrested. News comes later of his death in Mexico. Cadigan, by this means, is spared needless bloodshed, thus qualifying for a fate much better than that of Faust's earlier lover of danger, Dan Barry. The final paragraph of the novel epitomizes the *Western Story* approach to final resolutions:

But Cadigan and Lou, although they began their life together with a very small cash basis indeed, felt that money had little to do with the life that lay ahead of them. They settled at the foot of Gorman Pass, where the hills spread wide and low, and where the grass grew thick and rich. And in the perfect fullness of their happiness there was only one shadow, which consisted of two old revolvers, laid away in a drawer and wrapped in oilcloth. But in that household, they were never mentioned; and no one in all the valley ever dreamed of asking why Cadigan never wore a gun. (223)

Trouble Trail

By mid-1926 Faust had produced more than 130 pieces, mainly novelettes and serials, for *Western Story*. Though he would write almost 200 additional stories for Frank Blackwell, the work must have become tiresome. Perhaps for this reason some of his later items are touched with irony and facetiousness, even comedy. *Trouble Trail*, a serial that began appearing in August 1926, is a good example of

Faust's lighter side, demonstrating a rare Mark Twain–like style in its witty first-person narration.

The story is told by its main character, Larry Dickon, an outlaw being pursued by Sheriff Wally Ops, a good-natured lawman with a plump wife, a beautiful daughter, and a genuine personal liking for the outlaw – Dickon – whom he pursues and captures. Another character of some importance in the story is Cherry Pie, Dickon's faithful horse, whom he describes early on in a manner reminiscent of Huck Finn: "I suppose that it was thinking of the beauty of Cherry, and wondering how it was that God ever should of trusted anything so good, so beautiful, and so wonderful to an ordinary, good-for-nothing, low-down gent like me – it was thinking of that, I suppose, that made me all the worse. And I begun to hate myself pretty hard, and love Cherry more than ever, if that was possible."[11]

The story develops after Wally Ops jails Dickon and gets him sentenced to seven years in prison. But Ops's daughter, who has fallen for Dickon, objects. Ops then lets Dickon go, pretending to have been overcome by him. The ploy fails, though, and Ops himself is jailed. This leads Dickon to hunt down the real villain, Dr. Graves. Dickon's own crimes, it turns out, were always justified – and ultimately forgivable. Graves, though, is a true badman, even a murderer, and when Dickon brings him in, the sheriff is freed from his own jail and Dickon is free to marry the sheriff's daughter. This is the point, of course, at which a *Western Story* tale should end, but Faust was not able to let things go yet, as he has his narrator explain:

> Life on a farm, and sowing and mowing and reaping; and marrying and having children; and house-building and such, well, they make good living, but they don't make good telling. I have noticed how most books end up with a marriage and the reason is that after a gent has got the right girl for himself, then there ain't anything for him to do except to be happy, and happiness ain't interesting to those that are outside the front door of your house. If it wasn't for panics, and murders, and robberies, and politicians, and such, newspapers would be terrible dull reading, you know. So here is where I have got to stop talking about myself and say a little about Doctor Graves. (235)

What follows is an odd coda to the story of Larry Dickon because it raises the stature of the character who, until then, had played the role of villain in opposition to Dickon. "A murderer, nacheral and plain and simple was what Doctor Graves was," Dickon says, "but along with all his faults he was brave." Moreover, Dickon has come to believe that "him and me was cut out for one another. He would of furnished the brains. And I would of furnished a scrap of decency that he lacked" (237).

Border Guns

Trouble Trail in effect concludes by chafing under an imperative that the hero be a nice guy in the end. Dan Barry had not turned out that way, and in many Max Brand heroes there is a touch of wildness (often symbolized through the closeness with animals, as in *The Untamed* or *Wild Freedom*), even a slight leaning toward the later male existential heroes of American literature. It is possible to understand this aspect of his fiction primarily as a reverse reaction to editorial expectations or the simple ennui of constantly tailoring new stories from the same old cloth. Christine Bold claims that as Faust continued to produce pulp stories, "the more overt were his hints about his unease at being locked into a repeating pattern" (Bold, 104). That Faust was also a romantic misfit, out of place in his times and within any genre, is an equally adequate explanation. But the evidence on the face of his *Western Story* fiction is as much that of variety as it is of formula.

Border Guns exemplifies the liberties that Faust took within *Western Story* expectations. This novel appeared first as the serial "The Brass Man" under the byline of George Owen Baxter in June 1928, after eight years of Faust's steady work for the magazine; it first appeared as a Max Brand book in 1952. In the novel Faust chose to create a contemporary but Gothic environment for a story in which one woman plays two parts, an automobile is challenged to perform feats generally expected of a horse, and the narcotics trade between Mexico and the United States is the basic criminal activity underlying the plot.

The protagonist is a nonchalant Anglo living casually, at the beginning of the story, in a Mexican border town; his real name is Lorimer Everett Weldon, but he goes by the resulting acronym, Lew. Lew Weldon is called, as he says, "Big Boy. Blondy. The Big Kid. . . . The world takes me easily. I take the world easily."[12] His ease is challenged when he is pulled into strange adventures after agreeing to protect a young invalid woman, Helen O'Malley, who is threatened by thieves looking for money left by her recently deceased father. Helen lives in the O'Malley home, a castlelike house on the American side of the border, separated by a river meant to be the Rio Grande.

The story is heavy with Gothic elements, including unexplainable drops of blood leading into Helen O'Malley's bedroom, the disappearance of her father's body from his tomb, and unexpected shifts of behavior by people who first seem friends, then enemies: "All seemed a great machine, and all the wheels were interlocking and grinding together, but what that machine was accomplishing, he, Weldon, could not guess" (197). One point of clarity, however, comes when Lew Weldon falls in love with Francesca Laguardia, a mysterious woman who seems linked to drug smuggling. When she tells Lew, "Believe that I love you – I love you!" his response is an unusually complicated one for a pulp story. It sounds, in fact, more like Nathaniel Hawthorne:

> He, all ice with cold wonder, looked before him and tried to see the truth, and then he glanced down at her. She was still waiting for an answer. And then belief grew up in him and unfolded like strange flower, poisoned with the very unbelief from which it had come, and all the more beautiful because of it.
>
> "I do believe," said Weldon.
>
> Now, if it was a cunning lie she had acted, what would she do? What would she say?
>
> She merely closed her eyes. (167)

In the end, Lew learns the central mystery of his adventures: that the erotic Francesca Laguardia and the apparently ailing Helen O'Malley are the same woman, who plays two roles in her effort to protect her dead father's fortune. As expected by *Western Story* readers, Francesca-Helen and Lew Weldon are united in marriage, but the union is not the typical one of strong hero and submissive woman.

In fact, despite the demands of readers and the careful, market-based editorial decisions of Frank Blackwell, little about Max Brand in *Western Story* can be described as "typical." The romantic ending of *Border Guns* suggests the editorial freedom available within the pages of *Western Story*. Even though the periodical had begun as a boys' magazine with "Big Clean Stories" in mind, the demand for western fiction in the 1920s provided the magazine's writers with a broader literary field than Frank Blackwell may have intended. In the 1930s the situation at the magazine changed, and Blackwell was forced to rein in its contributors, Faust included. In the 1920s, however, *Western Story* provided Faust with an editorial environment that nurtured his storytelling by giving it the literary equivalent of the free range over which many of his western characters rode.

Chapter Seven

Life and Poetry on a Grand Scale

Yes, we went touring through the Aegean and it is the cream of the cream. I would have to talk like a lousy painter to describe the effects. Let it go at an ocean that can really be "wine-dark," as Homer describes it, and on this purple sea scatter islands from blue to brown, and on the islands paste in some white cities, and over the whole drink pour a decoction of thirty days of flawless sunshine, and put in a dash of crystal clear air – and then in spite of this mixed metaphor you may get an idea of the happiest month of my life. The mainland was almost as beautiful. Its beauty is a matter of light and shadow and distance, plus a temple here and there and a flock of glorious names. Nothing can describe Greece.

– Letter to G. W. Fish, 1931

There were at least two sides to Frederick Faust. On the one hand, he was the writer of pulp stories, a diligent worker on his typewriter, enjoying the discussions with editors about story ideas, intrigued with his success not only in magazines but also on Hollywood's silver screen, and eager to accept his payments for work completed. He gave generously of his advice to other would-be magazine writers and sometimes even served as a silent partner for some of his compatriots in the trade. He admired those, like his Street & Smith editor, Frank Blackwell, who had good instincts for the market. Later called "The King of the Pulps," Faust was a full participant in the business of popular fiction.

On the other hand, having by 1922 seen almost 50 of his serials and novelettes published in magazines, Faust had relinquished few of his larger ambitions. Ever since his high school years, possibly even before, he had high expectations for himself. At Berkeley these had been attached primarily to literature, especially the traditional Western European classics. He had a genuine compulsion to admire literature. While staying in a San Antonio hotel in 1919 during the western trip arranged for him by Bob Davis, he wrote to his wife about his interests. "Nothing else matters," he said, "nothing but

Greek and English poetry. And maybe Goethe and Dante as exceptions to a rule."[1]

In reality, of course, many other things mattered, including his
wife, his growing family, and his style of life. In the 1920s, and continuing several years after the stock market crash in 1929, Faust con-
ducted his life on a grand scale. The means of doing so were, of
course, the earnings derived from millions of readers of pulp magazines and moviegoers. By the end of 1921 Faust had suffered a serious heart attack, even though it failed to slow him down. In the years
thereafter he discovered Europe, eventually settling in Florence,
hoping to make his home there permanently. He also continued to
write poetry, "the God of my worship," he said in 1925, thinking
always that his real talent lay not in prose but in verse.

From New York to Italy

Faust seldom allowed tranquility to disturb his domestic life for long.
After his dramatic marriage to Dorothy Schillig in the spring of 1917,
he and his new wife began their constant relocations from residence
to better residence in New York City. Their first child, Jane, arrived
in April of 1918; a son, John, followed in the fall of 1919. While
awaiting the birth of Jane, Faust tried again to become a soldier.
Finally, in the early summer of 1918, following surgery to remove a
swollen testicle, he was allowed to enlist in the U.S. Army, only to be
sent to Camp Humphreys, Virginia, not far from Washington, for the
duration of the war. He wrote continuously while at Camp
Humphreys, turning out a virtually undiminished supply of stories
for Bob Davis. Money was on his mind then and later. In the two
years following his discharge after the Armistice, he returned to New
York except for his trip west at Davis's bequest or to visit in
California.

The pace of Faust's life included not only his incredible pulp
productivity but also constant work on verse, frequent drinking
bouts with old friends from Berkeley and new friends in the city,
long conversations, attendance at a variety of sporting events, and
constant reading. John Schoolcraft recalled that during one winter in
New York City, the Fausts – Heinie and Dorothy – read aloud in the
evenings many plays of Shakespeare, all of Sophocles and Aeschylus,

some of Aristophanes, and all of Spenser's *The Faery Queen* (Schoolcraft, FP). For Dorothy, marriage to someone of such energy was a mixed blessing, especially with young children to worry about. According to Robert Easton, she suffered the first of several nervous breakdowns shortly after giving birth to John Faust in November 1919.

Faust decided thereafter that a trip to Europe without Dorothy would do them both good. Consequently, in the summer of 1921 he and his old college friend, Dixie Fish, now a physician, sailed for France. The trip lasted until August, with Faust writing frequently to Dorothy to assure her of his affections and to ease her fears about money. To maintain his life-style, Faust had to write constantly during the trip, which reinforced his long-standing interest in European places and culture. He returned to New York and to Dorothy with completed manuscripts and the hope of returning to Europe someday on a permanent basis.

Faust maintained a gargantuan schedule of work and play despite a serious health problem. He had been told when he enlisted in the Canadian Army in 1915 that something was amiss with his heart; in the fall of 1918 while at Camp Humphreys he had suffered an attack of flu that may have further damaged his coronary system. In any event, in November of 1921 he suffered a heart attack. It was a time of particular stress as he was trying to pull his family out of the debt that their spending habits continually created. Alcohol was also a factor. His doctor noted that he was "under nerve strain . . . after a drinking bout."[2] The problem was erratic fibrillation of the heart and a resting pulse rate of 155. The condition was treated then and thereafter with doses of digitalis. At his age of 29, it was a powerful reminder of mortality to Faust, and for the rest of his life he lived in dread of heart failure and suffered frequently from feelings of suffocation, especially at night. As the years passed after the initial attack, Faust's heart became a reason for ever more work, more squeezing of pleasure and significance from life. Within a year after the attack, he was playing golf regularly, sometimes also sparring with friends in a boxing gymnasium, and living outside the city in Katonah, New York, where he bred dogs, rode horses, and led his own version of the life of a country gentleman. Robert Easton vividly describes the scene, day and night, at Katonah:

As for peace and quiet, a chance visitor might have thought it the training camp for a heavyweight contender. White bull terriers, symbols of combat, overran the yard. Here was the woodpile where Faust did his chopping. There was the lane where he did his roadwork. In good weather a punching bag hung from a tree limb. Dumbbells lay everywhere. Sudden strain was bad for the heart, but regular exercise was a necessity. He had come to believe in the virtues of sweat with a faith that bordered on the religious.

Visitors entering the Katonah household at this period received unforgettable impressions. One recalled hearing Faust yell at Dorothy, "Cry, damn you, cry!", with tears of emotion streaming down his face as he stalked the living room declaiming Desdemona's final lines from *Othello*, holding the book in one hand while tearing at his hair with the other. Dorothy had mastered the art of letting a tear glisten in the eye and not fall, but he wanted a commitment equal to his own. Despite his great personal charm, there were moments when some observers thought him mentally disturbed. Others said that he lived in a make-believe world. (Easton, 95-96)

Alcohol was still a problem. "Dorothy never knew whom to expect for dinner – a distinguished editor, a drunken cab driver delighted at the huge fare and the several drinks collected en route, a young and impoverished poet of great potential, or just her inebriated husband whose next tottering step might be his last." And so it went, but with Faust still able to turn out the stories, $60,000 worth of them in 1922 alone (Easton, 94-97).

The Fausts had decided, however, that Europe would be far preferable even to Westchester County. In the summer of 1923 Faust again went alone to Europe, including heart specialists in his itinerary this time. His hope was that life in Europe, perhaps in Italy, would be a refuge from the frenetic activities that he could not avoid in the United States. Also, Italy held for him a clear esthetic attractiveness, as the home of Dante and Michelangelo, that nothing in America could match. For years he had dreamed of living in Italy.

In the summer of 1925 he went again to Europe, this time taking Dorothy and his two children, touring England by automobile and then moving on to the Continent. Still worried about his health, he consulted with a number of doctors, including Carl Jung.[3] The Fausts remained in Europe throughout 1925, spending the winter in France and crossing into Italy in the spring of 1926. The family settled in Florence, leasing for a year a villa to the south of the Arno River. In 1927 the Fausts moved to a villa north of the river owned by Arthur Acton, a wealthy Englishman. The new place had several acres and a number of American and English neighbors. Faust immediately began pouring his own money into the property, enlarging the house eventually to 22 rooms and improving the grounds to include a swimming pool and tennis courts. He named it Villa Negli Ulivi, the house among the olive trees, and maintained it as his family's principal residence for the next 10 years.

Faust had long thought about living in Italy. "I feel more and more," he had told John Schoolcraft in the summer of 1918, "that we will set up shop somewhere in Italy, probably in Florence."[4] Italy was his dream of a ideal life, pursued with dedication and great expense. Servants were hired, as were special tutors for the children. Guests were always welcome and wonderfully entertained. Faust took special pleasure in the delights of Florence and its renaissance treasures. The grandeur of Florence was a fitting context for his expansive dreams of personal and artistic grandeur, deriving as they had from their unlikely origin in his San Joaquin childhood. When Martha Bacon, Leonard's daughter, wrote after Faust's death that he had lived in Florence "like a medieval prince," she hardly exaggerated (Bacon, 73).

Poetry

Italy was also a place of poetry, and poetry was what Faust had long pursued. As a college student he had seemed to his literature professor Leonard Bacon to be "poetry incarnate." Bacon's daughter Martha recalled of Faust during his Italian years that he was still obsessed with the idea of being a poet. "Alive in him like a nerve," she wrote, "is the instinct for poetry. He spends long, painful mornings, not wooing his muse, but ravishing her." It was as though Faust was determined to have poetry, possess it, as he had insisted on having Dorothy or living in Florence. Bacon continues, "But she resists, and though he masters tennis and Greek and makes success his slave, the muse evades him" (73).

No portrait of Faust can fail to observe his obsession with poetry and his assumption that poetry was the greatest of the arts. Unfortunately the scale of his own poetry was less than he hoped. His models were clear, as he often indicated to Leonard Bacon and others, and he knew what he did not like: Wordsworthian romanticism and virtually all modern poetry – with the exception of Edwin Arlington Robinson's Arthurian poems and Bacon's efforts to revive the epic tradition. In his own practice, Faust dabbled in lyric, dramatic, and narrative modes of poetry. But in all cases he wrote for few readers, even in his early years. By contrast, his stories were the equivalent of crowded Saturday mornings at the local moviehouse, the customers gasping at the hero's narrow escapes. His poetry was a solo stage performance in a grand but empty theater.

In 1922 G. P. Putnam's Sons published a collection of his poems, *The Village Street*. Even though Putnam had by then published four Max Brand novels, the firm agreed to publish the poems under Faust's own name with no reference to his famous pseudonym. The volume is dedicated to Thomas Downey, Faust's high school principal. It consists of 21 poems, four of which were previously published. Of these four, two had appeared at Berkeley under different titles, one was "The Secret" (first published in the *Century*), and the fourth was "The Legend of St. Christopher," which had the distinction of having appeared in 1918 as a Max Brand poem (one of three under that byline during Faust's life) in *All-Story Weekly*. Of the new material, including the title poem, most were short lyrical poems on a variety of themes. The book also included a section of six poems for children, including "The Secret," which in its evocation of a funeral hardly seems like typical children's verse, and a long Arthurian poem, "Balin." Anyone looking for consistency of theme or style would not have found much in *The Village Street*.

Most of the poems are unremarkable, even though the language is often touching and some of the themes seem to have autobiographical connections. The best poems in the book are "The Secret," with its veiled reference to the death of Faust's father, the Saint Christopher poem, and "Balin," the latter two because of Faust's narrative skill. The Saint Christopher piece is a retelling of the legend of Offerus's ferrying of a child across a river, and "Balin" is a dark medieval tale whose hero, the knight Balin, resembles Dan Barry in his anger and violence, which, in this case, leads to the death of a woman whom the knight has championed.

In Faust's effort to be a poet, "Balin" is an important work. It contains some remarkable imagery, especially of dead leaves blowing in the wind, a constant reminder of death, and makes good use of blank verse. The poem ends with Balin sadly reconciled to the death of Nerys, the woman who, Juliet-like, assuming his death, had wasted away to death herself:

> At night the stars looked through the naked forest
> And he was open to the cold eyes of God.
> He thought in vain of glories old, and praise.
> The horns that sounded once on famous fields
> Blew thin and far. The knights in noble ranks
> Rode shadowlike upon his memory.
> Nerys was dead, and through his fingers poured
> His life, loose sand.[5]

The poem was a serious effort by Faust to put his poetry before the public. He was encouraged, no doubt, by Edwin Arlington Robinson's success with his Tennysonian *Merlin* (1917) and, especially, *Lancelot* (1920); also, he must have seen the Balin story as a way to recoup some of his Arthurian efforts that had gone for years into the never-published Tristram poem that he had started in 1915. In writing "Balin," however, Faust was occasionally uneasy about the results he saw in front of him. "I'm very uncertain about it," he told John Schoolcraft in March 1921. "A few passages are real poetry, I hope. But God knows the bad places are frequent and close together and long." Nor did he feel particularly good about the entire collection, thinking it "such bum junk, so thin and sentimental and flabby from beginning to end."[6] Still, as the volume neared publication, Faust admitted that with "Balin" included – and occupying almost half of the book – it was "the first thing I ever cared about very much. So I look forward to its publication . . . with fear and trembling."[7]

When *The Village Street* appeared, William Rose Benét gave it a few polite compliments in the *Literary Review*, as did Richard Le Gallienne in the *New York Times*, but the book attracted little attention. Faust had hoped that it would establish his reputation as a poet and pave the way to future publications. In reality, it had an opposite effect. Disappointed, Faust ceased virtually all efforts to write poetry for a popular audience. In fact, after 1922 he published only two poems in magazines – in 1933 and 1942, both times in *Harper's* – and never returned to the Arthurian material that he had loved since childhood.

He did not stop writing verse entirely, of course, but he shifted his efforts away from Malory and toward the Mediterranean and its classical heritage of mythology and drama. Also, he proceeded with fewer illusions about reaching readers, concentrating instead on the matter and material of his most admired masters: Homer, Dante, Shakespeare. On occasion Faust realized his problems of excessive derivation. In 1925, for instance, he sent Leonard Bacon a poetic drama entitled *Rimini* for his opinion; Faust had been working on the play for at least two years, having told Bacon in 1923 that he hoped it might be purchased by some producer in Manhattan. Bacon offered candid criticism that Faust found hard to swallow at first. "Your letter about the play hits the sore point," he told Bacon. But he admitted his own failings:

> *Rimini* is now at such a sufficient distance that it is no longer the pound of flesh nearest my heart. Your letter, I suppose, only took off a leg or two. But I am not much in doubt that the members will grow again. Every one of us who writes possesses an enormous egotism, and though someone occasionally steps upon our faces, we are soon up and about again, shouting our conviction forth in blank verse or something worse. Not that your criticisms were anything savage in their nature, but they ring the bell with me. I think that you are quite right. . . . I find it hard to distinguish one from another the moments when my emotions are real and the moment when my emotions are footnotes on reading I have done long ago. I do not think imitation is bad; not when it has something to do with mere form. But one should not borrow the substance inside the form.[8]

As a poet Faust found it hard to develop substance for his borrowed forms. Once he moved to Italy, where he could write in the luxury of his Florentine study, he retreated even further from the modern world. The only bridges between his prose and his poetry were some common elements of heroism and mythological allusion. Otherwise, the separation was obvious, even in his style of composing, with Faust turning to special paper and a quill pen for his poetry, symbolic gestures showing how his prose success gave him only the poetic freedom to write without needing an audience. By contrast, eager to speed his prose into print, he always wrote his stories on a typewriter. In Florence, Martha Bacon and others saw a problem: "He is split by two necessities," Bacon observed, "what the public will read and what he longs to write. The split is an agony, and he drinks to soothe it, until he cannot tell friend from foe"

(Bacon, 73). As early as 1921, working on poems for *The Village Street*, he had said to John Schoolcraft, "Of this I am certain – that I have sold my soul. I can no longer write decent verse."⁹

Dionysus in Hades

Surrounded by books and Renaissance art in Florence, writing verse almost as an antidote to the furious composition of stories, Faust continued his efforts to create poetry out of traditional themes and narrative materials. He even took up the study of Greek to enrich his appreciation of Homer, thinking that some essential, retrievable poetic treasure was locked in the language of the *Iliad* and the *Odyssey*. Likewise, he read widely in Greek mythology, stalking the sources of Sophocles and Aeschylus, hoping to make the Greek muse his own.

In 1931, following a tour of Greece with Dorothy and friends, including Walter Morris Hart, a Berkeley professor, Faust prepared for publication the 2,000-line poem *Dionysus in Hades*, on which he had worked for several years, often drawing advice from Hart. The poem was a retelling of Dionysus's visit to the underworld to free his mother, Semele, once the mortal lover of Zeus. The significance of this mythology for Faust lay in its ambiguous treatment of mortality and divinity, with Semele ultimately released from the underworld to assume a role as goddess of joy and Dionysus himself the child of both mortal and god. Dionysus's search for his mother and, in Faust's account, his confrontation with Zeus, his father, also must have evoked Faust's memory of his own long-dead parents.

Whatever the exact motivation, Faust was drawn to the Dionysus story, and from it he thought that he had created a powerful contemporary poem. Writing to Dixie Fish in July 1931, he said, "I've been pushing out some verse that may be pretty hot . . . and my trust is that the wise guys will see that I've set the clock ahead of them while they were sound asleep."¹⁰ A month later he confidently sent the manuscript to Carl Brandt, who had been serving for several years as his agent for book publications and movie rights, asking him to find a publisher. Faust was certain that the poem was good. "If you have two spare hours," he told Brandt, "take a look at the manuscript. At least I think it is a new *kind* of cheese. . . . Anything

you can do to hasten the printing along will be much appreciated. I
am like a kid waiting for his first long pair of pants."[11]

In the United States, however, a depression was in progress, and
no one was interested in publishing the book. Faust finally paid Basil
Blackwell in Oxford to print 500 copies of *Dionysus in Hades*. By
December 1931 Faust had sent some of these to friends, hoping for
reviews. The results of Faust's long labor on the Dionysus matter
were hardly noticed by the world of letters.[12]

The poem suffers from what Robert Easton calls "murkiness," a
common problem in Faust's verse, suggesting that he was often too
close to his material to portray it with clarity. Yet *Dionysus in Hades*
deserves notice if not for intrinsic virtues at least for its reiteration of
themes implicit in his popular prose. The poem ultimately stresses
the values of action rather than contemplation and of mortal life
rather than divinity. To the mythological narrative, Faust adds a
meeting between Dionysus, god of wine and revelry, and
Prometheus the Titan. Dionysus realizes that he and Prometheus
have given similar gifts to humanity: hope from the Titan and, from
Dionysus, the divine madness of laughter and wine. For Faust,
Dionysus affirmed human aspirations for a kind of divinity in human
life (in other poems Faust sometimes referred to "the god-in-man")
and stood in contrast to Apollonian control of emotions. In the
poem no less an authority than Zeus tells Dionysus "that in deeds,
however blind, / There is an end of doubt."[13]

In the final lines of the poem, then, Dionysus finds his peace not on
Olympus or in the temple of Apollo but in nature and in action. It is
the same philosophy that President Wheeler had excoriated in his
1915 commencement address. Although *Dionysus in Hades* is alternately foggy and archaic, its central theme was a fitting expression
for a man driven to think, talk, travel, exercise, compose verse, drink
heavily, and spend money – all while suffering from a weak heart and
writing magazine fiction at the rate of a novel a month.

Chapter Eight

Singing Guns
and *Destry Rides Again*

The hunger Westerns satisfy is a hunger not for adventure but for meaning.
— Jane Tompkins, *West of Everything* (1981)

Although Faust favored poetry over prose, he preferred even his pulp stories to most fiction of his time. His faith in human aspiration, the "god-in-man" quality he saw in the figure of Dionysus or in Saint Christopher, was particularly missing, he felt, in the realism praised by critics in the 1920s. Sinclair Lewis was especially distasteful to him. "I think *Main Street* is the worst book ever written," he told John Schoolcraft. "It is so ugly that everybody thinks it must be important. That's the way nowadays. The world won't let you show a man with the skin on. But when you've torn the skin away and shown the world the torn and bleeding insides, the world says: 'Jesus! How true! What art!' I got so mad . . . that I actually hurled the book across the room. I was so mad that I picked it up again and went on reading and cussing. I invented new cuss words that would have lifted a team of mules right through their collars."[1]

More than fiction bothered him. He also attacked a John Masefield poem (*Dauber*) in which the protagonist comes to a sad end: "People who read western fiction don't read *Dauber* and would hate the poem if they did. The sadness of poverty and the sadness of life don't appeal to the horny handed sons of toil. . . . They have enough grimness stuffed down their throats every day." Moreover, he claimed, "The ones who want the bitter junk in stories are those who eat strawberries and cream every day of their lives; that makes them appreciate the sour."[2] Although Faust had no quarrel with classical tragedy, he felt that art had an obligation to be heroic and positive. He found fault even with Michelangelo because, in his opinion, the Italian artist "couldn't forget anatomy any more than Rubens

81

could forget fat." His statue of David bothered Faust because it lacked ideality. Michelangelo, he felt, had "carved a young man rather than a young god. And stone ought to do gods, not men." "The trouble," Faust said, "was that his *taste* was wrong. He was in a period that was becoming decadent."[3] In short, Faust equated realism with decadence.

He had no patience with such decadence, preferring, as he once said, heroes who are 50 feet tall. While he once admitted to his son-in-law that it was possible to read half of a published story, imagine how it might continue to the end with some changes in details and characters, and then to that imagined plot graft a new first half,[4] his own view of the heroic generally shaped his work. This is especially true of *Singing Guns* (1928) and *Destry Rides Again* (1930). Both novels, usually assumed to be among his best, have thematic depth that others lack. In *The Untamed* Faust created a character who stood out from other humans because of his atavistic, nonhuman rage when hurt. In other stories, such as *The Smiling Desperado*, Faust relied on heroes who simply become very skilled in the art of violence; in still others, such as *Wild Freedom* or *Border Guns*, he placed primary emphasis on plot rather than on the character of the hero.

In *Singing Guns* and *Destry Rides Again*, however, Faust strove for a combination of growing self-awareness and idealism in his heroes. In doing so, he drew on elements of character that appear in his *Dionysus*. Both novels also incorporate a degree of philosophical speculation, setting them apart stylistically from other stories that use the same spare, action-oriented style. *Singing Guns* and *Destry Rides Again* are not short on action; in fact, it was as an "action-packed" story that the second novel found its way to Universal Studios and a career on the screen. But in both cases the action demanded by the pulps, especially by Frank Blackwell, coexists with complex thematic elements and Faust's requisite heroism.

Singing Guns

Singing Guns may have begun as a clever way for Faust to make use of Celtic material from the *Mabinogi*. He had been long interested in Celtic and Welsh material as it had become part of Arthurian legends and tales. In *Singing Guns* he used obvious Celtic lore in the naming of his protagonist, an outlaw with a golden heart, Annon Rhiannon. Rhiannon is, however, a feminine name in Celtic mythology, a fact that raises some questions about Faust's conscious use of literary sources. The second most important character in the novel is named Caradac, also Celtic, perhaps taken from the Arthurian knight Caradoc.[5] Although these names are very Welsh, the characters who bear them inhabit an unspecific western American landscape.

The novel begins when Caradac, sheriff and bounty hunter, seeks an infamous outlaw, Rhiannon, on Mount Laurel. On the mountain, behind a secret hole-in-the-wall rock formation, Rhiannon has been living a hermitlike existence. When he is surprised by the sheriff, however, he uses his pistol and wounds Caradac badly. Out of compassion for the man he has shot, Rhiannon nurses Caradac back to health and establishes a bond of strong friendship, even love, with him. Caradac in turn convinces his new friend to shave his dark beard and return with him to the lower country; there Caradac sets him up as the manager of a farm that he, as sheriff, had repossessed. Rhiannon, living under the assumed named of John Gwynn, shows amazing agricultural prowess and soon has the property in full production of alfalfa and butter.

Up to this point *Singing Guns* is hardly a typical western, even for Max Brand. For almost half its length, the story moves slowly through the Rhiannon-Caradac relationship and the growing of crops on the farm. There are some hints of possible future action, especially in a mysterious young woman named Nancy Morgan, a named adding definite Arthurian overtones to the story, whom Rhiannon discovers often on his property. Also, a man named Richards, hired by Caradac to help Rhiannon with the farm, behaves very suspiciously at times. Finally, on the adjacent property lives a family named Dee, whose members seem to Rhiannon to exhibit "an enormous kindness" to themselves and to others.[6] Rhiannon's admiration for the Dees is important because their presence seems to suppress his older, outlaw tendencies. Earlier in the story, before coming down from the mountain, he had told Caradac his reason for choosing to live apart from other people: he has "smoke" within himself. When angered, he says, "I get hot. My brain, it fills up with smoke. I got no right to live around among people" (18). But in the first half of the novel, as the story wanders without sure aim, this – living "around among people" – is what he learns to do again. His story is Dan Barry's in reverse.

Halfway through the novel, Faust finally shifts the action into a mode appropriate for pulp fiction. Visiting the Dees' home, with no sense of impending danger, Rhiannon is suddenly in the middle of violence: "A door crashed in the unused wing of the house. There was a sound like the screech of a window thrust violently up, and then a scream rang terribly across the patio!" (318). Rhiannon next discovers that Richards is also a Morgan, related to Nancy, and that the Morgans are the traditional enemy of the Dee family. As things work out, Richards and Nancy Morgan are part of an elaborate plot designed to trick Rhiannon into revealing the hole-in-the-wall passageway to Mt. Laurel, where treasure is reputed to be located. At a pace now typical of Max Brand fiction, these and other matters now come to light as Caradac, with Rhiannon's aid, finally captures the conspirators. At the end of the story, with Rhiannon's identify revealed far and wide, the governor pardons him for the past crimes that had made him a fugitive. With freedom also comes romance, because young Isabella Dee has fallen in love with him.

Singing Guns introduces themes not often found in Max Brand westerns or else handled more covertly in other stories. Chief among these is the extraordinary friendship between Caradac and Rhiannon, as the following passage clearly exemplifies:

> "Your way is my way," said Caradac Quietly. "Your life is my life, and the trail you travel is the trail that I ride."
>
> To this announcement Rhiannon could not make a rejoinder. Once or twice, in the moments that followed, his lips parted. Then he got up and began to pace the veranda in his usual restless way when his mind was full. At last he paused behind the sheriff's chair and rested his big hand for a single instant upon the wide shoulder of Caradac.
>
> That was all. Then he resumed his pacing, but whole volumes had been communicated from one to the other by a sort of nervous wireless that traversed the air in silence. (127)

This extraordinary affection between the two men – one a fugitive, the other a bounty hunter – contributes to the general ironic tone of the story. The irony is reinforced by Rhiannon's pastoral inclinations when he pursues (as does Shane, in Jack Schaefer's later western) life as a farmer.

The novel is weakened by indirection and uncertainty, especially in its treatment of Rhiannon's personality. Given the behavior of such Max Brand heroes as Dan Barry or Danny Cadigan, the "smoke" inside Rhiannon hardly shows itself; the proclivity to rage that he says had forced him to choose life apart from humanity is never really active in the story.

In her book on westerns and hard-boiled detective fiction, Cynthia S. Hamilton claims that Max Brand heroes often have the status of underdogs and victims. Such characters, in Hamilton's view, are like tricksters in folktales, surviving by thwarting established power; their primary values are those often associated with the working class: "loyalty, mercy, wily cleverness and endurance" (Hamilton, 115).[7] These values are particularly evident in *Singing Guns*, where Rhiannon's stature as a famous outlaw renders him more of a victim than a villain, forces him to adopt a false identity, and leaves him at the story's end dependent on the mercy of a distant governor.

Rhiannon ultimately is rewarded not only with the land he has made productive and a pardon from the governor but also with the love of Isabella Dee. Yet the central feature of the novel is not its melodramatic system of rewards but, as Hamilton points out, the contrast between Rhiannon's character and Caradac's: "Caradac lives a double life. On the one hand he maintains his position as sheriff and continues to pursue criminals; on the other he harbours a known criminal" (Hamilton, 106). Rhiannon, although a fugitive from the law, provides Caradac with a moral example through his understanding of his own behavior.

Destry Rides Again

No evidence exists to show that *Singing Guns* attracted much attention when it was first published. It appeared first in December 1928 as a serial in *Western Story* under the byline of George Owen Baxter, the "author" attached to more Faust westerns at time of publication than any other save Max Brand. The story did not reappear for 10 years. In 1938, however, it was issued as a Max Brand hardcover novel by Dodd, Mead & Company, which in 1927 had begun publishing several Max Brand westerns a year.[8] In 1942 it was the first of many Max Brand novels published as paperbacks by Pocket Books. In 1947 it was produced as a radio drama by CBS and in 1950 was the basis for a Republic film of the same title (Nolan, 155, 157). But the visibility of *Singing Guns* hardly matched that of the most famous Max Brand title, *Destry Rides Again*.

Destry Rides Again is without a doubt the most famous of all Max Brand titles, thanks primarily to Universal Studios and some of its actors, especially Tom Mix, James Stewart, Marlene Dietrich, and Audie Murphy. The story appeared first under the title of "Twelve Peers" as a six-part serial in *Western Story* beginning in February 1930. Six months later Dodd, Mead published it as a hardcover with the new title. Within a year the first printing of 7,000 books had sold. Eager for money at the time, Faust agreed to sell the movie rights to Universal in 1931 for $1,500. Thirteen more reprintings of the book appeared in 1931 and 1932. Thereafter, *Destry Rides Again* became a Hollywood fixture of sorts. In April 1932 it was issued as a Universal film starring Tom Mix, recently returned to the screen for sound appearances. In 1939 the screenplay was rewritten by Felix Jackson and made into a film starring James Stewart and Marlene Dietrich. Its final Hollywood version appeared in 1955, with Audie Murphy playing the character of Destry. The story was also adapted for radio, stage, and television versions. Aside from the 1932 Tom Mix film, the adaptations of Faust's story retained little beyond the skeleton of his plot and the last name of his protagonist.[9] Yet the attention by the entertainment industry suggests that Faust captured in his novel a powerful germ of popular sentiment.

Destry Rides Again is certainly a candidate for what Cynthia Hamilton claims it to be: Faust's best book (Hamilton, 119). It stands out in his career as a *Western Story* serial that in many respects violated the demands of the pulp market by providing explicit philosophical commentary and developing its protagonist through a form of defeat rather than victory. As such, it defies the opinion stated by Christine Bold and implied by others that the more pulp stories Faust wrote, the more "rigidly conventional" they became (Bold, 184). Although Faust relied on a traditional form of adventure story – the revenge plot – he added distinctive touches to typical elements of pursuit and suspense.

The protagonist is Harrison Destry, who is framed for a robbery by Chester Bent, presumably his best friend, and sentenced by a jury composed entirely of men who dislike Destry because in his youth he had bested each of them in one way or another, in fighting, shooting, racing, or romancing. When the judge explains that he has been sentenced by his peers – and that the term *peers* means "equals" – Destry rejects the idea that any of the 12 are his equal and he vows revenge for what he sees as a miscarriage of justice. Six years later he returns to the town of Wham, so named Wham because of the frequency of fighting and the sound of blows being struck. His years of incarceration have narrowed his purpose in life to a single, sharp point: to exact reparations from the jury. Meanwhile, Chester Bent succeeds in feigning friendship while continuing to plot against Destry. Two other characters are especially important. Charlotte Dangerfield, called "Charlie," is a steadfast friend who ultimately falls in love with him. Willie Thornton is a boy who worships Destry as a hero. Destry himself is largely defined by his relationships with each of these three persons.

Much of the plot is taken up by Destry's clever efforts to do in his "peers" who sent him to prison – efforts that are generally successful owing to Destry's working against these men's moral weaknesses. As he proceeds, however, working for a while behind a lawman's badge provided through Charlie Dangerfield's efforts, he is frustrated by the sense of some evil genius working against him. The reader knows that this is Chester Bent, but Destry's self-confidence erodes when he is unable to discover the source of his frustration. In disgust, he leaves Wham and secludes himself in the Crystal mountains. Bent then kills one of the jurors himself, doing so with Destry's knife in an effort to frame him once again. This time, however, young Willie Thornton witnesses the crime, and then flees for his life from Bent's now murderous rage and from his mongrel watchdog. He finally reaches Destry and collapses in Destry's arms as he reveals the treachery of Chester Bent.

The thematic climax of the story occurs when Faust performs the strange rhetorical feat – for a pulp story – of having his western hero reflect philosophically on his own humanity. Previously, Destry had assumed that he was better than others and had, in effect, no peers. Following the humbling experience of prison and then the bewilderment of being duped by Bent upon his release, Destry faces a crisis of identity. With the almost lifeless boy in his arms, and suddenly

feeling "all of paternity, all of motherhood," he experiences a
moment of extraordinary self-awareness:

> He became to himself more than a mere name and a vague thing; he for the
> first time visualized "Destry" as that man appeared before the eyes of others,
> striking terror, striking wonder, filling at least the eyes of a child with an ideal!
> Knowing this, he felt a sudden scorn for the baser parts that were in him,
> the idler, the scoffer at others, the disdainful mocker at the labors of life. He
> wished to be simple, real, quiet, able to command the affection of his peers.
> It seemed to Destry that, through the boy, for the first time he could real-
> ize the meaning of the word "peer." Equal. For all men were equal. Not as he
> blindly had taken the word in the courtroom, with wrath and with contempt.
> Not equal in strength of hand, in talent, in craft, in speed of foot or in leap of
> mind, but equal in mystery, in the identity of the race which breathes through
> all men, out of the soil, and out of the heavens.
> So it was that hatred of his enemies left him.[10]

This epiphany has few parallels in popular western fiction, such
events generally having been reserved for easterners who are transformed by their contact with the West. But Faust shifts the character
of his hero – originally a revenge seeker somewhat on the order of
Dan Barry in *The Untamed* – to a quasi-Christian sense of common
experience; he also allows the remainder of the story to reinforce the
shift in character. In a final showdown with Chester Bent, Destry
discovers that he is not a better fighter than Bent, who now seems to
wield diabolical skill as well as intent. In the end Destry kills Bent
only through a lucky rifle shot after Bent has taken off laughing on
Destry's horse, leaving Destry himself beaten and sprawled in the
dirt. The shot hits the horse, and Destry watches from a distance as
Bent is thrown from the saddle. Destry sees Chester "lurch from the
saddle of the flying mare – lurch, so to speak, from the white cradle
of the moon. Both his arms were flung out; he dropped at once from
view against the rock of the cliff-face." Destry hears the impact:
"horrible, distinct, like huge gloved hands smitten together" (292).
    The simile of the giant hands carries mythic overtones. Destry
and Bent fight, it would seem, some ultimate, titanic duel before an
unearthly audience. But the final evolution of Harrison Destry moves
away from myth. Whereas Dan Barry's status as half-man, half-animal,
a "Pan of the Desert," renders him ultimately incapable of human
society, Destry comes to accept his role as an ordinary person.
Thinking at one point about the remaining jurors, Destry realizes,

"He, too, had been a child; so were they all, men and women, children also, needing help, protection, cherishing, but capable now and then and here and there of great deeds inspired by love and high aspiration" (269). At the end of the novel Destry proposes marriage to Charlie Dangerfield, who accepts. The impending marriage, also a sign of Destry's internal changes, "meant the end of the old days and the beginning of a new regime in Wham, for Harrison Destry had put away his Colt" (296). Faust thus gives Destry two lives, as David L. Fox has noted – "one the perfect embodiment of the two-fisted vindictive champion, the other the peace-loving reluctant hero" (Fox, 10).

In her *West of Everything* Jane Tompkins says that the essence of the western is seriousness. The experience of the hero is a contrast to the sense that life under ordinary conditions has little meaning. Thus the hero "never fritters away his time. Whatever he does, he gives it everything he's got because he's always in a situation where everything he's got is the necessary minimum."[11] These are the general terms of *Singing Guns* and *Destry Rides Again*, especially of the latter. Whether *Destry*, the most famous Max Brand novel, is also the best one will no doubt remain in dispute. In writing it Faust hit a peculiar form of paydirt, as the Hollywood versions of the story attest, but he was not motivated to use Harrison Destry in other stories as he had with Dan Barry and did with many other characters. Destry rode again only on the silver screen. For Faust himself, his most famous western hero may have represented an effort to break free of the pulp western format by turning to a more reflective character embracing – with high rhetorical flourishes – his own humanity and "the identity of the race which breathes through all men." It was an unusual effort for Max Brand.

Chapter Nine

Pulp Problems

Blackwell to-day refused the first novelette that I handed him. This time, he said the plot was all right but that the writing was "dated." He picked out a page that he thought was bad and read it aloud to me. He said it was old-fashioned. It wasn't a good page, but on the other hand I didn't think it was a bad page. He simply has come to a point where he cannot find anything good about my work.

– Letter to Dorothy Faust, 1932

Faust's most comfortable years as a writer were in the late 1920s and early 1930s, when he wrote almost exclusively for Frank Blackwell at *Western Story*. Out of 23 published titles in 1928, for example, only one appeared in some other magazine. Moreover, Blackwell seldom turned down a manuscript. At 5 cents a word, western fiction for Street & Smith was steady and lucrative work, earning Faust at least $50,000 a year. In Italy, where costs were low, the Fausts lived in great luxury.

Things began to change in 1932. By then the Depression had begun to affect even pulp magazines like *Western Story*, and the western market in general had begun to decline. Always financially overextended despite his incredible earnings, Faust now faced a desperate need to develop new outlets for his prose. His pseudonyms had to be attached to better westerns or to other kinds of stories, perhaps even in slick magazines.

Storm Warnings

Even while he was enjoying life in Italy, Faust never saw himself as anything other than an American writer. "No matter how long I stay on this side," he told his friend Dixie Fish in 1926, "I shall never become one of those Europeanized bastards." "But," he added, "it seems a lot more pleasant to be patriotic at a distance than at the front door of the Great Republic."[1] He maintained his distance for four years after leaving New York City in 1925. Not until 1929 did Faust return to the United States, doing so then to take an automobile trip across the country with Bob Davis, his old Munsey editor. Faust jumped at the opportunity to do so because he believed that the trip would help him to expand his material and his market. Even with steady acceptances by Blackwell, he seldom moved out of the realm of red ink. The solution, always, was more money.

Writing to Dorothy in February 1929 in response to her plea that he cut his American visit short and return to Florence the next month, Faust explained in lavish terms what he hoped to accomplish in the States. He said, for instance, that he needed to see the West again. But he also said that America in general offered him a great opportunity: "Return by the middle of March, indeed! You don't understand, old pie, that I am here not only as a gentleman farmer of western estates (ahem!) but also as a prospector looking for gold. Chunks and lumps and thick veins of it." He was impressed by the prosperity he saw in the months preceding the stock market crash. "With all this prodigious current of boiling gold running down the streets," he wrote Dorothy, "I don't want to leave before I've tried to dip out a bucketful without burning my hands off." His purpose was, as usual, to assure himself a comfortable life. "Then to get back to Florence, my family, my friends, and the knowledge that a long stretch of easy living and hard working lies ahead of me." For the time being, however, he wanted to absorb as much of America as he could: "There is more blood circulating in the arteries of America than in all the rest of the world, I believe."[2]

To some extent, these ambitious statements had been the product of Faust's meeting with his new agent. In 1925, when Bob Davis decided to move into semi-retirement, Leonard Bacon had recommended that Faust engage the services of Carl Brandt, who served as Stephen Vincent Benét's agent. Bacon was especially impressed with Brandt's literary acumen and believed that Faust would find him both capable and congenial. Faust took Bacon's advice and turned to Brandt for many of the services that Davis had been providing. But as long as Frank Blackwell took the vast majority of Faust's work for *Western Story*, there was little left for an agent to do other than handle the details of copyright assignment for books and films. When he met with Faust in 1929, however, Brandt told him that he should think about expanding his opportunities beyond Frank Blackwell.

Brandt no doubt stressed the booming film industry where "talkies" were now all the rage. For a moment, at least, Faust was caught up in the Hollywood myth of money and success. He told Dorothy that he wanted "to take a good hard look at Hollywood." He was jealous, in fact, of some success enjoyed by his old college friend, Sid Howard, who would eventually write the screenplay for *Gone with the Wind*. He told Dorothy that he would do better than Howard. Relying on the usual ethnic stereotype of Hollywood filmmakers, he wrote, "I am going to make some moving picture Jew thank God that he has met me, and I'm going to thank God that I've met the Jew."[3]

Nine years later, Faust would become a Hollywood fixture, but little developed out of his interest in 1929. He knew how to produce interesting stories for the pulps, at which he worked with great diligence. As long as the pulp market – namely, *Western Story* – was good, even if it did not make gold run down the streets, Faust had little incentive to change his work habits. He could crank out the fiction for Frank Blackwell, stay a step or two ahead of expenses, and still have some time for writing verse.

But the Great Depression changed things, even though its effect on Faust was not immediate. In fact, in 1931 Blackwell published more Faust material, at 5 cents a word, than he had in either 1929 or 1930. But clouds were gathering on the horizon of the pulp magazine business. The first inkling came to Faust in the summer of 1931 when one of his checks bounced because Blackwell refused a serial and therefore failed to deposit a payment that Faust had expected. It was, Faust told Dixie Fish, "the first serial he has rejected in nearly three years, and he only let me know six weeks later about the rejection."[4] Things soon got worse. By January 1932, according to Robert Easton, Blackwell had rejected an additional 300,000 words of Faust material. Moreover, Blackwell had cut Faust's rate to 4 cents a word. The cut reflected falling revenues from subscriptions. The rejections were a sign of Blackwell's hope that improving the quality of fiction would boost sales of the magazine.

Faust was not overly concerned about this turn of events at first, thinking that it reflected only a temporary downturn. Even Carl Brandt thought that the market would improve before long. "After all," he told Faust in August 1931, "we can't stay in the doldrums forever."[5] In early 1932, Blackwell did in fact restore Faust's rate to 5 cents a word.

Carl Brandt

Faust began 1932 only slightly worried about the problems with Frank Blackwell. He was flushed temporarily with another kind of success, the completion and publication of *Dionysus in Hades*, which he celebrated by arranging a trip to Egypt early in the spring. The only distinctly bad news – from America – was Tom Mix's mediocre performance in the first film version of *Destry Rides Again*. Faust thought that the difficulty with Blackwell could be worked out at long distance. Back from Egypt on 6 April 1932, Faust wrote Carl Brandt to discuss a new request from Blackwell, who had indicated to Brandt that he would like to see more novelettes and fewer serials. Faust wanted to make sure that the wordage would be sufficient. "Usually he takes 80,000 words per serial," he told Brandt. "You say twenty-five thousand words for novelettes but usually he takes thirty thousand. Will you make sure? 20 novelettes at thirty thousand is 600,000 words; 8 serials at 80,000 is 640,000. That makes 1,240,000 words for a year. Will you bear down on that point to make sure?"[6]

Blackwell had continued, however, to reject much of what Faust sent him. Brandt insisted that Faust come to New York, meet personally with Blackwell to resolve the editorial difficulties with *Western Story*, and work directly with Brandt himself to develop material for other magazines. Brandt knew that *Western Story* and other pulps were slipping. Therefore he told Faust, "you have got to provide the cure for its aliments, or we will all go down the drain together. We are fighting with our backs to the wall" (quoted in Easton, 161).

Brandt also wanted Faust to develop a market among the so-called slick magazines – generally printed on glossy paper – that had been growing in number, circulation, and prestige throughout the 1920s. Brandt knew better than Faust that the standards for the slicks were different than for the pulps. Whereas the primary purpose of the pulps was to sell stories to a mass reading audience, the slicks were more heavily funded by advertising revenue. They devoted a greater percentage of page space to advertisements and maintained more selective editorial policies. To some extent, the editorial judgments were intended to build an increasing middle-class base for advertising. Fiction in the slicks tended to be shorter than in the pulps and somewhat more sophisticated in style and subject matter. While not excluding western and adventure fiction from their pages, neither did the slick magazines invite it. Brandt was optimistic about Faust's prospects in the slicks, but he knew that Faust would have to make a concerted effort to shift his style and material in the direction desired by the magazines.

Faust was aware that slicks paid better, and in the early 1920s had placed a few pieces in *Country Gentleman* and *Collier's*. In 1927 Bob Davis reminded Faust of the slicks' rates when he bragged that he had sold one of his own stories to *Collier's* for 30 cents a word.[7] But with *Western Story* taking such huge quantities of his wordage, Faust had little reason to aim stories at other kinds of magazines. In 1930, according to a letter to Bob Davis, he sold a story to a slick magazine. "Perhaps it's the beginning of a new era for the old Jewish cowboy," he said.[8] But nothing followed at that time.

In late April of 1932 he arrived in New York City to work closely with Brandt. "I am seeing Brandt regularly," he wrote to Dorothy on 10 May. "He knows his business. I am getting a tremendous lot out of what he has to say."[9] Faust was especially taken by the idea of writing higher quality fiction for better magazines. "Oh," he told Dorothy, "think of the day when we need not be ashamed of what we write."[10] Even the pulp editors, Blackwell included, stressed the need for better prose. "For fifteen years I have simply given my typewriter the rein and let it gallop through many millions of words," Faust told Walter Morris Hart of the University of California, "but now it appears that I must rein in the trusty typewriter and turn out words that have a meaning and a weight of their own. . . . Can it be that the depression has stimulated the brain of the pulp paper reader? I hope not, but the editors tell me that is the fact."[11]

After a month in New York, Faust returned to Florence. On the ship with him was Cass Canfield, the president of Harper & Brothers, who discussed with him the possibility of Harper publishing a series of hardcover westerns under the pseudonym of Evan Evans. Faust liked the idea. The Harper imprimatur would encourage him to write at a different and the guarantee of a book publication might allow him to sell magazine versions somewhere other

than *Western Story*. His discussions with Blackwell had apparently
not gone well. In July Faust wrote to his agent in seeming desperation: "Brandt, can you find *no* editor with a magazine, no matter
how small, who would like to take my output, or a great part of it? If
Blackwell is, as I think, trying to ruin me or, what is worse,
'discipline' me, I'll work for a cent a word and love in order to help
any rival he may have."[12] To his friend Dixie Fish, however, he admitted that if he lost Blackell he had "only small markets and uncertain
ones to turn to." "As for the hard paper and the dollar a word stuff,"
he said, " God knows if I ever can do it. . . . Sometimes I think that
the great river of words which I have had to turn out during the past
fifteen years has washed away all my brains."[13]

To Brandt he admitted that his trip to New York had been "a
fool's trip." "In personal contact," he said, "there is something
about me that irritates people. . . . My only out is to live like a hermit,
which is the sort of life I lead in Europe." But Brandt would hear of
no such thing, and he insisted that Faust return as soon as possible
to New York. Faust knew that his situation was desperate. "I am living on borrowed money now," he told Brandt, "and that money is
now used up. . . . This is certainly the sink or swim moment with
me."[14] Thus on 5 September he boarded a ship again for the United
States. As he explained to Dorothy, "I *must* secure the pulp paper
market to give us security while we are paying off our debts, at the
least. But even while working on the pulps, I shall be grinding at the
hard paper stuff."[15]

He spent more than two months in the States in the fall of 1932,
renting a cottage in New Canaan, Connecticut, where he wrote
steadily, taking breaks only to visit with Brandt and editors in New
York. He patched up his relationship with Blackwell to some extent
and introduced himself to Kenneth Littauer, the fiction editor at *Collier's*. He knew, however, that slick magazines posed a challenge for
him. What they wanted was "editorialized" fiction – "that is to say,
stories to cheer up the depression, stories   .enounce divorce, etc.
etc."[16] Although Faust was willing to giv such material a try, and
did, he was more successful in turning ou. new and better material
for Blackwell. As he told Dorothy, "I m   set my teeth and agree
that he must have better writing from r   everything I write, I
must try to screw the standard up to   was particularly pleased when Blackwell accepted   about

a character named the Montana Kid, a manuscript that Harper would publish as a book. Faust also worked with Howard Bloomfield, the editor of Munsey's *Detective Fiction Weekly*, to develop a number of ideas for crime stories. Throughout his stay he wrote furiously, keeping three to 12 typists busy at the offices of Brandt & Brandt (Easton, 165).

According to Robert Easton, Faust was forced "for the first time in his life" to revise and rewrite even his pulp material (Easton, 165). This was especially true in the case of the *Silvertip* stories that he began for *Western Story*, where Frank Blackwell long had been interested in a series of short novels about the same character, with each novel to be published in a single issue of the magazine. Faust complied with stories about a character named Silvertip, a young man with tufts of gray hair above his temples. He had developed the idea during his first trip to New York in 1932, thinking that the series would provide him with steady work for Blackwell. But Blackwell rejected the first novel late in the fall of 1932. As the editor explained to Brandt, "A general objection of mine to the story . . . is that the entire story is clothed, in its manner of telling, in a very old world atmosphere. There is no American Cowboy 'relief' in it, as it were."[18] In reality, this was a common feature in many of Faust's westerns, but it had never been a problem when the market for pulp westerns was strong. Now, however, Faust had to change the medieval atmosphere of his story. By mid-December of 1932 he had rewritten his manuscript, which Blackwell then accepted, setting the stage for 12 additional Silvertip novels and steady income from Street & Smith throughout 1933, when 12 of the 13 novels were published in *Western Story*.

The two trips to America in 1932 represented a major turning point in Faust's career. He had done well for more than a decade on the strength of the pulp market in westerns and his own internal counsel. With changes in the marketplace, he, too, had to change. "Keeping Faust going financially," Robert Easton has said, "was like keeping a small nation afloat" (Easton, 166) – and the process now required constant attention to an increasingly variegated market. In the next five years Faust would achieve some success in the kind of "editorialized" stories demanded by the slicks. In the immediate future, however, he had to continue his close work with Brandt. As 1932 closed and he spent the spring of 1933 in Florence, he worked feverishly to provide material for Blackwell, for Howard Bloomfield at *Detective Story Weekly*, and for Dan Moore, the editor now at *Argosy*, attacking these pulp outlets with renewed vigor as his best hope for reducing his debt and sustaining his beloved style of life in Europe.

Slick Success

The quantity of Faust's publications in 1933 shows the success of his efforts. Robert Easton calculates his total for that year as more than 1.8 million words in print. He published 12 Silvertip novels in *Western Story* in addition to seven serials and seven novelettes. He also saw three serials appear in *Argosy* and two in *Detective Fiction Weekly*. His wordage in 1933 was, in fact, the highest of his career, and as the year progressed and the checks came in, Faust's financial concerns eased somewhat. But a rate cut at *Western Story* in March – lowering his payments to 3 cents a word – meant that his total income was at least $10,000 less than the year before. Even though pulp fiction – western, crime, historical adventure – was what Faust could produce with the least effort, not even he could take up the slack of an ever-declining market. If he did not fully realize this, his agent did. "You are almost on the spot of doing these hard-paper stories," Brandt told him. "What you need is to have Ken Littauer or me or both sitting next to your elbow just for a time" (quoted in Easton, 171).

In other words, Faust needed to be back in New York again, and for a longer stay than before. In the summer of 1933 he explained his plans to Leonard Bacon, saying that he might have to be in New York for as long as a year, "until I've definitely gotten into the hard paper market or have definitely failed." At the moment, he told Bacon, "the pulp market holds up amazingly well and there is no gun at my head as there has been when I made other trips to the States," but "I find it increasingly difficult to turn out the action stories – difficult to the point of nausea." His production of such stories in recent months had been greater, after all, than ever before. Yet he was now ready to assault the slick market aggressively, "to gain both in money and in self respect." His plan for the New York stay was "a simple life and nothing but work from morning till night."[19]

A year before, rationalizing his difficulty with slick material, he had found the stories in the *Saturday Evening Post* and *Collier's* to include "no more substance . . . than there is in a wild west by Max Brand, except that people are not falling over cliffs all the time."[20] Yet he yearned to join the crowd of writers who wrote for the slicks. "Will the day ever come," he asked Brandt, "and I have brains enough, to write hard-paper stuff?"[21] Determined "that Maxie can and must turn the trick," he departed for the United States – accompanied by Dorothy this time – in mid-September of 1933, having made arrangements for the children to stay behind with a governess and the servants in Florence. Dorothy's presence was a necessary precaution against the temptation of alcohol and the weaknesses of his heart, both physical and emotional. The year before, alone in New York, Faust had included a disturbing passage in a letter to Dorothy: "Bad news, my dear. I fell off the wagon and for two days I have been drinking too much. I didn't get really boiled and I kept away from females, but I had a lot too much to drink, and now I'm shaky, the heart has the blind staggers, and I feel horrible despair. My work is behind, my time has been wasted, and, as always when I'm sunk, I most desperately want you and it seems to me that I cannot face the oncoming of night. I wonder why I can be forty years old and such a fool."[22] The couple rented a house in Katonah, New York, and Brandt arranged for Faust to occupy an office down the hall from his own in the city. "With Dorothy at hand to guard him from excesses" – as Easton phrases it – and Brandt next to his elbow, he set out to discover his place in the world of slick magazines (Easton, 173).

The Fausts stayed in the United States for nine months, spending the last month in Virginia. The results of Faust's efforts during this period were mixed. With bills to pay, he and Brandt continued to work the pulp market for whatever it was worth but aimed an increasing number of stories at magazines other than *Western Story*. *Argosy*, for instance, took five serials for publication in 1934. Although his success with the slicks was modest, Faust managed to break through with 1934 stories in *Liberty*, *American Magazine*, and *Collier's*. He also wrote two stories, published under his real name, for the highbrow *Harper's*, receiving $250 per story. The largest gain from his American stay in 1933 and 1934, however, was a much expanded visibility for Max Brand. With the byline beginning to appear in the slicks, Brandt thought he might be able to leverage additional magazine acceptances, new book reprints, and possibly the sale of more film rights to Hollywood.

Faust and his wife returned to Italy in late May of 1934. He hoped somehow to continue living there while making gains in the New York magazine market. In late October he made his first big sale to the slicks, a novel-length society story taken by *Liberty* and published as a serial titled "Name Your Price"; the magazine paid $5,000, more than twice what he was getting from the pulps for a serial. But such acceptances did not come easily. "The hard-paper markets treat me kindly enough," he wrote to Bob Davis, "but they take six weeks to make a decision, unlike R.H.D. [Davis] who would have a complete opinion ready on Friday morning for a serial received on Thursday."[23] Yet the slicks appeared to be his only future. By 1935 the *Western Story* market was a thing of the past; only two novelettes appeared that year, for which Faust received merely 2 cents a word. *Argosy* and *Detective Fiction Weekly* were still taking his stories (a total of eight serials and 13 novelettes in 1935), but rates were not high and the prospects for the future were, at best, uncertain.

Remaining in Italy was problematic under such circumstances. Brandt was good at selling his work, but Faust needed to be in closer contact with editors. Thus, after a year of uninterrupted residence in Italy, he decided to attack the New York market in person one more time. In August 1935 he brought Dorothy and the three children with him to the city for a ten-month stay. The months in New York were well spent, resulting in stories taken by *Collier's*, *McCall's*, *Cosmopolitan*, *This Week*, and, eventually, the *Saturday Evening Post*. Faust's first sale to *Cosmopolitan* was drawn from the experiences of Dixie Fish, now a respected urologist in New York. Titled "Internes Can't Take Money," the story introduced a young doctor named Kildare to the reading public.

By June 1936, when the family returned to the villa in Florence, Faust had indeed succeeded in redirecting his career. No longer a single-genre writer as he had been during most of the 1920s, he was now familiar in pseudonym to a much wider audience and knowingly capable of satisfying the editorial expectations of even a highbrow magazine like *Harper's*. For the moment, at least, he was also free of debt, and while his life would never again be as settled as it had been during his first five years in Italy, he could see some ways out of the Depression. The slicks were one way. Hollywood might be another. Moreover, his efforts at the typewriter for the past five years had also pushed his pulp work in new directions: historical adventures, American Indian stories, detective and spy fiction, and fresh approaches to the western. Max Brand, by 1936, was a much more versatile American author than he had been in 1931.

Chapter Ten

Indian Stories

Rusty leaned forward on his left hand; and with the right, he thrust out the length of the knife into the body of Major Arthur Marston. . . .
"God!" breathed the major. "A – a damned – a white – Indian."
— Max Brand, *Frontier Feud* (1934)

In his early westerns Faust almost never used Native American characters, nor was the presence of Indians an important element in the settings of his stories. Unconcerned with the usual mythology of the frontier, he was free to envision the West as merely a stage for action rather than a setting endowed with special historical, geographical, or cultural features. Indians were therefore no more necessary than were grand vistas or ghost towns. Faust wrote about them only when they were part of the white hero's adventure. As a result, his early stories seldom insist on a particular point of view about Native Americans. In 1932, however, as he was struggling to redirect his prose away from complete reliance on *Western Story Magazine*, he approached Indians as subjects in a new way.

Early Stories

Indians generally serve as an exotic, romanticized experience for his white heroes in such *Western Story* pieces as the "Border Bandit" series, three 1926 novelettes in which a New England-born hero is kidnapped by Comanches. Some Faust stories resemble James Fenimore Cooper's Leatherstocking series in their emphasis on intertribal conflict, especially between Cheyennes and Pawnees. More rarely, they draw a moral distinction between good and evil Indians. Edgar Chapman has noted that *Tamer of the Wild* (1931), for instance, was one of the earliest popular stories in America to portray Apaches in a sympathetic light.[1]

Such general facts do not provide much evidence of a carefully considered judgment of Indian-white relations on the frontier. Yet Faust's Indian stories adopt popular attitudes and attempt to bring Native Americans into the climate of opinion that sustained magazine fiction and mass-audience novels. These two features – popular images of Indians and Faust's own shaping of those images – often work together in his stories. In *Lucky Larribee* (1932), for instance, a story mainly about the capture of a proud wild stallion, a Cheyenne chief explains why his people kill the horses of dead warriors; while his words give some credence to the perception of Indians as childishly superstitious, they also tweak whites for their absence of spirituality. "They are killing three horses," Shouting Thunder says. "So, you see, the souls of the dead men will be able to ride over the thin blue prairies above our heads. That is what we believe, though I know that you white men believe nothing except the flesh in the meat pot and the fire that boils it."[2] This passage also indicates the sense of pride that Faust's later Indians generally exhibit. Typically they are not the "underdog heroes" that his white protagonists often are.

Faust's own motivations for writing about Indians were varied. To a large extent, he simply needed new material for his narratives, although some evidence indicates that his interest ran deeper than that, especially in the early 1930s. Before then, most noticeably in *The White Cheyenne* (published first as a *Western Story* serial in 1925), a story about a giant white man raised by Cheyennes, Faust's portrayal of Indians often fell prey too quickly to stereotypical images. In that narrative, the white Cheyenne, named Lost Wolf, is eventually returned to white culture. Although the narrative pays a certain degree of respect to Cheyenne culture, it draws a definite moral line between Indian and white. A minister in the novel, Charles Gleason, explains this in no uncertain terms: "Your Indian gets his greatest glory out of a night attack, and the safe throat-cutting of a sleeping warrior. A woman's scalp looks as well as a man's, and a child's is as good as a woman's in Indian logic. That's why their ideas can't fit in with those of Lost Wolf."[3]

New Intentions

A few years later Faust was influenced by his reading of George Bird
Grinnell and J. W. Schultz, both sympathetic to native cultures.[4]
Grinnell, an amateur anthropologist, wrote sensitively of such matters as Plains Indian tales and rituals. Schultz's *My Life as an Indian*,
first published in 1907, was drawn to Faust's attention by Bob Davis
in 1926.[5] These two writers and possibly others (in the late 1920s
Faust amassed a considerable library of western Americana) encouraged Faust to approach Indians as subjects with a new seriousness.

In late 1932, when Faust was working hard with Carl Brandt and
various editors in an effort to reshape his fiction for the slick magazine market, he also turned to *Argosy* as a possibility. It had been
seven years since he had placed work in that magazine. During his
fall visit to New York, however, he discussed a new story idea with
Dan Moore, *Argosy*'s editor at the time. In December 1932 he
expanded on the idea in a long letter to Moore. The chief character
was to be "a white boy kidnapped and raised by the Indians." For
Faust, this was hardly a new idea, but he wanted the story to express
both a white and an Indian point of view. Even though he said he
might "show the naïveté of the Indian culture contrasted with that of
the white man," he also wanted, if possible, to "point out how completely the two races failed to understand one another." The main
character, caught between white and Indian allegiances, would thus
express a "tragic viewpoint." A central part of the story would
involve an "enchanted valley" held sacred by the Indians but desired
by the whites; such a valley, Faust said, would serve as "a symbol of
the wilderness which white men pollute."[6]

For Faust himself, the idea of such a story – possibly a series of
stories, with each conclusion "dissolved again by the double pull on
the hero" – had genuine appeal, as he explained to Moore:

> You know about what I can do, though I don't think I've ever sent you any
> careful writing. I hope you'll be able to look through this sketch and into it
> and tell me just what situations seem to you promising and what ones do not.
> It is true that a goldrush, a couple of Indian wars, and the strife of ideas
> between two races may seem too broad a canvas to work on for an action
> magazine, but I'm tired of writing drool and would really like to get my shoul-
> der under a weight worth lifting. The melodrama and bloodshed I don't mind.
> I like it. And there are other aspects of the story . . . that appeal to me a lot,

and particularly the sense of the Indian life which was naked to nature, and the white man's life which was closed away from it with walls. The attempt will be much more ambitious than anything I've ever undertaken, and as a matter of fact I didn't know that I could get all boiled up with excitement about a prose theme, but for the moment, at any rate, I'm keen to go ahead. I've written about a million and a half words or more of Indian stuff, but I've never before gone at the thing on such a scale.

The only possible problem, Faust thought, "may be that this is stronger meat than an action magazine can stand."[7]

To some extent his fear was borne out by Moore's return letter. Even though the *Argosy* editor told Faust to go ahead and build "a novel which will be pleasing to your own artistic soul," he suggested that the writer tone down the anti-white elements he had mentioned in his sketch. The hero can be half-Indian and half-white, Moore said, but "the white should dominate," and in the end the hero should keep the friendship of Indians but live with whites. "I think you want to watch the danger of enlisting your sympathies too much on the Indian side," he added, reminding Faust that *Argosy*'s readers were, after all, white. He thought that Faust would have "a great book" if he wrote a story satisfying to himself "yet avoiding the pitfalls of too much Indian propaganda and blackening the white expansion unjustly."[8]

Red Hawk and Rusty Sabin

Faust proceeded over the next two years to write not one but three novels based on his original concept. The central character of these stories is the white Indian, a young man adopted by Cheyennes after the massacre of his mother. His Indian name is Red Hawk; his white name is Rusty Sabin. The stories about this character are in some ways less than what Faust had anticipated when he sketched his plans to Dan Moore in 1932, but they still represent a far more complex treatment of Indians and the matter of western expansion than anything in his earlier fiction. Also, while the three serials seem to incorporate Moore's admonition not to overemphasize "Indian propaganda," their depiction of whites is ambiguous at best and often highly critical.

The stories involve, first of all, some confusing problems of titles because they were republished under different titles and pen names. The first serial appeared in *Argosy* under the Max Brand byline and titled "The White Indian," but it was published a year later (in 1934) as the George Owen Baxter novel *Call of the Blood*. In 1973 it was reissued by Dodd, Mead and then as a Warner Books paperback with the Max Brand byline restored and the title (a third one) of *War Party*. The second serial was originally "Brother of the Cheyennes," by Max Brand; in 1935 it appeared under the same title as a Baxter book and then in 1973 as Max Brand's *Frontier Feud*. The third serial, "The Sacred Valley," became *Cheyenne Gold* when it was published as a book in 1972, with the authorship credited to Max Brand. These matters of title and republication are furthermore complicated by the decision of Dodd, Mead to reprint the third serial (in 1972) before the first two. For the sake of convenience, however, the Red Hawk-Rusty Sabin stories are best identified by means of the most recent and available titles: *War Party*, *Frontier Feud*, and *Cheyenne Gold*.

While the series was conceived and written during a time in Faust's career when he was redirecting his prose toward the slick magazine market, it is rich in traditional pulp magazine features. The three novels include mistaken identities, close brushes with death, trickery by characters whose behavior is unalterably evil, and an ongoing romantic triangle. In the first and best of the novels Faust also heightens the conflict by including a variant of the Oedipus story in which Rusty Sabin almost kills his own father, whom he does not recognize as such until the end of the narrative.

In that first novel, *War Party*, Faust develops his white Cheyenne hero almost exactly as he had outlined the character to Dan Moore. Rusty Sabin, known only as Red Hawk in the beginning, finds that he is unable to endure a Cheyenne manhood ceremony. He is then trained in white ways after he is rejected – though only temporarily – by the Indians who reared him. He regains the respect of the Cheyennes, however, on his capture of a great white stallion. In the important, *Oedipus*-like subplot, he meets Wind Walker, a legendary frontiersman feared by the Indians, who turns out to be his own father, still mourning the massacre of his wife and presumably his son years before at the hands of an unredeemable Cheyenne named Dull Hatchet. The plot is further complicated by two attractive

women: a half-white Indian named Blue Bird and Maisry Lester, a
white with whom Rusty Sabin eventually falls in love. At the end of
the novel Rusty recognizes Wind Walker as his father – Marshall
Sabin – and settles the question of his own identity as the white
Rusty Sabin, not the Indian Red Hawk: "When his mind cleared, . . .
it was as though the Cheyennes had withdrawn to a distance. Yes, it
was as though the great red tribe had been seen marching off into
the horizon, with the White Indian, Red Hawk, among them."[9]

In the other two Rusty Sabin novels, Faust makes much less of
the conflicts within his protagonist. In *War Party*, despite the melodramatic action and coincidences, Sabin's internal conflict is real. He
truly does not know whether he is Indian or white. His consciousness includes shards of memory from early childhood, including the
massacre of his mother, and his Cheyenne upbringing. Not until the
end of the story does he solve his problem of self-identity, and even
then the solution is not easy.

But the other stories are fueled by specific actions of other characters rather than the internal conflicts of the hero. In *Frontier Feud*
and *Cheyenne Gold* Rusty Sabin becomes a go-between for both the
Cheyennes and the whites. In the second novel, for instance, he
temporarily assumes command of Cheyenne warriors in what he
assumes will be a last-ditch effort to stop white westward advances.
The conflict is avoided, though, when Sabin forces the villainous
leader of the white troops, Major Marston, to fight him alone. Edgar
Chapman has observed that Faust's portrayal of Major Marston in
Frontier Feud "is a harshly satirical caricature of the military mind"
and seemingly "modelled on an imaginative conception of Custer"
(Chapman, 37). In fact, the novel generally focuses on western mili-
tarism even though Faust allows the evils of military behavior in the
American West to be represented by a single reprehensible character
who claims, "I'm going to write my name in Cheyenne blood – write
it so damned deep that it will never come out of the earth."[10] In the
end, however, Marston himself dies a bloody death at the hands of
Rusty Sabin.

Throughout the first two Rusty Sabin novels, the divided nature
of Sabin's allegiances is one of blood versus emotion. He is white by
blood, which is the main point established by the Wind Walker-Mar-
shall Sabin subplot of the first novel. The 1934 book title of the
novel – *Call of the Blood* – identifies its theme far better than either

the title of the serial or the 1973 reissued book. The first story concludes with the protagonist stating his intention to obey the call of
his white blood that has been made known to him through the discovery of his father. In the second novel he is called back to his
Cheyenne values largely by the duplicity of white leaders. *Frontier
Feud*, the second novel, is undivided in its sympathy for Indians,
omitting Indian villains (such as the evil Dull Hatchet of the first
novel) from its cast of characters. In fact, it is the power of Sweet
Medicine, the name given to the spiritual power associated with the
Cheyenne's sacred valley, coveted by whites, that miraculously heals
Rusty Sabin from the wounds he suffers at the hands of Major
Marston.

The Indian-ness of Rusty Sabin, while powerful, is never complete. If his spiritual affinity for Cheyenne values prevents him from
fully participating in the ethos of white civilization, his blood ties
make it impossible for him truly to be a Cheyenne. He is even more a
divided man than is Cooper's Leatherstocking, who maintains a
steady commitment to white Christian values. By contrast, Rusty
Sabin's ties to white culture are more emotional – and are symbolized by his unavoidable romantic attachment to the white woman,
Maisry Lester. This attachment is made clear in conventional sentiments at the end of the first novel. At the moment when love is rec-
ognized, "Rusty felt that they were rushing together out of the world
of flesh, and that they were sweeping through a measureless domain
of the spirit" (188). In the last paragraph of that novel, Rusty Sabin
and Maisry Lester are headed east on a riverboat. With them is the
great white stallion that Sabin has captured. But he, too, is a captive,
for Maisry stands at the rail of the boat "with the look of one who
has plucked a wild bird out of the sky and has made it her own
forever" (189).

In *Frontier Feud* Sabin is pulled back temporarily from Maisry,
who becomes a pawn in the villainous deceptions of Major Marston.
Maisry is not a particularly well-developed character, especially in
contrast to the half-Cheyenne Blue Bird, which again illustrates the
general sympathy for Indians that Faust felt as he wrote the serials.
In the final novel, *Cheyenne Gold*, the conventional romantic expectations represented by Maisry are pushed further into the background. Instead, the conflict focuses directly on the Cheyenne
sacred valley ("The Sacred Valley" being the title of the original

Argosy serial). Again there is a white villain, this time a would-be settler named Galway who learns that there is gold in the valley. Obviously, Faust based his story loosely on the historical struggle for the Black Hills, sacred to many Plains Indians, where gold was discovered in the 1870s. Prior to Galway's effort to steal the sacred valley from the Cheyennes, Sabin had appeared destined to marry Maisry Lester and "settle down to a white man's life in some eastern city, wearing hot, stiff, containing clothes."[11] The plot of *Cheyenne Gold* ensures that he need not worry about such a fate.

In a series of dramatic events, Sabin helps the Cheyennes to repel Galway and 100 whites who assist him in the attempt to gain the valley and its gold. Sabin must kill Galway himself. Much of the story develops around a suspenseful subplot in which Blue Bird, daughter of a Cheyenne woman and a white trader, is captured and held hostage by Galway. This part-Indian woman begins to tug on Sabin's emotions, freeing him of his previous emotional attachment to Maisry. In neither of the first two novels does the white hero respond in such a manner to Blue Bird, but his newfound desire for her in *Cheyenne Gold* is an essential element of the story. Largely because of this, the novel ends with Rusty Sabin truly divided in his sentiments, the conclusion truly "dissolved," as Faust had explained his intentions in his 1932 scenario, "by the double pull on the hero." In fact, the last words of the story come in the form of a letter from the hero to four other characters who have been present in all three novels: Maisry Lester, Blue Bird, her white father, and Sabin's Cheyenne blood brother, Standing Bull. Like another divided American hero, Sabin decides to light off by himself. Signing the letter with both of his names – Red Hawk and Rusty Sabin – he leaves the following message:

> O my friends, where I go among you I bring sorrow. The red men sharpen their knives against one another. The white men commit murder. No trust comes to me.
>
> My own heart is divided, for if my right hand held that of Maisry, my left hand would go out to the Blue Bird. These things cannot be. . . .
>
> Farewell. My heart aches. My heart is colder than a winter morning. To die is not great sorrow; but it is not the will of the god that I should live among you. The red of my heart and the white of my skin have cursed me. (158)

It was an unusual conclusion for an *Argosy* story. Faust's editor had wanted the white side of the hero to dominate and had expected the story to avoid "Indian propaganda." Faust was torn between editorial expectations and his own vicarious sympathy for Indians, prompted no doubt by his reading of George Bird Grinnell's work on Plains Indian cultures. As a result, the Huck Finn–like ending of *Cheyenne Gold* may have been Faust's only honest way out. His original intention, after all, was to "point out how completely the two races failed to understand one another." In this he succeeded – while still meeting the demands of a pulp magazine for exciting adventure.

The Red Hawk–Rusty Sabin series, whatever its stylistic and structural flaws, stands out among Faust's pulp-magazine fiction as an effort to approach western material from a historical and critical perspective. In fact, the three serials were revisionist efforts intended, with a degree of seriousness unmatched by any of Faust's other pulp work, not only to change readers' minds about Indians but also to correct his own earlier perspective. In *The White Cheyenne* (1925), writing without benefit of Grinnell or Schultz, whose *My Life as an Indian* is in part the story of his marriage to a Blackfoot woman, Faust created an entirely different kind of "white Indian" story, one where Indian-ness is not a virtue. The Cheyennes in the 1925 story are monstrous in battle and dance, and the most admirable characters are white. But from 1932 to 1935, as he produced the *Argosy* serials about Red Hawk, he redirected his sentiments, indicting whites for the tragic consequences of western expansion, and wrote a trilogy of stories that looks forward to Thomas Berger's *Little Big Man*. As literary works, the Rusty Sabin novels are flawed, but as Edgar Chapman says, they are still good enough "to make one wish that Brand had forgotten all commercial considerations and written for once with high art as his only aim" (Chapman, 38).

Chapter Eleven

Last Westerns

"He means," said Buck, "that now and then a man can get in a good quick snapshot. He don't mean that people can shoot nowadays the way that they used to when the old timers were stepping high. Maybe the liquor we drink ain't so good for the nerves. Maybe we take to beer too much. Maybe prohibition done something to all of us. But we ain't the same as the old timers."

– Max Brand, *The Streak* (1936)

When Faust wrote the first Silvertip novel for *Western Story* late in 1932, he was desperate to develop material for Blackwell and boost his sagging income. Perhaps it was his desperation that prompted him to reach back to *The Untamed* for a way to end his story. Jim Silver, the hero, facing the possibility of marriage to the beautiful woman to whom he is attracted, is instead called away Dan Barry – like by the sight and sound of wild geese. Taken at face value, this repetition of a earlier deus ex machina suggests that Faust had run out of new ideas for westerns. In fact, writing to Dorothy from New York in September 1932, he admitted the same: "When I come to the writing of western stories, I have so thoroughly exhausted most of my possibilities that I don't find new stones to describe, or new emotions, or a new lingo for new ideas."[1]

In reality, as he wrote fewer westerns after 1932, groping for effective approaches and revising more than usual to meet the stiffened editorial expectations of a declining pulp market, Faust found at least an occasional new idea for a western, perhaps even a "new lingo" in a few cases. This is especially true of the work that he did for outlets other than *Western Story*. The Red Hawk – Rusty Sabin series is one example. In more traditional stories, those containing what Frank Blackwell called "the American cowboy 'relief,'" Faust tended after 1932 to write in a much more self-conscious, even facetious, style than he ever had before. It was almost as if he wished at the end of his career as a "western writer" to turn the conventions of the western into its subject.

The Montana Kid

One of Faust's ideas for reviving his income had been a series of western novels for Harper & Brothers. He had developed this idea in the late spring of 1932 when he returned to Europe on a ship where Cass Canfield, the president of Harper & Brothers, was a fellow passenger. Canfield was interested in Faust because Zane Grey novels, the publisher's primary western staple, were no longer selling well. Faust convinced Canfield that some of his own work, published under a fresh pseudonym, could help Harper to gain a new dominance in the western book market (Easton, 160-61).[2] Faust lost no time in pursuing the opportunity. Within a few months he had completed the first of three novels that Harper would eventually publish under a new pseudonym: Evan Evans.

The three novels present the exploits of a single Anglo hero in Mexico. The hero is known only as the Montana Kid. The first story, *Montana Rides*, was published as a serial in early 1933; the second, *Montana Rides Again*, appeared more than a year later in April of 1934; and the final story, *The Song of the Whip*, did not see print until 1936. Harper published each of the novels as a book a few months after its magazine appearance, with a Harper book thus appearing in 1933, 1934, and 1936.[3] The three novels are an important part of Faust's work for several reasons. First, they represent sustained work aimed at a new kind of audience: readers of hardcover novels. Second, they demonstrate Faust's interest in both exploiting and exploring ethnic stereotypes. Finally, the sense of development from the first to the third novel suggest that as the 1930s progressed, Faust grew increasingly uneasy with the expectations of the western. As a result, he sought to revive the genre by incorporating elements of class conflict. In the last novel, *The Song of the Whip*, he produced a story that could be read, certainly to his own surprise, as an example of proletarian fiction.

The name of the hero – the Montana Kid – is unexplained in the stories but conjures up associations with the Texas-to-Montana cattle drives. This cowboy, however, has nothing to do with cows. In fact, he does not even know how to use a lariat. His job is to ride both point and drag on mystery and adventure but still be a sensitive humanitarian within his rough western exterior. The first novel begins in a Texas border town where the Montana Kid first appears as an insouciant saloon patron, laconic in speech and semi-tough in behavior. He is convinced by con men to pose as the long-lost son of a local rancher until he suffers an attack of conscience and decides to find the real son in Mexico, from whence a few rumors have come during the 20 years of the son's absence. His search is also motivated by his romantic feelings for Ruth Lavery, the sister of the lost brother. Most of the novel is taken up with search-and-pursuit action as the Kid discovers Dick Lavery, the brother, deep in Mexico, where for two decades he has lived as the adopted son of a Mexican bandit named Mateo Rubriz.

Two aspects of *Montana Rides* deserve attention. First is the initial and blatant stereotyping of Mexicans, which is as egregious throughout the first two-thirds of the novel as it is in any work by Faust. The Mexicans are "greasers," violent and untrustworthy. Eventually, however, Faust provides a form of redemption for his own racist portrayal of the Mexicans, a redemption that continues throughout the remaining two novels of the series.

In *Montana Rides* this change from racism to empathy occurs through a strong father-son theme, common in much of Faust's writing and an important aspect of this novel. The Montana Kid helps Dick Lavery to escape Mateo Rubriz, his foster father. Initially this escape is precisely that, a removal from harm's way and a return to his rightful Anglo place in life. In the end, however, Mateo Rubriz tracks down the Kid and Dick Lavery with a vengeance motivated more by fatherly affection than by ill will. Montana realizes that the real passion in the Mexican is fatherly and that he had become Dick Lavery's father in all respects except blood. Moreover, Lavery himself, who has been living under the name of Tonio Rubriz, realizes that his experiences in Mexico have given him a Mexican heritage for which he feels pride rather than disgust. In short, at the end of the novel, the Mexican villain and most of what he had stood for in the first part of the novel is translated, for the reader's benefit, into surprisingly sympathetic terms.

The other two novels suggest that the conclusion of *Montana Rides* was, in effect, an act of discovery for Faust, for in them Mateo

Rubriz shares the hero's billing with the Montana Kid. The second novel, *Montana Rides Again*, seems almost carefully calculated to dispel the "greaser" image of Mexicans created by the first story. Mateo Rubriz is now a Robin Hood–like *bandido* working on behalf of the church and the peasantry of northern Mexico. There are even occasional allusions to the Mexican Revolution in the novel, and Rubriz bears a slight resemblance in portrayal to Pancho Villa. With such a shift in the depiction of a character whose relationship to the Anglo hero was once that of a degenerate villain, the role of the Montana Kid becomes problematic. The first novel ended in classic western fashion with hints of a romantic union between Montana and Ruth Lavery. The second novel sets out to free Montana from this entanglement. Ultimately Montana leaves Ruth on the morning of their planned wedding, doing so with a touch of hardness quite unusual in a Faust character: "She only stared at him. Her lips were parted a little. She looked older; she seemed to be squinting at a bright, distant light. The future, as like as not. Montana tried to feel sorry, but couldn't."[4] Following this cold departure from an Anglo woman, the hero not only joins up with the Mexican bandit Rubriz but finds himself attracted to a woman named Rosita, a Mexican.

In addition to rearranging the ethnic sympathies of the first novel, *Montana Rides Again* also plunges into graphically violent action. It is a very bloody story, rivaling even *The Sword Lover*, and drawing its sanction for violence from class conflict. Opposed to the bandits are the Mexican government forces who are also the obvious oppressors of the poor. The Montana Kid is given the opportunity, for instance, to see helpless women and children beaten by the government forces.

The final novel of the series, *The Song of the Whip*, takes Faust's Mexican setting and imposes on it a plot of furious action. The title refers to the sound of a whipping that Montana hears at the beginning of the story as a Mexican peon is flogged by government officials. By the time the novel ends the count of battles and deaths is staggering. Brother Pascual, a Friar Tuck–like figure associated with Mateo Rubriz's gang, sums things up in comments to Montana – "El Keed" to his Mexican compatriots – in the closing pages:

> "When you come south," said the friar, "there is trouble. . . . A peon is flogged, and that was too bad . . . and to help the peon you crossed the river

into danger. . . . How many men have died since then because a peon was flogged?"

Montana could not speak a word.

"Young 'Tonio' [Dick Lavery] has left his father's ranch; a dancing-girl has been riding under gunfire," said the friar. "A lady of great place has damaged her name – who can say how much? . . . A famous hacienda has been looted; a peon has been turned into a bandit; every Rurale in Mexico has been turned into a savage beast; an outlaw has passed into fire and out again; and a poor friar has left his flock and gone wandering far into sin, I greatly fear . . . because El Keed rode south! Because he heard 'The Song of the Whip'!"[5]

Such is the scope of Faust's last pulp western novel, his final effort at reaching out with a western adventure serial to the readers of magazines like *Argosy* and *Western Story*. In this case it was *Argosy*, which had also published the second Montana Kid novel, following the appearance of the first one in *Western Story*. Even though Faust wrote the series under the expectation of the Harper imprint in hardcover novels and the vague hope of appearing first in slick magazines, the stories appeared as pulp western serials, the last of their kind for Faust. He left the pulp western business on a high note, with all stops pulled out.

In *The Song of the Whip* the Montana Kid is again portrayed as a person of strange nonchalance, physically involved in action yet at times almost carelessly distant in mood. His responses to the affections shown by women – the dancing girl Rosita and an upper-class Mexican named Dorotea – is especially careless. This is explained by another character, who says, "There's nothing in the world that he cares about except a horse to carry him into trouble and a gun to fight his way out again" (61). His response to social injustice is more direct and immediate even though it, too, is occasionally hidden behind a screen of indifference in the Montana Kid's mood. Yet none of this inhibits Montana from assuming the role of a revolutionary hero when he leads a force of peons and bandits against the hacienda of the rich and corrupt Lerraza family. Montana is also a singer, expressing his views in the lyrics of his songs. The title of the novel, in fact, refers not only to the song of the actual whip as Montana hears it being applied to a peon but also to a song he sings. This "Song of the Whip," with the whip itself as persona, states the unusually strong lower-class bias of the novel:

I am weary of slaves;
Their hides are too tough;
Many blows have thickened their skins;
I must cut deep, very deep,
To open the peon's heart
And let out the screaming.

But I could make music flow
From bodies more tender.
A song of howling, a shriek
From delicate lips could draw.

Give me no more the tough back of a peon,
A Juan or Jose, a Pedro or Leon,
But give me a lord from a lordly terraza,
A Diaz, Angeles, or a Lerraza. (5)

The most unusual aspect of the *Song of the Whip* is its free-wheeling pleasure in dealing with Mexican life. Even though the novel is rich in stereotypes of Mexicans, reflected even in the depicted pronunciation of "El Keed," it presents its lower-class characters with considerable respect. The two women in the story are particularly strong characters, Rosita with her proletarian hardness of mind and Dorotea Lerraza with her loyalties divided several ways. At the end of the story, when Dorotea has sided with the peons and bandits in resistance to her own family, Montana questions her motives, stating, "But after all, you're a Lerraza." Her reply is, "After all, I'm a Mexican" (69). The respect for things Mexican also shows up in the interaction between the Montana Kid and Mateo Rubriz. Whereas in *Montana Rides* Rubriz was originally portrayed as an ethnic villain, he emerges in *The Song of the Whip* as a co-hero. His stature in the novel is communicated in his own words at the end when he tells Montana, "My God! amigo, what a wonderful thing it is that in such a little world there should be two such men as you and I" (189).

New Ideas

In 1932 Faust had doubted that he could find "a new lingo for new ideas" in the western. Certainly the Montana Kid novels were told in a new lingo. In *Smugglers' Trail*, originally published as an *Argosy* serial in 1934 seven months after *Montana Rides*, he had also used some of the elements apparent in the Montana Kid stories: a pro-Mexican flavor and a bias in favor of the lowest social classes. In *Smugglers' Trail*, however, the ethnic focus is complicated by the inclusion of Chinese who are portrayed as victims of a drug smuggling operation between Mexico and Texas. Although some of the Chinese characters are portrayed in stereotypical ways – as mysterious and inscrutable – their values and manner are respected. "Perhaps the whole majesty of the timeless orient was speaking now from the tongue of Sam Li," thinks the Anglo hero (named Ripley) at one point, "and what did Ripley comprehend except houses, beef on the hoof, ropes, and saddles and guns?"[6] The villains in the story are whites.

In addition to different ethnic contexts, Faust sought other "new ideas" in the last years of his career as a writer of westerns. In *The Streak*, first published as an *Argosy* serial in January 1936 immediately before *The Song of the Whip*, he produced a story that takes many humorous liberties with the conventions of the western. *The Streak* is a story in which the hero faces accusations of being a great gunman when in reality he is so poor with a gun that he packs it around with no bullets in it. His fame derives from an incident in which he accidentally fired a single shot into the air and, by so doing, frightened off several would-be bank robbers. The only real talents he possesses are a general likableness and an ability to fall in love.

The Streak is a comic western, entirely different in mode and mood from many other Faust novels. In the Dan Barry series, the hero is driven by natural, primitive forces within him to seek revenge. Barry is a superhuman hero whose most faithful companions are two superanimals. The hero of *The Streak*, Blondy Jim Terrance, is not super anything. Even his reputation is wrong. "The Streak" is the name given him because people presume that he streaks toward danger and adventure. In reality he streaks away from danger whenever possible.

But the differences go beyond character. *The Streak* is antimythological in many ways. Its western hero is created by default, not by heroism. Dan Barry expresses the wildness of a mythological west where the villainy of villains is almost as great as his own

Achilles-like heroic potential. But in The Streak the hero is falsely accused of having murdered a local money lender. When a townsman demands that Blondy be killed, the gunman hired for the job is Calico Charlie, a strangely nonmasculine badman who wears perfume and whose valet is a huge black man named Shine. The novel could have been written by E. L. Doctorow.

Furthermore, *The Streak* is set in a day of automobiles and Prohibition. There are still horses around, but the story makes it clear that the legendary West has passed. In the opening scene of the novel, in fact, Blondy and two of his pals are listening to a phonograph machine.

Ultimately *The Streak* plays games with the same western mystique that Faust helped create in *The Untamed* and other early westerns. Nowhere is this more apparent than when Blondy realizes what Mary Layton, who had fallen in love with him earlier, thinks of him after his accidental and undeserved acquisition of gunman status: "She thinks that there's something dark in my past. . . . She thinks that some day terrible things will be known about me and then what sort of heritage would she have for our children, besides being widowed when she's young?"[7] There is no darkness in Blondy's past; he is the light and comic reverse side of such characters as Dan Barry, Zane Grey's Lassiter, and Jack Schaefer's Shane.

Dust across the Range

By 1936 Faust's problem as a writer of westerns was clear. Work such as the Montana Kid novels and *The Streak* represented new directions for the genre. But the market was gone. His most trusted outlet, Frank Blackwell of *Western Story*, published four novelettes and four serials in 1934, two novelettes in 1935, and nothing at all in 1936. *Argosy* continued to accept westerns but with less frequency than before. The pulp audience for western stories had receded beyond Faust's reach, leaving him to consider whether or not he could adapt the western for slick magazines. Eventually he decided that he could not. In the interim, however, he produced one long western aimed directly at the slick market. Its title was *Dust across the Range*, a progressive, "modern" western quite unlike anything

Faust had ever tried before. It was published in November 1937 as a serial in the *American Magazine*, a slick.

In *Dust across the Range* the hero comes riding in to the rescue mounted not on a horse but on a caterpillar tractor. The source of heroism, moreover, is eastern knowledge rather than western experience. What saves the day is not some allegiance to atavistic values of individual combat and honor but technology, formal education, community values, and the desire to avoid a fight. The story pits an eastern-educated protagonist who is determined to practice soil conservation in the face of a traditional rancher's refusal to change his ways. As such, the story places the values of technology and government action (the hero has a Civilian Conservation Corps crew working for him) against the ethos of the Old West. Harry Mortimer, the hero, born in New England and trained in the scientific management of land, is ultimately vindicated when a great, feared dust storm roars across the range, ruining all of the ranches except the one on which he has worked to protect the soil by plantings, terracing, and other good land practices.

Within such a story Faust added a believable love story in which Mortimer is ultimately joined with the daughter of the old rancher. His scientific hero – "with a brain crammed full of college-bred agricultural theory and a missionary desire to teach the ranchers new ways with the old range" – is also a good boxer and able thereby to prove himself in typical western ways.[8] But the typical western ways do not prevail in the story, which salutes technology, education, progress, and community. For Faust, *Dust across the Range* was obviously a New Deal western, quite in keeping with its times.

The *American Magazine* earlier had published four shorter stories by Faust. The magazine favored realistic fiction set in the present. Unfortunately, *Dust across the Range* was both the first and the last purchase of a book-length story from Faust. Given the topical nature of the story, especially its relevance to the great dust storms of the 1930s, the serial should have been of interest also for book publication. But it was not picked up at the time and, in fact, was never reprinted later until it appeared in edited form in 1981 in *Max Brand's Best Western Stories*.

Whatever the reason for lack of attention to the story in 1937 and shortly thereafter, *Dust across the Range* was Faust's last western novel. He produced a few western short stories afterwards but never again a long western story. Both the content of the book and the title may serve symbolically to mark the end of Max Brand as a western writer. The range of the story's title is largely destroyed by the dust storm within its pages. Faust could not have chosen a more apt situation for his last western, and the title could have applied just as well to the drying up and blowing away of the pulp western market.

Chapter Twelve

Detectives and Spies

"Do you know the Doctor?" asked Witherby.

The glance of the district attorney went down to his desk again. The eyelid fluttered.

"The Doctor?" he said. "What Doctor?"

Witherby rose.

"That's all I wanted to know," he said.

"I don't understand," said the man of the law, rising in turn, looking baffled.

"I do, though," said Witherby.

"Doctor? Doctor? What doctor are you referring to?"

"The murdering crook who pays you such a fat lot of coin," said Witherby. "That's the one I mean."

– Walter C. Butler, *Cross over Nine* (1934)

"What a good time I am having writing this crime stuff!" Faust wrote to Dorothy from New York City in the fall of 1932. "What a really good time, and what a load off my mind, with the Western junk out of the way at least temporarily!" He was referring to work begun after meeting with Howard Bloomfield, editor of Munsey's *Detective Fiction Weekly*, during his quest to find new markets for his fiction. "Bloomfield thinks my style is perfect for his magazine," he had said a few days earlier. A month later he reported, "The Crime Story, God be praised, is accepted. Not only is it accepted, but with enthusiasm. Not only with enthusiasm but with prolonged shouting and cheering." For the moment, at least, it seemed as though Faust's problems with Frank Blackwell and *Western Story Magazine* would be overcome by switching from westerns to detective stories. "Writing forever seems easy," Faust said in the midst of writing his initial serial for Bloomfield. "I feel as though the world were a pleasant place to roam in and scribble about."[1]

His excitement in the fall of 1932 was partly a matter of returning to the scene of earlier successes. "Convalescence" (1917), his start as a pulp writer, reputedly written on the spot of his first meeting with Bob Davis, had been a tale of recovery from crime rather than pursuit of it, but it took its characters from the urban underworld. In several stories written before *The Untamed* Faust wrote about city crime. The most elaborate was *Who Am I?*, the serial that placed an orphaned woman in a world of gamblers and criminals. In *Children of Night*, published immediately after *The Untamed*, Faust told of a young wall street broker who is drawn away from his orderly and "frictionless" routine by a woman associated with the underworld. The woman and her circle represent a kind of urban eros; they are "the people of the night, the lovers of the dark . . . who could live a lifetime between evening and dawn."[2]

Shortly after beginning his long run with *Western Story*, Faust digressed from western themes long enough to produce eight novelettes for another Street & Smith publication, *Detective Story Magazine*. These stories, all appearing in 1922, the first under the pseudonym of George Owen Baxter and the rest under Nicholas Silver, are not classic detective stories. They all turn on matters of plot, however, including some amazing coincidences, that involve the solving of crimes. In "Sealed for Fifty Years," for instance, the protagonist finds himself in a strange family house only to discover that he is the true heir of the estate, having been given away illegally as a young child by a distant relative who sought the estate for himself. In "Stolen Clothes," arguably the best of the Nicholas Silver stories, a young dressmaker is mistaken as a jewel thief's accomplice when she masquerades as a socialite, wearing the clothes she had made for a wealthy customer. The story rises above others because the woman, once she is mistaken as a criminal, actually relishes the idea of stealing the pearls from around the fat, undeserving neck of a society matron. In the end, however, all's well that ends well when the pearls are returned and the jewel thief himself decides to go straight.[3]

For 10 years after 1922 Faust found all the pulp work he wanted in Frank Blackwell and *Western Story*. He published one final Nicholas Silver story in 1923. Only one crime title appeared in 1924 and another in 1925. Not until the collapse of his relationship with Blackwell in 1932 did he re-enter the detective field. All along, of course, he wrote "crime stories" in the form of westerns, because the western virtually demanded the breaking of laws, but he kept his pages free of cops, hoodlums, and other elements of city crime. Beginning in 1933, however, these kinds of characters and their stories became regular features in the works of Max Brand. For good measure, in 1935 he turned to spy stories as well. Many of the stories that he later wrote for slick magazines were also stories of crime or espionage.

Detective Fiction Weekly

Faust found the world "a pleasant place . . . to scribble about" in late 1932 because the market for crime stories was flourishing. Ellery Queen had been invented in 1929. As Faust was starting his work for Bloomfield, Erle Stanley Gardner was writing *The Case of the Velvet Claws* (1933), which would sell more than 15 million copies. In the pulps, led by *Black Mask*, a new hard-boiled school of crime fiction had emerged in reaction to the genteel settings and characters epitomized by Mary Roberts Rinehart. The hard-boiled writers sought, as Raymond Chandler later said, "to get murder away from the upper classes, the weekend houseparty, and the vicar's rose garden, and back to the people who were really good at it."[4] In 1930 Dashiell Hammett's *The Maltese Falcon* had appeared, followed by *The Glass Key* in 1931. While the demand for westerns had declined, urban crime stories were big sellers, and *Detective Fiction Weekly* needed good material for its growing number of subscribers.

Carl Brandt, Faust's agent, made the connection with Howard Bloomfield in 1932. Faust responded warmly to the editor. "Dorothy, he's unbelievably keen at making a plot," Faust wrote to his wife in late October. "I think I can get more out of him than out of anyone I've ever talked with about stories."[5] Bloomfield's narrative bent was indeed strong and sure, as it had to be with his magazine constantly besieged by manuscripts.[6] Working closely with Bloomfield, Faust turned out four serials published in *Detective Fiction Weekly* in 1933 and 1934: *Steel Cut Steel, The Dark Peril* (published in book form in 1936 as *The Night Flower*), *X the Murderer*, and *Cross Over Nine* (published as a book in 1935). By the end of 1934 the Munsey Company had moved Bloomfield to *Adventure Magazine*, but Faust impressed the new editor, Duncan Norton-Taylor, not only with his detective stories but also with an idea for a series of stories about a master spy. These appeared in the magazine throughout 1935. During the next two years four additional detective serials appeared: " – *Murder Me!*," *The Granduca* (published as a book in 1973), *Seven Faces*, and *The Face and the Doctor*. Thereafter Faust published occasional crime stories in other pulps and in some slick magazines. One serial, *Six Golden Angels* (also published as a book in 1937), was taken by the high-paying *Collier's*. *Mister Christmas*, the last work published before Faust's death in 1944, was also a crime story.

Of the detective stories he wrote for *Detective Fiction Weekly*, two stand out as better than the rest and as examples of the two directions in which Faust tried to take his "crime stuff." In the first, *The Night Flower* (originally *The Dark Peril*), Faust went as far with the hard-boiled tradition as his temperament would allow. He conceived the story as one focusing on a young woman who had made herself into a perfectly shaped and tuned gold-digger through years of education and concentrated effort. Thus she would "flower" at night in her attractiveness to rich men but live a schizophrenic life torn by more admirable desires. After showing the scenario for such a story to his old mentor, Bob Davis, who did not like the idea, Faust shifted the burden of the story away from the woman, born as Mary Carthy but posing as Jacqueline Leigh, to the central male character.[7] Charles William Pursivant admires a political boss named Richard Franklin (born Riccardo Francolini) even though, unknown to Franklin, he killed Franklin's younger brother years ago. As the complicated story develops, Pursivant helps Franklin solve the theft of some jewels and in the course faces the sudden threat of having Franklin learn, as he eventually does, that he was responsible for the death of Franklin's beloved brother. That earlier killing, it turns out, was a matter of self-defense, but knowledge of it turns Franklin against Pursivant. Meanwhile, Pursivant and Jacqueline Leigh are attracted to each other.

Ultimately Faust's strong characterizations of Pursivant, Franklin, and Carthy-Leigh, the "Night Flower" of the title, are threatened by his own plot as it works its way to a resolution in which evil is punished, Franklin regains his respect for Pursivant, and Leigh agrees to marry Pursivant. Before that resolution, however, Faust provides the sharp, clipped details of a hard-boiled urban world. Pursivant is an honorable character but also a killer. Franklin, the political boss, practices graft but meets the city's need. Good and bad are not clearly distinguishable categories. Faust's language in the novel is also tough at times. "I've got you, Pursivant," a blackmailer says, "and I'm going to drag you down into the slime until it closes over your lips. You're going to snuff the filth up your nose and throttle on it."[8] Nor does the story shy away from gory details; when one character finally dies from a gunshot wound to the stomach, "He pitched over on his face and began to kick himself around in a circle with the last mechanical flurry of his strength. He looked like a headless thing, like a butchered chicken struggling beside the chopping block" (295).

While the hard-boiled story had some appeal to Faust, his Gatsby-like sense of "the promises of life" alienated him from the truly dark streets of Dashiell Hammett and Raymond Chandler. While Faust has his hero in *The Night Flower* feel "that he was moving through nothingness, among the ghosts of things" (199), he preferred lighter tales of crime, such as " – *Murder Me!*" (1935), probably his best long effort in the detective genre.

The story, never published in book form, begins with a metaphoric description of the protagonist, Richard Willett, driving in a rainstorm:

> All the way from New York his car hit the rain like a fist, knocking it into a dazzle before the headlights while Willett lounged at ease behind the wheel. When the road was straight it had a winter look, a black, polished river that flowed under the wheels without carrying the machine back; but when the lights swung around a corner they gave him reassuring glimpses of spring, a horn of abundance filled with the bright rush of the rain but with the summer green about to flow into it.[9]

This passage presages the movement of the plot as the reader rounds corners and begins to see beyond them, and as darkness ultimately turns into light for Willett and the other characters. The mystery is solved, moreover, by the work of an unlikely team of detectives, Sergeants Campbell and O'Rourke. Angus Campbell is a thin, acerbic Scot while Patrick O'Rourke is a fat, grafting Irishman whose sense of humor offsets Campbell's lack of the same. The constant, seemingly malicious banter between the two detectives gives the story a comic lightness of tone even when its chief business is murder.

Like *The Night Flower*, " – *Murder Me!*" is about love as well as crime, but the success of the love affair depends on finding out who killed the murder victim discovered in the early pages of the story. In fact, the would-be lovers suspect each other of the murder. "It hardly matters whether one or the other did the thing," Jacqueline Barry tells Richard Willett. "The point is that we *could* have done it, either of us."[10] With a bow in the direction of Mary Roberts Rinehart, the story ends with the crime solved and the two lovers driving away "into a new horizon . . . ready for a new start."[11]

Spy Stories

The protagonist of Faust's sixth pulp story in 1917, "The Sole Survivor," is a German secret service agent. But there is no evidence before 1934 of any other interest in international espionage. Yet in 1935 Faust published in *Detective Fiction Weekly* eight novelettes and one serial – all by Max Brand – relating the exploits of Anthony Hamilton, an American secret agent in Europe and Central America. These magazine stories were soon published in book form as three novels by Frederick Frost: *Secret Agent Number One* (1936), *Spy Meets Spy* (1937), and *The Bamboo Whistle* (1937).

Why Faust chose to write spy stories is unknown. The Anthony Hamilton stories he produced departed from public taste, for the mid-1930s were a time of economic depression and international isolation. Hollywood was busy hawking movies about G-men fighting crime in the cities. Not until Edward G. Robinson starred in *Confessions of a Nazi Spy* in 1939 did the public turn its interest to international intrigue. Faust was ahead of the times, particularly in the basic, personal conflict carried forward by the spy novels. Anthony Hamilton, the American secret agent Number One, is pitted against a clever, often disguised antagonist named Henri de Graulchier, who is the top secret agent of imperial Japan. Moreover, even in the first novel the story raises the specter of a second world war resulting from Japanese imperial aims: "The Philippines were close to them, an ideal extension of their empire; Hawaii was not very far away."[12] Faust wrote these words sometime in 1934.

While the geopolitics of the Anthony Hamilton novels are fascinating – and surprisingly prescient – the narratives are successful primarily on the basis of character. Hamilton himself is a Max Brand hero not unlike some of the later western heroes. He adopts a studied nonchalance, hiding his role as a spy behind the mannerisms of a vacuous fop. His motivation, explained in his own words on request in the first novel, is clear and unsentimental: "A pat or two on the shoulder from a few men in Washington, a chance to smash the plans of Japan and prevent a world war that would make the last one look like thirty cents, and an odd feeling that my country is being served by the way. That's about all" (171).

Following Faust's established pattern, the novels combine love with adventure. The romantic element in the Hamilton stories develops slowly, however, out of the actions of two women. In the first novel, Anthony Hamilton falls in love with Mary Michelson, a beautiful American-Russian woman who works unwittingly with Henri de Graulchier, hoping only to free Russia from Communist control. The sexual allure of Mary Michelson is a genuine complication for the American secret agent. "Suppose," he muses, "that the girl warms your heart, and then you discover that her talents are all bent towards a scheme that will smash your country between the eyes?" (76). Hamilton's task throughout the three novels is not only to save his country but to save Mary from her own misguided intentions. All the while a second woman, Louise Curran, an American agent, is in love with Hamilton. This romantic triangle is ultimately resolved in the third novel as the patient but intent Louise Curran, her wits always intact, finally replaces the other woman in Anthony Hamilton's affections. In his closing line Hamilton says that they will "be happy together to the end of time."[13]

With his secret agent happily joined with his co-worker and de Graulchier eliminated, Faust had no more to do with Anthony Hamilton. Two years later in the pages of *Argosy*, he attempted one further spy novel, *War for Sale* (published in 1973 as a book entitled *The Phantom Spy*). This time the subject was German aggression, especially a planned invasion of France. But neither the characterization nor the plot is up to the standard set by the *Secret Agent Number One* series.[14]

Short Crime Stories

With some exceptions, Faust handled short crime stories better than long ones. Novel-length efforts invited overcomplicated plots and strained romantic resolutions. *Flower of Hell*, a 1938 story about the use of marijuana, begins brilliantly, as Faust's stories typically do, only to trail off into a murky plot that reveals only on its final pages that all the strange previous behavior was caused by the drug.[15] *Dead Man's Passport* (1941) begins with an exotic Shanghai setting, including the dangerous running of guns by the Japanese, but ends unconvincingly with a marriage in Westchester County, complete with a hefty inheritance.[16] In short stories, however, where Faust's plots are necessary limited in situation and work toward a unitary effect, often without the need for romance, his crime pieces are impressive. "Bulldog," one of two stories published in *Black Mask* in 1937, ironically places a corrupt policeman in the role of solving a crime he committed and thus betraying himself. Betrayal as a theme occurs frequently in the short crime stories, especially those published in slick magazines.[17]

One of the best short stories deals with the cold facts of multiple betrayal. In "A Silence in Tappan Valley" (1938) a loutish husband, Ashton, grows jealous of his wife's friendship with another man who shares her love of classical music. He kills the other man, Newberry, as he walks through the woods in suburban Tappan Valley toward the train station, shooting him in the head at close range and then throwing both his revolver and Newberry's body into a stream, Tappan Creek, that will carry it out to sea. That night, with his wife, he tries to appreciate Schubert, Mozart, and Bach, hiding from her his hatred of the music: "When he compressed his lips to keep from cursing she thought he was being moved to the soul by the beauty of the music she loved." The next morning, after an especially cold night, his wife goes out for a walk. When she does not return, Ashton follows her trail to the creek, where to his horror he discovers that the creek is frozen. "A yard below the surface the body of Newberry lay with his face turned up and the great wound still visible, still red upon it." Ashton sees that his wife's footsteps lead away from the creek and toward town: "Then the silence, greater than the cold, pressed in upon him until he was listening to his own breathing and seeing the vapor of it whiten in the air, like a fine symbol of life."[18]

The spare style of such a story, close to the hard-boiled school, often shows up in the longer crime stories, but its consistency of effect does not. The serials, including the early *Children of Night*, sometimes demonstrate brilliant conceptions of characters trapped by opposing compulsions (as Ashton is moved to both murder and love) and facing both external and psychological threats to their initial or desired stability. With some exceptions, however, the sheer length required of serials tempted Faust to provide labyrinthine adventures and fruitful romances that have the effect of vitiating his characters' internal dilemmas. Nevertheless, the excitement he felt in 1932 in writing "crime stuff" was a true indication of his talent for such work as well as its rejuvenating effect on his career as a magazine writer. But Faust did not give to contemporary crime his most intense interest as a writer of adventure stories. That interest was reserved for history.

Chapter Thirteen

Historical Adventures

And now from the wounded and the dead the blood spread across the floor in
widening pools that interlinked and made little flowing streams.

— George Challis, "Claws of the Tigress" (1935)

When his *Western Story* market began to fail after 1932 Faust
returned not only to crime stories but also to his very earliest genre:
historical romance. The first fiction he published, in the pages of the
Modesto High School *Sycamore* in 1910, was an Arthurian adventure
fashioned loosely after Malory. Later the romantic tragedy of Tristram
and Isolde occupied center stage for several years in his literary
imagination. It was entirely logical, therefore, that when he was freed
by necessity from the constant writing of westerns that he would
turn again to stories set in the distant past. At odds in some respects
with his own times, his imagination easily moved his settings and
characters into a romanticized past where opportunities abounded
for heroic if not noble action. The continuing viability of *Argosy*
magazine in the mid-1930s gave Faust an additional and very practical reason to pursue historical tales, which he did frequently from
1934 to 1937, drawing his settings from seventeenth-century piracy
on the Spanish Main, Machiavellian intrigues in Italy, the life and
times of Richard III, and finally the French Revolution. These efforts
were not as successful as his westerns and not as numerous as his
crime stories, but they were true to some of Faust's deepest interest
and open, in their telling, to expressions of historical nostalgia and
degrees of violent action not often conveyed in his other genres.

Early Historical Adventures

What Faust produced in historical adventure stories in the 1930s was
an extension of themes and subjects that he had explored at the

129

beginning of his career. *The Sword Lover* (1917) began as an eighteenth-century historical novel, with Colin Ornald fleeing to Virginia from the long arm of the English crown. In "One Glass of Wine" (1917) Faust had been even more explicit in his use of historical material, setting the story amid the details of Addison's *Spectator* and other features of London society in 1711 and 1712. In "A Rendezvous with Death" (1918) he drew sometimes amusing caricatures of English Puritans and Cavaliers and based his plot on a young woman's resistance to the dictates of her Puritan father. In all of these early stories, Faust created characters who embody to some degree the particular tensions of their historical eras. *The Double Crown* (1918), co-authored with John Schoolcraft, is a particularly good instance of this, with a conflict between monarchy and democracy expressed by the emotions of the protagonist as well as the action of the plot.

In 1919 Faust had attempted a complex novel involving Renaissance Italy. Titled *The Hammer* and published as a serial in *Argosy*, the story described the successful efforts of an English artisan – a swordmaker – to become an artist by studying sculpture under an Italian master and then emigrating to Rome. The hero of the story, driven by his artistic yearnings, seems to represent Faust's own desires to be something more noble than a prose artisan. Although the plot of *The Hammer* eventually falls victim to a series of implausible contrivances and coincidences, it is rich in historical details that draw a contrast between the low state of English art during the reign of Henry VIII and the elevated artistic culture in Italy.

Faust's early historicals differ considerably from his westerns of the same period. Although his personal library contained many books on the history of the American West, he seldom based a western on such actual events as the Johnson County War in Wyoming (the backdrop of both *The Virginian* and *Shane*) or the exploits of famous outlaws. His westerns are, in fact, virtually antihistorical, refusing to celebrate either western geography or history. Whereas his early historical fiction reflects historical tensions even in the personality of main characters, his westerns depict conflict that is more universal or mythological in nature.

The Splendid Rascal

With his own invention of Max Brand as a western alter ego and his entrance into the lucrative work of writing for *Western Story*, Faust generally avoided historical adventure fiction from 1919 to 1934. There were some exceptions, however, especially a 1926 novel about English buccaneers on the Spanish Main.

This novel – *The Splendid Rascal* – has particular significance in Faust's career. First of all, it was a departure from the mainstream of his work – westerns – in the mid-1920s. Also, its subject matter has absolutely no relationship to any of his personal interests at the time, when he was establishing a residence in Italy. The novel seems to represent a free choice by its author, undictated by events in his life or by the pulp magazine market. In fact, *The Splendid Rascal* was never published in a magazine; it stands out as the only work of fiction during Faust's lifetime published first (and only) as a book. It appeared in May of 1926 in hardcover as a Bobbs-Merrill novel by George Challis.

The greatest significance of *The Splendid Rascal* lies in its content, to which Faust would return eight years later. The novel includes concrete details of seafaring, piracy, and Caribbean geography; it also includes gratuitous violence and a hero who lacks most of the usual heroic qualities except expertise in fighting, good luck, and a belated awareness of his mistakes. In *Destry Rides Again* Faust's definition of heroism is "great deeds inspired by love and high aspiration" (269). In *The Splendid Rascal* this definition applies only in part. The hero commits "great deeds," but the aspiration behind his actions is uncertain.

The novel's hero, Louis Madelin, first appears as an unscrupulous English con man and gambler in Belgium. His only apparent virtues are skill as a swordsman and dedication to the exiled Charles Stuart. Nothing in his past or his values seems heroic, and his first actions in the story are to betray a young woman who loves him and, in a swordfight, to fatally wound a sea captain on the streets of Antwerp. But Faust soon places Madelin in a situation where he is forced to join a group of English pirates as they return from Antwerp to the Spanish Main on their privateer, the *Careless*. In fact, the vessel belongs to the man Madelin has stabbed. Then, amid the geography of the western Caribbean, Panama, and Peru, Faust proceeds to spin a tale of piracy, slave rebellion, and the Spanish Inquisition – with Louis Madelin and the English pirates at the center of violent action resulting in the deaths of hundreds but the rescue of an Englishwoman who had been sentenced by a Spanish Inquisitor to burn at the stake. The scenes of violence and injury range from the brutal keelhauling of a sailor to the slow roasting alive of rebellious African slaves. Blood flows constantly.

Such a story demands a particular suspension of disbelief by the reader, for the redeeming motive for such carnage is not always apparent. At the end of the novel Louis Madelin emerges as a sympathetic character largely by virtue of his skill as a killer and as a leader of other killers whose primary moral claim lies solely in their identity as Englishmen. Beyond this, Madelin is motivated by a mistake he makes early in the novel: serving as a judge aboard the *Careless*, he decrees that a captured Spaniard has the right to freedom and to possession of the Englishwoman, Mary Winton, provided he can raise a large ransom once he returns to Peru. When Madelin rescues Mary Winton from the horrors of the Inquisition in the closing pages of the novel, he absolves himself of his own poor judgment earlier.

Adventure in *The Splendid Rascal* thus lacks the revenge motif of most Max Brand westerns, replacing it with a strain of redemption. While Louis Madelin's redemption hardly redeems the novel for its gore and torture, the book closes with a nighttime scene of peace and resolution. Madelin and the crew of barbarous buccaneers are headed to England in a stolen ship loaded with Spanish treasure, referred to as "Dew of Heaven." Madelin knows that Mary Winton, safe now from the Inquisition, "would waken to love him and with all her heart." In the final paragraph, with love in his future, Madelin senses that even the past battles and pirated treasure are fading from significance:

> A drunken sailor went past him to take the wheel, growling out the last of a ditty; but when he saw the group, he went by them on tiptoe. The ship became quiet, saving now and then for the rush and whisper of a bow-wave curling down the side. In the waist the buccaneers slept with the flagons in their grimy hands. Their wounds grew cold and stiff unheeded. The gold slipped from twenty sacks upon the boards and as the moon rose higher, silvering the broad yellow pieces, it became dim – a ghost of money – the Dew of Heaven, indeed![1]

One of Faust's longest novels, *The Splendid Rascal* sparkles with such prose, almost as if it had been a welcome diversion from *Western Story* work. It also bears a political message, unusual for Faust, in its sympathetic treatment of slaves and Central American native peoples.

The Naked Blade

Faust used the George Challis byline for one other story in 1926, *The Tyrant*, a historical novel with a French protagonist and enough western elements for *Western Story* publication. But after his Louis Madelin saga, Faust put both the Challis pseudonym and the historical genre aside for the next eight years while he concentrated on stories that Frank Blackwell would buy without question. In 1934, however, desperate for new markets to replace *Western Story*, he returned to the Challis byline and the Caribbean setting of *The Splendid Rascal*. This time he had a magazine outlet as well: *Argosy*, which had been running his white Indian stories about Rusty Sabin. For *Argosy* he produced two stories about piracy: *The Naked Blade* (1934) and *The Dew of Heaven* (1936), each incorporating as a character the real-life Welsh pirate, Henry Morgan, and recounting the exploits of a fictional hero, an Englishman named Ivor Kildare, whose last name would soon find use in a far different kind of story about a young physician.

Of the two Ivor Kildare novels, *The Naked Blade* is clearly superior, plunging with its first paragraph into the world of Faust's earlier Caribbean story:

> The dream of Ivor Kildare swiftly accommodated itself to facts. The devil that had been breathing hot steam upon him seemed to leap suddenly upon his back and drive a spur into his ribs; so Kildare, wakening, saw the gaoler leaning over him with a long, sharp-pointed staff in his hand, and realized that he was a prisoner in the hands of the Spaniards and lodged in the prison hut of Porto Bello. The Indian woman was whimpering, as usual, and the man who groaned at every breath was the Negro who had been flogged the evening before.[2]

In this novel Ivor Kildare falls in love with a half-English, half-Spanish woman, Ines Heredia, and eventually leads a group of buc-

caneers in an attack on the Spanish stronghold of Porto Bello, where
she is held, on the north coast of Panama. As was the case with *The
Splendid Rascal*, Faust uses his historical setting as a stage for
incredible acts of violence and bloodshed. Hundreds of persons are
killed, often horribly. Heads are decapitated by cannon balls, and
entrails fall from men wounded in the abdomen. Kildare himself
produces some of the gore, especially when he kills one of his adver-
saries, an ironically named Captain Tranquillo: "he stabbed Tranquillo through the hollow of the throat. Again, and again, he buried
the daggerlike fragment of his sword in the breast of the buccaneer"
(269). Moreover, it appears that Kildare's dashing and death-dealing
ways are part of what attracts Ines Heredia to him, allowing the
novel to end on a scene not of violence but of resolution and future
peace. The broken sword of Kildare, used to kill Tranquillo and others, is now symbolically a cross and a benediction for the hero:

> So Kildare sat forward with the girl, where the motion of the ship was like that
> of a jumping horse that flies across country. . . . He idly kept thrusting his
> broken sword into the gunwale until at last he forgot that, also, and left it
> standing on the bows of the canoe like a cross. And the girl said nothing at all,
> either. In the hollow of his shoulder lay her head. Looking down he could see
> her brow and her smile, but her eyes were only a shadow. He could not tell
> whether the pulse that he felt was the beating of his heart or of her own.
> (272)

Regeneration through violence is a blatant theme in *The Naked
Blade*.

The *Dew of Heaven*, by contrast, is disorganized, lacking the narrative control of the first Ivor Kildare story.[3] In both, however, as
with the earlier story about Louis Madelin, the villains of the New
World are the Spaniards. A large part of their villainy – which justifies
English piracy in Faust's telling of the matter – lies in their subjuga-
tion of African slaves and New World natives. In *The Splendid Rascal*, Louis Madelin becomes a guerilla leader of Indians and Blacks
against the Spanish colonial powers.[4] In *The Naked Blade* Ivor Kildare's moral superiority over Spaniards is represented by his constant companion, a Mosquito Indian named Luis, who is to him what
Chingachgook is to Natty Bumppo in Cooper's Leatherstocking novels. Although Cooper's pattern is ultimately violated by Kildare's love

affair, *The Naked Blade* flirts with the beau ideal of American heroism, the isolated male more at home with nature than civilization.

Machiavellian Violence

After writing *The Naked Blade* and while working also on crime and
spy stories for *Detective Fiction Weekly*, Faust turned to yet another
arena of adventure: late-fifteenth-century Italy, a time of warfare and
intrigue, especially in Tuscany. Italy itself was a subject dear to Faust,
as must have been the writing of stories involving city-states around
Florence. As a result, he wrote several *Argosy* serials and novelettes
relating the adventures of an English-born swordfighter named Tizzo
and called "The Firebrand" in reference to his red hair. Among the
supporting characters of these stories are Cesare Borgia and Niccolo
Machiavelli as Borgia's political advisor. In 1950 and 1951 Harper &
Brothers published this material as two George Challis novels, *The
Firebrand* and *The Bait and the Trap*.[5]

As action fiction, these Italian stories are among Faust's best.
They move swiftly; the plots are unified by the sequential adventures
of Tizzo, and the details of intrigue and deception are cleverly
arranged, especially after Cesare Borgia enters the story. Faust takes
liberties with history, of course, and uses such central Italian places
as Perugia, Forli, and Urbino primarily as set pieces. *The Firebrand*
and *The Bait and the Trap* move from one fight – generally with
swords or axes – to the next, with Renaissance Italy as the stage for
such violent action.

Tizzo is a character mainly of action, showing little sophistication
of thought or motive beyond his allegiance to a code of honor. As his
story continues he also emerges as a person of great vitality who sees
much joy in life. In *The Firebrand* he is depicted as a compendium
of human accomplishments and interests during one interval of several days between battles, when

> time was used by young Tizzo in adoring his Lady Beatrice, in drinking wine
> with boon companions – for the entire camp was his companion – in playing
> dice, in riding races against the other youngsters on their finest horses, in
> fencing, wrestling, running, leaping, practicing with his great blue-bladed ax,
> and twanging a harp and composing songs to his own music, in the reading of
> a curious old Greek manuscript which Giovanpaolo, knowing his taste, had

presented to him, in thumbing out little models of clay – for one day he swore
that he would be a sculptor like that great broken-nosed genius, Michelangelo – in sleeping, eating, laughing, laboring, and filling every day to the brim
with his abundant activities. For every moment his flame-blue eyes were open,
they were employed with the first object or the first thought that came his
way. (219-20)

In *The Bait and the Trap* he is noted as "a fellow . . . all aflame,
without fear, never still, and who fills his days with so much action
that he'll hardly take time to sleep in between for fear of missing
another adventure" (74). He has, Cesare Borgia notices, "a certain
noble carelessness"; this same quality allows others to use him at
times – as "bait" – for their own devious purposes. Throughout his
story Tizzo is attracted to Beatrice Baglioni, a member of the ruling
family in Perugia, who often joins him in battle, but his romantic side
is given little development. Tizzo is the embodiment of adventure,
not eros.

Although Faust includes interesting peripheral matter in the
Tizzo story – including the characters of Alessandro Bonfadini, Borgia's personal poisoner, and Henry Melrose, whom Tizzo discovers
as his real father – the central feature of both *The Firebrand* and *The
Bait and the Trap* is violence. In accord with much of Faust's historical fiction, the novels depict the sacking of three towns, the
deaths of hundreds, frequent vivid bloodshed, and even widescale
raping by the forces of Cesare Borgia when they storm the city of
Forli. Although Borgia's actions late in the second novel finally place
Tizzo in opposition to him, he is earlier allied with the young hero,
making it difficult to draw the kind of moral distinctions that are possible with Faust's Caribbean novels. The carnage in his Italian stories
seems primarily a reflection of the hero's enthusiasm for action,
unconnected to any larger purpose, straining only to outdo itself.

The Golden Knight

The Tizzo stories have an air of youth about them. Tizzo himself is
hardly past adolescence, certainly not to the point of sexual maturity
in his relations with Beatrice, and he functions in the novels as the
son of an older man. A sense of youth runs throughout the telling of
the stories as well, an innocence about violence and death, a pre-

sumption that such things are primarily a matter of sport and excitement. Almost as though he realized such deficiencies in his Italian adventures, Faust set out immediately afterwards to write a novel about an older historical figure, Richard the Lion-Hearted of England on his return from the Crusades in Jerusalem. Already king of England, Richard had been 35 at the time. With this and other historical facts to weave into his story, Faust's task was much different from the sheer invention required of the Tizzo stories. The result was *The Golden Knight*, Faust's only novel based on the actual events of a historical figure as protagonist. It was published first as an *Argosy* serial, by George Challis, beginning on 20 June 1936, and then in 1937 as a novel by the Greystone Press, which retained the Challis byline.

The Golden Knight sticks to the basic facts about Richard I, including his companion, the minstrel Blondel, and his eventual capture by Leopold V of Austria in 1192. But Faust adds some unusual features to the historical record, the most significant – and unusual – being the romantic interest represented by a young woman named Elspeth, with whom both Richard and Blondel fall in love. The presence of Elspeth allows for two lines of plot development: one is the conflict with Leopold and his henchmen, who are desperate to capture Richard on his return from the Holy Land; the other is the odd romantic triangle of Richard, Blondel, and Elspeth. To the triangle Elspeth brings not only some affection for both men, though ultimately she is in love only with Blondel, but also her peculiar family background as an assistant to her father, a torturer. Torture is presented as an art she has learned well. Why Faust would give his romantic female lead such strikingly incongruous experience, including a delight in having done her gruesome work well, is a puzzle without an answer. But Elspeth seems to have a life of her own outside the control either of the two Englishmen or the author. That she offers freely to be Richard's mistress in order that she might remain close to Blondel suggests that her characterization lies outside the boundary of most stereotypes in popular American fiction. Blondel refers to her at one point, innocently, as "this sweet little thing, this blond-headed girl, this supple young witch of an Elspeth," but she is much more than that.[6]

The novel is in fact more than it appears to be, certainly more than a historical narrative. Like most if not all of Faust's fiction, it involves an implicit contractual relationship with readers, self-consciously promising good entertainment in return for the readers' suspension of disbelief. In this case, the telling of the story also reveals – perhaps more than any other – Faust's joy in being a story-teller. Even as he speaks, Richard seems to know that he is not only a historical character but also, for the moment, an actor in a popular entertainment. When he faces death or torture, he does so happily, as though he, like the narrator, knows how things will work out in the end. "I shall dive into death as into deep water and heal my hurts all in a moment," he tells Elspeth, "and all the book accounts and all the records of St. Peter will never be enough to bar my way through the golden gates" (248). In this respect, even though he is King of England and a man in full adulthood, he shows the ebullience and playfulness of youth – and so renders useless the potential seriousness of his situation and of the story Faust tells. *The Golden Knight* locates its own value in its performance as a tale, not in any recanting of history or scrutiny of human nature.

The French Revolution

After *The Golden Knight* Faust moved from the twelfth to the eighteenth century, writing a novel about revolutionary conditions in France. Unlike most of his other fiction, this story touches on matters of American attitudes and values. Although he aimed at serialization in a high-paying slick magazine, where patriotic historical themes were valued, he settled once again for publication in *Argosy*, where the story began running in February of 1937. But the nationalistic intent of the story was captured in its title: *The American*. It was a fitting conclusion to his career as a writer of historical fiction.

As Faust's novels typically do, *The American* begins with a brilliant situation and a unique set of characters. Its protagonist is a young Virginia adventurer, John Hampton, who finds himself in France, where he is mistaken for another American whose business dealings had gained him possession of a French village. When the other American is killed in a tavern brawl, Hampton is first amused at being confused for the new American lord of Charlevain, the village. Then he is appalled at the oppressive conditions under which French peasants must live and, determined to make improvements in their quality of life, continues to pose as the rightful owner of the village. A believer in value of the common man, Hampton soon grants new freedoms to the residents of the village. His idealism ultimately comes to ruin, however, when the peasants are incited by revolutionary rabble-rousers to revolt in bloody conflict against the local aristocracy.

Faust takes considerable pains here to sketch in the social background of the times. When Hampton first enters Charlevain, for instance, he is troubled by what he sees: "Charlevain was a lovely name towards which he traveled; now the unhappy reality walked straight into his heart." The villagers look "like beasts out of caves, scratching their bodies through their rags, and turning hopeless eyes, without curiosity" as Hampton approaches.[7] Hampton serves to remind the French aristocracy how America's "damned democratic ideas have returned to pollute our own land."[8] Hampton frequently cites the sentiments of American democracy in the first half of the story, believing, as he tells himself that "if the common people cannot be trusted, there's nothing left to trust."[9] Meanwhile, the omniscient narration of the story alerts readers to the violence brewing in Paris and soon to engulf Charlevain.

Despite the apparent simplicity of opposing political ideas, *The American* presents extraordinary complications for its hero. To begin with, he is torn between two women: a peasant innkeeper's daughter and a daughter of the aristocracy. Moreover, as the story develops, the peasants turn violent and irrational, suggesting that perhaps they cannot be trusted to govern themselves and casting some doubt on Hampton's democratic ideals. In the end, the novel presents scenes of horrific bloodshed when the peasants storm the château above their village. Hampton leads them in: "It was as though his axe had opened a way through the barrier of centuries, and let the new time flood roaring in." But the roar of the flood is the noise of death as well: "The first step to this new liberty, this new freedom, was murder."[10]

The novel traffics in moral complexity, even ambiguity, at a level quite remarkable for a pulp story. Faust eventually works John Hampton into a liaison with the aristocratic woman, Marguerite de Freron, and away from the violence. Since the peasant woman – Julie Marceau – is a more fully developed and deserving character, this resolution weakens the novel somewhat. In the final pages, however, Faust manages a strangely effective denouement when he links Julie with the revolutionary zealot responsible for the violent uprising.

The American was Faust's last effort at long historical fiction; it was also his best effort and an indication of his ability not only to tell an interesting story but to explore historical complexities as well. Even though the novel was published as an *Argosy* serial and contains many scenes reminiscent of the Tizzo novels, it leans away from pulp traditions and toward more sophisticated literary expression. In the context of Faust's career, it was one of many available signs that his tenure as a pulp writer was coming to a close. In fact, judging strictly from its content – its nationalistic overtones, the large historical significance of its events, and a struggle between two women for the heart of the hero – one might easily claim that *The American* was written with Hollywood expressly in mind.

And Hollywood was where Faust was headed at the time.

Chapter Fourteen

Hollywood

This is not California. This is Hollywood.
– Letter to Dorothy Faust, 1938

At times in 1936 things seemed to be looking up for Faust. In March, for instance, Paramount Pictures paid him $5,000 for film rights to the story "Internes Can't Take Money," which was soon to appear in *Cosmopolitan*. In August his agent, Carl Brandt, was almost beside himself with happiness over the acceptance of a Max Brand serial by a slick magazine. The serial was a mystery, *Six Golden Angels*; the magazine was *Collier's*, which paid $5,000. Even though the story seems less distinguished than several of Faust's other detective stories, Brandt saw it as an augury of good things to come: "I can't help but feel the most complete sense of achievement on your part. It is a thing that I've wanted and struggled for – to have you have a serial in a first-class magazine. It's only the beginning – I know it – and all my faith goes behind that statement."[1]

Brandt's faith was not misplaced, for Faust was on something of an upswing at the time, but the loss of the *Western Story* market was hard to replace for regular, stable earnings in the amount that he required. The one *Collier's* sale demanded extensive rewriting in the months ahead to meet the expectations of fiction editor Kenneth Littauer. While Faust was proud of the acceptance, it was a departure from the write-and-mail mode of production he had enjoyed so long under Frank Blackwell.

There were other problems as well. For one, his heart continued to trouble him. "The old heart lay down on me in Paris," he told Brandt in July 1936, "and I had to have twenty-four hours of camphor injections and what-not to carry me through."[2] At the time of the attack he was returning somewhat dispirited from another visit to New York. "I feel more than ever that I can never live happily in my own land," he said to Brandt.[3] But at home in Florence he was not much happier. His marriage, he felt, had lost its vitality. As a result, during a fall trip to New York he began an intense affair with a wealthy and recently divorced younger woman named Mary Churchill. Dorothy Faust sensed something, and her husband admitted the relationship but expressed an interest in continuing it with Dorothy's approbation, which she refused to give. The resulting tension in the marriage was wracking to both Fausts as they tried to make it through the winter of 1936-37. "It was a long, long winter for me," Faust told Brandt later.[4]

Although Faust's personal problems dominated his mood, he was also worried about Italian politics. While he had never complained openly about life under fascism, the increasing alliance between Mussolini and Hitler made him uncomfortable and raised the possibility in his mind of a general European war. In short, he was ripe for change, and Hollywood, it appeared, was one means of achieving it.

MGM

During his visit to New York in late summer of 1936 there had been some talk about a studio job in California. Faust did not assume it a sure thing, however, and, as a guard against disappointment, claimed he was unable to live happily in his own land. "As for the Hollywood business," he told Brandt a few months later, "it probably will blow over and nothing come of it at all, as everything from that direction has blown over during the last ten years."[5] It did not blow over, though, and by late January 1937 Brandt was discussing the matter with a Hollywood agent, saying that Faust needed a minimum of $1,500 a week to make it in Hollywood. In April Faust was in Hollywood discussing matters with Edwin Knopf, an MGM executive.

Although no deal was struck at that time, it was clear to Faust that he had been warmly received by MGM, and he was heartened by the meeting. In fact, with Hollywood as a possibility, *Internes Can't Take Money* doing well as a Paramount film starring Joel McCrea and Barbara Stanwyck, and a novelette just published in the *Saturday Evening Post*, Faust was suddenly very upbeat about his prospects. "Darling," he wrote to Dorothy in April 1937, "I really think that we have turned the corner on the dark days and that from now on everything will be rosy."[6] By "dark days" he meant the time since the failure of his *Western Story* market. (Because he was still involved with Mary Churchill, however, there were still dark days ahead for Dorothy Faust.) Having ended 1937 with total earnings of more than $42,000 – and this in a Depression year – Faust obviously had some reason for happiness. To maintain progress, especially in New York magazine placements, as well as to keep tabs on the movie situation, he decided to remain in the United States in the fall of 1937, taking up residence in Katonah, New York, with Dorothy and their youngest child, Judy, while the two older children attended school in Vienna.

By the spring of 1938 Faust was working for Metro-Goldwyn-Mayer. He had finally arranged to write for the studio at a weekly salary of $1,000; a raise above that figure would depend on his success. He retained the right to sell to magazines and book publishers anything he wrote on studio time, while continuing to write for magazine and book markets on his own time. Initially, at least, Faust was excited about his prospects, telling Brandt, "This is a time when Hollywood is pulling in its horns and growing dissatisfied with its present staffs in all directions. It might welcome new blood, even forty-five year old new blood."[7] He also believed that the weekly salary would remove some pressure from him and, as a result, give him more time to write poetry.

He began his Hollywood years as Hollywood began to explode with success. What he found was "an array of low-lying buildings and streets and people on the northern edge of Los Angeles, a community that was partly an industry, partly a technology, partly a style and a quality of mind, partly a negation of all those things, partly just a hunger for money and success."[8] His college classmate Sidney Howard was a fixture there, having written the original script for *Gone with the Wind*. In fact, it was Sid Howard who gave Faust some hope that he could learn the ropes in Hollywood, offering to show him around to the various people whom David O. Selznick had set to work on the 1939 film *Gone with the Wind*.[9] That Hollywood was increasingly a refuge for European intellectuals, including Thomas Mann, whom Faust soon befriended, made his new working environment somewhat acceptable, at least at times. "Dearest," he said to Dorothy, "big, easy fruitful things are going to come out of this business."[10]

Ironically, however, Faust chafed at the studio's emphasis on profit and mass appeal, its art-for-money ethos. In Italy he had enjoyed several thousand miles of actual and esthetic distance from the marketing and distribution of his pulp stories. In Hollywood he was now face to face with commercial popular culture, much of which had been sustained by his own work. Although he began his residence in Tinsel Town with high enthusiasm and hopes for "big, easy fruitful things," he soon complained about the atmosphere.[11] Collier Young, a Hollywood associate of Carl Brandt, noted that Faust was "alternately wildly excited about working for pictures and alternately depressed." For a while, though, at least in his upward mood swings, he thought that Hollywood would give his artistic potential more room to reveal itself. He wrote glowing letters to Dorothy and others indicating how amazed MGM was with what he could generate in story ideas. He thought he could breathe life into scripts that MGM had purchased but was unable to use. He thought he could write screenplays for particular actors. "It is like Heinie to stop, in midair, and think up a story for Joan Crawford," wrote Young, "then the next minute he is planning to do a story involving the life of Offenbach, and God knows what else." In reality, the studio wanted him to concentrate on one thing: another movie about Dr. Kildare. "I have stressed the fact he needs one good screenplay," Young reported to Brandt. "The quickest way I see is KILDARE."[12]

Eventually Faust got the message. Referring to two MGM producers, he told Brandt, "Wilson and Cohn are all heated up about the Kildare yarn, and finally I have what they want – an exciting story."[13] In order to give his employers the same opportunity Paramount had exploited with "Internes Can't Take Money," Faust wrote an entire novel about Dr. Kildare, the central character of the "Internes" story, and then from his novel created a script. Shortly thereafter, while Faust returned to Italy to close up his villa permanently and bring his older children to the United States, MGM turned the novel over to two seasoned screenwriters (Harry Ruskin and Willis Goldbeck), who produced a second script, the one used for the production of *Young Dr. Kildare*. In October, two weeks after Faust returned from Italy, the movie premiered as an "A" picture at Radio City Music Hall in New York to considerable success. Just as *The Untamed* in 1918 and 1919 had sealed his fate as a pulp writer, his first MGM film guaranteed his position in Hollywood and, in fact,

increased his MGM salary to $1,250 a week, not including a $2,500
bonus for the first Kildare story for the studio.

Brentwood

Ultimately Faust was better for Hollywood than it was for him. In the
summer of 1938 he purchased a house at 317 Burlingame Avenue in
Brentwood, west of Beverly Hills. "California will have to be paradise
enough," he told a friend, "even with men so busy out there spoiling
the things God gave them."[14] Brentwood was a quiet and exclusive
neighborhood filled with Hollywood people. Faust took some satisfaction in the property, leaving behind after his death in 1944 a yellow legal pad with a list of 42 changes made to the exterior of the
house and 39 to its interior. But he was not given to stable domestic
life in Brentwood or anyplace else in the United States, despite
protestations to the contrary. His youngest child, Judy, later said that
"317 Burlingame was his final American defeat on all levels."[15]

"Paradise enough" was the problem. Faust always found it difficult to compromise his dreams, preferring in various ways to rail
against the restrictions life placed on him. Having made the decision
to relocate in Hollywood, for instance, and promising a bright future
to Dorothy, he continued for almost two years to contact Mary
Churchill. Faced with a profit-minded environment in the studios, he
turned his poetry toward the figures of Jesus and Saint Francis.
(Leonard Bacon found this poetry to be "bookish," and even
friendly Professor Hart at Berkeley said that the verse seemed to be
"of books rather than of reality.")[16] Needing to apply himself to the
various tasks at hand, he turned instead, as he often had before, to
the bottle.

The trouble with alcohol in Hollywood began early. On 5 May
1938 Collier Young told Carl Brandt that Faust was "very strictly on
the wagon," adding that he had "never seen him quite so fit."[17]
Three weeks later Faust provided Brandt with the following account
of a weekend:

It makes me grind my teeth to confess it, but I've been off the reservation and
boiled as an owl for thirty-six hours. Three months was the limit of my term. I
wonder if I'm to become a relapsing drunkard, one of the fools who get on a
tear once in three months? They are almost the worst type of all. Anyway, I

dropped a couple of hundred dollars into the desert sands of Mexico. . . . I
went down to Ensenada and the look of the waiters in the hotel, the sallow
face and the black eye, made me think of Italy and red wine, and pretty soon
the red wine was inside instead of outside, and the weather was totally
altered, and then – oh, you know. Sure, there was that, too; and in Mexico it's
dangerous because they wear guns. But I escaped without being shot. Damn
Mexico. Damn Booze. Above all, damn all the Heinies in the world.
    Yesterday I lay in a semi-trance, full of hypodermics.[18]

Collier Young's explanation was simpler: "Heinie's beautiful behavior collapsed. . . . He went to Ensenada over the weekend and drank
it dry!"[19] Although Faust made light of such events to Brandt, who
also had serious problems with alcohol, the drinking binges were
obviously signs of stress and malaise. They continued on occasion
throughout his years in Hollywood.

The drinking was no doubt connected to Faust's marriage. He
could not let go of his extramarital relationship, even taking trips to
New York to see Mary and insisting that his daughter Jane meet her.
Dorothy, in response, grew increasingly depressed, faced with a
husband who called her "Dearest" and claimed to love her while
demanding at the same time his right to have an affair with another
woman. Eventually she attempted suicide by taking an overdose of
sleeping pills. Dorothy's life was saved by the prompt action of the
family doctor, who pumped out her stomach. According to Jane
Faust, "Life at 317 Burlingame Avenue became a kind of hell. . . . It
was a miserable time for all of us."[20] Even when Mary Churchill –
desperate herself for a life with a future – broke off her relationship
with Faust sometime in 1940, the unhappiness continued. The
younger daughter, Judy, considered her parents "two badly mated
people,"[21] but neither parent could choose divorce as a way out of
the problems.

Faust also faced the continuing uncertainty about his heart. In
one Dr. Kildare novel a young woman, ultimately returned to health
by the young intern, suffers from a frightening, recurrent dream of
being buried alive by sand.[22] Faust suffered from sleeplessness and a
sense of weight on his chest, especially when supine. When he did
get to sleep he was tormented by nightmares of being buried alive
(Easton, 239). Family members and friends remember that during his
Hollywood years he seemed to avoid sleeping or only slept upright
in a chair.

Nevertheless, he pressed on with his work for the studios, at first interested in being "a screen playwright more than a screen super-story mind," the latter being his chief value to Hollywood.[23] By the end of 1940, after a year and a half of work for MGM, six Dr. Kildare films had been released by the studio, each based on a Faust story and starring Lew Ayres, Lionel Barrymore, Lana Turner, and Robert Young. In addition, Universal had released the Marlene Dietrich and Jimmy Stewart version of *Destry Rides Again* in 1939. A seventh MGM film based on a Faust story appeared in May of 1941. Max Brand was a genuine Hollywood success in 1940.

Faust yearned, of course, for other kinds of recognition. Hoping to find a way to be the writer he wanted to be and tired of Dr. Kildare, he quit MGM in May of 1940 and went to work for Columbia Studios, where he wrote the story for *The Desperadoes*, starring Randolph Scott, Glenn Ford, and Claire Trevor. Carl Brandt constantly encouraged him to keep at magazine work while trying to produce what the studio bosses wanted. Faust wanted either genuine respect for his Hollywood work, which he felt he did not get, or work easy enough to allow him time for serious writing. Soon he moved from Columbia to Warner Brothers, where he came in contact with a number of other writers, including William Faulkner, who had been lured to Hollywood by Jack Warner. In fact, at Warner's in August 1942 he was assigned to work with Faulkner, whom he greatly admired, on the screenplay for *The de Galle Story*.[24]

During the years following his departure from MGM and the steady Kildare work, Faust also worked for RKO, Universal, and Fox, never feeling satisfied with his studio writing. After 1940 he produced little of his own fiction for motion picture use, applying his talents instead to scripts based on the writing of others. He had originally been hired by MGM for such a purpose, as a "script doctor," but yearned without success for ways to break out of that role.

Other Efforts

During his Hollywood years Faust was unable to accomplish two literary goals. One, as usual, was to gain recognition as a poet. The problem, as he explained it to a friend in 1944, was simple: "I wanted to write good verse and in fact my greatest happiness has been in writing it; but what I day-dream about is making money, and that is what I really have been doing."[25] In 1942 he did publish a poem under his real name in *Harper's* (he had published one earlier, in 1933). Titled "Distance," it evoked the theme of human isolation, ending with the lines "Even while our bodies burn/ To incense high and sweet of ecstasy,/ The soul is closed in space immaculate."[26] None of his other poetic efforts, including long works about Jesus and Saint Francis, reached print or stood any chance of doing so. "It is a pity," he told Dorothy, "that the themes in verse which interest me are so difficult, so dead, and dull to others."[27]

The second goal was to continue his work and maintain his reputation as a writer of magazine fiction. Brandt warned him of the problem in 1940, citing other writers who were "solidly placed" in magazines before they went to Hollywood and found, for a while, "too easy money." As a result, he said, they have been "squeezed of their juice by Hollywood" and now "have neither a movie *nor* magazine market."[28] Faust at least maintained some effort directed at the magazines and produced a few stories each year between 1938 and 1944. The best to appear in print was "Miniature," a 1939 *Good Housekeeping* piece about an exiled Russian count in New York City. He also wrote a sensitive short story, "Our Daily Bread," about a family of Jewish grocers in New York's Lower East Side, providing a subtle attack on stereotypes of Jews as penurious and greedy. The story, surely based on Faust's own contact with Jewish families in 1916 and 1917, was not taken by a magazine but did see publication in a 1940 collection of Max Brand stories, *Wine on the Desert*, published by Dodd, Mead.

Rather than direct his nonstudio prose toward magazine stories, however, Faust began in 1940 an entirely new venture. Perhaps encouraged by the success of *Gone with the Wind* (and Sidney Howard's work on the movie script), he started a Civil War novel, placing high hopes on it as his first serious work of fiction. To Grace Flandrau, a St. Paul, Minnesota, writer with whom Faust corresponded extensively from 1942 to 1944, he said that he had in the Civil War story "the good, deep soil for a yarn that might mean something to the world in perhaps more than a small way."[29] He worked on the book several years, doing extensive reading in Civil War history and finally producing 200 pages of manuscript by 1944, when Harper's Cass Canfield found little to encourage in the work. Canfield's rejection was "a hard blow" to Faust, and the book remained unfinished at his death (Easton, 238).

He was also disappointed at that time by the way another of his books was received. Once the United States entered World War II, Faust turned much of his attention to the conflict. First he was an air-raid warden, and then, when wounded sailors and soldiers began to return from battle, he visited them in local hospitals. He devised several schemes for getting himself to the war as an observer, once even hoping to be parachuted behind the lines in Yugoslavia so that he could write about the resistance movement there. In 1943 he spent much time at his Brentwood house interviewing Marine flyers who had fought in Guadalcanal and were now stationed at a base in El Toro. From the experiences he heard, he created the book *The Squadron*, certain that Harper would take it. In March 1944 it too was rejected – on the basis, Faust said, of containing too much detail about aerial combat.[30]

Faust had better luck in the year of his death with magazine work. The last story published during his lifetime, a serial in the *Brooklyn Eagle* in early 1944, was a return to his earlier pulp mode. Ostensibly a crime story, *Mr. Christmas* involves a young down-and-out man, living a life of shame due to an act of cowardice in the past, who redeems himself through heroism. It was, in some respects, a reflection of Faust's wishes for himself at a time when he was hoping to find a way to get out of Hollywood and, somehow, into the war.

The best pieces of magazine prose resulting from Faust's years in Hollywood were two stories published posthumously. One was a serial, *After April*, that began in the *Saturday Evening Post* in June 1944, the month after his death. Set in wartime France and England and reflective of Faust's emotional experiences in several ways, the story tells of a young Dutchman's search for a beautiful woman who reminds him of his lost wife.

The second story, not published until 1948, was a more direct reflection of his experiences in the film capital. Titled "The King" and fewer than 2,000 words long, it is narrated by a screenwriter who tells of an older actor, famous for his earlier portrayals of King Arthur and Richard the Lion-Hearted, who turns up one evening in an elegant Hollywood restaurant. There a brash producer, reeking of success and wealth, offers the old man a huge sum of money to play Shylock in a movie version of *The Merchant of Venice*. Etherton, the actor, turns down the money. When the narrator and the producer go to the actor's apartment later, they find that the man has killed himself with a medieval dagger. "Understanding grew in me," the narrator says:

> Those rare appearances of Etherton on the screen had not been a casual amusement but the nerve center of his whole life. His parts never had been large but they had made him a king, and with a child's pitiful sincerity he had enclosed himself within a dream. Rather than step outside it, he had starved. I could imagine with what care he dressed himself this evening, borrowed the last possible dollar from a pawnbroker and went out for the final time to see if Hollywood once more would give him a shadowy throne. Instead, it preferred to see in him the wicked moneylender, so he came home and erased himself from the page.

The narrator's melancholy reflections are interrupted by the sudden excitement of the producer, Rudy Zandor. "Zandor was triumphant." The reason for his excitement embodies all that Faust detested in Hollywood's exploitation of human sentiment:

> "He wanted to be a king or nothing, you see?" roared Zandor.
> "So he came home and ended his reign. You get it? It's big stuff. It's new. It's a picture. And it's mine."[31]

In the end Faust found little to appreciate in Hollywood. Although he seemed to enjoy some aspects of his life there – the conversations with other writers, the care of his Brentwood house and garden, the relative closeness to old friends and relatives in California – the constant pressure he felt to produce only what the studio bosses wanted he found oppressive. He yearned for opportunities to deal with grand themes, especially war. In reality, as had always been his fate, he was far better at less grand matters, especially the "casual amusement" represented by his popular stories about a young medical intern named Jimmy Kildare. While Hollywood was the closing curtain on Frederick Faust's life, it gave life in abundance to the most famous Max Brand hero.

Chapter Fifteen

Dr. Kildare

One chance remained. He called for adrenalin, reached for a syringe, and tore the dress of the girl open at the breast. High on the chest he located the Angle of Louis which marks the second interspace between the ribs and counted down to the fourth interspace, over the heart. Nurse Lamont had the syringe ready for him as he swabbed the skin. Laterally from the internal mammary artery he had to make the injection. He selected the exact spot and drove the needle right in toward the heart.

> – Max Brand, *Calling Dr. Kildare* (1939)

There are three ways to look at Dr. Kildare. The first is biographical: the character was the means by which Frederick Faust made his entrance into Hollywood and sustained his six-year career there. Second, the Dr. Kildare stories show, once again, the creative powers by which Faust could fashion sentimental stories of wide appeal at a particular historical juncture. Finally, the general success of the stories – partly a matter of pulp literary style and partly a matter of Hollywood imagemaking but pure Faust throughout – is a significant part of American social history.

All three perspectives are important. Together, they underscore Dr. Kildare as Max Brand's greatest legacy and Frederick Faust's largest impact on his society. Other writers have produced hundreds of western heroes, among whom even the best of Max Brand are sometimes hard to discern. But in the transformation of a physician into a culture hero, Max Brand stands virtually alone.

From Dixie Fish to Richard Chamberlain

The fictional character of Dr. Kildare – Jimmy Kildare, a young Irish-American physician – had its origins in the experiences of Dixie Fish when he was an intern and resident at Roosevelt Hospital in New York City from 1923 to 1925. Dr. George Winthrop Fish was Faust's closest friend from their days as Berkeley undergraduates to Faust's death. During Fish's years at Roosevelt, Faust was in constant contact with him, hearing of his adventures in the hospital wards and of his work under a famous internist named Evan Evans, whose name was later honored by use as one of Faust's pseudonyms. Fish's experience lay dormant in Faust's imagination for over a decade, perhaps rising to consciousness in the mid-1930s in connection with the Evans byline.[1] Fish's explanation for the delayed birth of Dr. Kildare was simple: Faust, he said, "had dozens of plots and characters in his mind at once. Even as rapidly as he produced stories, it might take him years before he ran out of plots for one character and decided to create another."[2]

Whatever the reasons for the time lag, Dr. Kildare first came to life in the pages of Hearst's *Cosmopolitan* magazine for March 1936. The story, it turned out, had a subtle double entendre in its title. Interns cannot take money as bribes nor do they take much money home as salary. With Jimmy Kildare, a straight-arrow M.D. making his way through big-city patients and temptations in the story, the story was an instant success both in print and, especially, in its 1937 Paramount release as a motion picture. As a film, *Internes Can't Take Money* was the key reason for MGM's hiring of Faust in 1938 and the studio's constant pressure on their new writer to turn out more Kildare material.

He did, and MGM soon began its production of seven Kildare stories by Faust. Both screen and print were thereafter flooded with Max Brand medical dramas. Under MGM's procedure, Faust first wrote the story, which was turned over to Willis Goldbeck and Harry Ruskin for the movie script, and then he sold magazines and book rights through Carl Brandt's agency. The public therefore could see a story first as a movie, then read it as a Max Brand serial in *Cosmopolitan* or *Argosy*, and then read it again as a hardcover Max Brand book issued by Dodd, Mead. For instance, *Young Dr. Kildare*, released in October 1938 as the first MGM film, appeared next as an *Argosy* serial the following month and then in February 1941 as a book.

All told, Faust produced Kildare material for eight motion pictures, two short stories, four single-issue magazine novels, four serials, and seven books – all of this appearing between March 1936 and January 1943. In those seven years Faust saw 34 story items involving

Dr. Kildare published or released, an average of one every two and a half months.

And this was not all. After Faust left MGM, the studio negotiated the right to use the name of Faust's characters and produced eight more Kildare movies. Although none of these were based on Faust's writing, they continued to keep his characters and basic hospital situations before the viewing public until 1947. In 1950 and 1951 a syndicated radio series, *The Story of Dr. Kildare*, was broadcast, featuring in 64 episodes the two actors who had appeared in all the MGM films: Lew Ayres and Lionel Barrymore. Finally, from 1961 to 1966 NBC produced *Dr. Kildare*, the television series starring Richard Chamberlain and Raymond Massey. By then Dr. Kildare had come a long way from Faust's original musings about his physician friend's experience in Roosevelt Hospital.

Kildare Stories

If the idea for Dr. Kildare came from memories of Dixie Fish in the early 1920s, the style of the stories was shaped by their first appearance as magazine fiction. Two stories – "Internes Can't Take Money" and "Whiskey Sour" – were published by *Hearst's International Cosmopolitan*, a monthly magazine for general readers. "Internes" was, in fact, Faust's first sale to *Cosmopolitan*, which continued to buy work from him thereafter. The sale came at a time when he was still struggling to expand the market for his work and working closely with Carl Brandt. Both "Internes" and "Whiskey Sour" were written specifically for the magazine, unlike later Kildare stories, all of which were written with a motion picture release foremost in Faust's mind and the MGM scriptwriters eagerly waiting for him to finish the initial manuscript. As such, the *Cosmopolitan* stories are relatively untarnished by Hollywood intentions and among Faust's best magazine work of the 1930s.

"Internes Can't Take Money" combines a young intern's personal concerns about his financial future with the ethics of the medical profession, the politics of a big city, the activities of a criminal underworld, and a number of esoteric medical procedures. Kildare himself is a relatively new intern, "an unpaid labor slave," working

under a famous doctor named Henry Fearson and often frequenting
Tom McGuire's neighborhood saloon.

The tone of the story, perfect for the Depression year of 1936, is
established by Kildare's fear that his poverty will force his return to
the country farm where he was raised: "The future to him was a
great question mark, and New York was the emptiness inside the
loop of the mark. Add a few strokes to the question mark and you get
a dollar sign."[3] The young doctor's economic dread stands in contrast to the heavily moneyed politicians and criminals in the Hell's
Kitchen area around the hospital where "there were men who lived
according to a new standard of morality about which Kildare knew
nothing" (134). He notices the difference even in the "perfection" of
clothes worn by such persons as the wounded Pat Hanlon, whom he
is asked to treat in the privacy of McGuire's saloon.

The sentimental resolution of the story brings together medicine
and the morality of the street, a reconciliation suggested early when
Kildare performs a virtually illegal operation on Hanlon, presumed to
be a hoodlum, assisted by the injured man's associates. The people
of the street and the saloon pay homage to Kildare even in their
physical attention to him after the operation: "Jeff and another man
. . . were rubbing the blood from Kildare's hands with painful care.
He surrendered his hands to them like tools of infinite value in the
trust of friends. A warmth flowed like strong drink through his brain"
(136).

A complication occurs, however, when Tom McGuire, owner of
the saloon and political boss of the local ward, later leaves $1,000
with Kildare for his services. As an intern, Kildare cannot take the
money, especially for work done outside the hospital, even though it
would mean his salvation and the continuation of his work under
Fearson. His problem is ultimately solved, however, when he learns
that Fearson owes a large gambling debt that is erased through
McGuire's assistance after Kildare performs another out-of-hospital
surgery, this time to save the life of a man Hanlon had shot. The
point of the story is the respect Kildare earns through his combination of integrity and medical skill.

The second *Cosmopolitan* story adds sex to Kildare's situation
and presents a tight fictional structure emphasizing Kildare's physical
weariness as an intern, his heroic reputation in the political ward
around the hospital, his friendship with ward bosses Tom McGuire

and Pat Hanlon, his human susceptibility to romantic love, and his great skill as a diagnostician and surgeon. "Whiskey Sour" begins with the admission to the hospital of a badly wounded man, Lafferty, accompanied by a red-haired woman. Lafferty insists that Kildare close his wounds. The woman remains, at that time, only as "a dim pleasure on the horizon of Kildare's Mind" (56). The story then shifts to the hospital administrator, Dr. Gloster, who is concerned about Kildare's rising reputation in the political ward – for a newspaper article even suggests that he would be a good candidate for public office – and tells him to stick to his hospital duties. Kildare then goes to tell his friends Pat Hanlon (who was his patient in "Internes") and Tom McGuire that he will no longer be able to see them. When he enters McGuire's bar, McGuire and Hanlon are trying to figure out how to keep the wounded Lafferty from revealing some false political dirt that will destroy McGuire. With them is the woman, Meg, who had brought Lafferty to the hospital. They agree, before they go out to speak with Kildare, that Meg can try to restrain Kildare and keep him from returning to the hospital in time to prevent Lafferty's death.

Meg's beauty tempts Kildare, who is fighting exhaustion from his round-the-clock duties at the hospital, and takes him for a drive in her car. He falls in love with her – hard, it seems – and talks to her about marriage. "We're going to burst out – like summer – like summer after winter – like blue heaven – you and I, Meg, when we're married," he says as he finally leaves her (39). Back at the hospital he notices something unusual about Lafferty, who is still alive and interested in telling his story to a stenographer. Kildare, completely unaware of his relationship to McGuire, asks him to rest, first, and then takes a phone call from Meg, who begs Kildare to come to her place. To do this he must violate a cardinal hospital rule by leaving when he is on duty. But he asks another intern to cover for him and goes to Meg's. There Meg introduces him to her husband, letting Kildare know that she had duped him. "I'm sorry I was such a fool, Meg," he says, and leaves. Hanlon and McGuire enter and accuse Meg of betraying them by breaking off so quickly with Kildare when she could have kept him away from the hospital. But all three of them realize their affection for the young doctor. "Well, to hell with us!" Hanlon says, "He's worth the whole pack of cards" (40).

Back at the hospital Kildare's absence has been noted, and Dr. Gloster tells him that his career is over. Kildare accepts the verdict but asks that Lafferty be operated on again, for he suspects that the man is suffering not from infection but from a blood clot resulting from a fractured skull. Gloster allows Kildare to perform the operation as his last act in the hospital. It is a success, described in considerable detail:

> He cut the bone of the skull on three sides and broke it off on the fourth. It would grow better that way, when the piece was inset again. The blood clot was exposed before him.
>
> Kildare lifted out the clot. From a small blood vessel blood was oozing almost inappreciably. With exquisite delicacy, Kildare picked up the ruptured blood vessel with small hemostats and tied it off. (41)

"That was a beautiful diagnosis . . . a beautiful operation," Gloster tells Kildare (42). Lafferty, when he recovers from the operation and learns that Kildare is one of McGuire's friends, asks Kildare to tell McGuire that everything is all right.

With Kildare's future in the hospital now secured by the brilliance of his medicine and the political threat to McGuire removed by the same, all that is left to tie up at the end of the story is the affair with Meg. She is waiting outside in her car, crying. Kildare now senses why she had to ask him to come to her house and learn of her marriage. In words that reinforce the story's basic connection between medicine with love, Kildare says, "I think I understand. It was an operation. You had to cut me out of your life." When Meg asks for his forgiveness, he replies, "A right sort of patient has to trust his doctor." (42)

Kildare in Hollywood

Both "Internes Can't Take Money" and "Whiskey Sour" were written before Faust went to Hollywood. Once there, after following a series of story leads that went nowhere, he returned in desperation to the idea of more Kildare yarns. Hollywood added two elements to his original mix of characters and situations. First, Paramount's screen version of "Internes" had inserted a romantic subplot involving Kildare's relationship with a nurse, an element completely missing in the two short stories. Second, MGM was seeking a way to make use of a partly infirm Lionel Barrymore, a situation which gave rise to Faust's invention of a gruff mentor, Dr. Gillespie, for the young Kildare. It was this invention, in fact, that assured Faust of his MGM job. "Max Brand has an idea for a doctor who has cancer," one MGM producer told another in the spring of 1938. "And he's a great doctor and he wants to impart as much information as he can to his young assistant before his time runs out." According to Faust, the producers were ecstatic about the idea, especially since Barrymore was Louis B. Mayer's favorite actor.[4]

With a love interest now within the hospital, along with the constant interaction of Kildare and his older mentor, Frederick Faust and Metro-Goldwyn-Mayer had a winning and highly profitable formula for medical stories. In fact, as Joseph Turow explains in *Playing Doctor: Television, Storytelling, and Medical Power*, Faust played a major role in shifting the image of the medical profession and turning the American doctor into a culture hero. What began with Jimmy Kildare continued at least through *M*A*S*H*. According to Turow, Faust's positive view of human nature and his belief in both heroism and science came effectively together in his fictional treatment of doctors and the profession of medicine. (Turow, 9). Also central to his success, though, were his finely honed skill in the creation of stories and his deployment of sentimentality.

It is theoretically possible to distinguish between the Kildare films and the stories because of the plot changes introduced by screenwriters Goldbeck and Ruskin. Faust may even have used some of the screenwriters' changes to his original story in later magazine and book editions. Overall, however, Faust's achievement – Max Brand as the premier American author of sentimental medical fiction – shows up clearly in his final printed stories, as virtually any example will illustrate.

Young Dr. Kildare, the first MGM story, introduced not only Dr. Gillespie, the gruff but humanistic mentor, but also Jimmy Kildare's past. In the pre-MGM magazine stories, Kildare's rural past is mentioned only as something to which he does not want to return. But for the wider audience now available through motion pictures, Faust added the Norman Rockwell–like details of a country doctor as Kildare's father. In order to pursue his own medical dreams, Kildare must turn away from his father's practice and, at a salary of only $20 a month, take up an internship at Blair General Hospital under the supervision of Dr. Gillespie. The fact that Gillespie is apparently dying of cancer makes it all the more important for Kildare to learn as much as he can as quickly as possible.

In *Calling Dr. Kildare*, a movie in 1939 and a book in 1940, Faust added an in-hospital romantic attraction in the person of nurse Mary Lamont, who became a standard feature in later stories. In this story Faust pays particular attention to the matter of Kildare's "heart," his development of a humanistic approach to patients. His failing, at the beginning of the story, lies in being too coldly professional. "Good grief, Kildare," Gillespie challenges him, "don't your patients have any faces for you? Are they all numbers and diseases?"[5] As the story progresses, Kildare shows true heart, convincing Gillespie that he has not only brainpower and knowledge but also the proper sentiments to become a great doctor. It is no surprise, therefore, that the American Medical Association praised *Calling Dr. Kildare* when it appeared on the screen (Turow, 16). In its printed form, the story was particularly effective in describing medical procedures in dramatic language, showing the detailed information Faust gained from Drs. Fish and Eickenberry (the Faust family doctor in Brentwood), and adding some scientific exoticism to the narrative. In one procedure, for instance, it is necessary to use "some of the bacterial antigen of brucella melitensis" (177).

But it is the human, not the scientific, interest that shows Faust's talent as a popular writer. *Calling Dr. Kildare* is peppered effectively with sharply drawn pulp characters: the local residents of Hell's Kitchen outside the hospital, a hospital switchboard operator, an ambulance driver, a bartender, and the like. There is also an understated romantic triangle that develops when Kildare is infatuated with a Hell's Kitchen woman named Rosalie, a contrast to the white-uniformed Mary Lamont. These characters all fit together in a plot where a life is saved, a murder is solved, and Kildare's heart is revealed for both Dr. Gillespie and the public to see. Such a story, according to Joseph Turow, meant that the American physician could be seen "as a member of a modern elect: a contemporary knight whose painful movement through the lists of training had shown that he had the heroic stature necessary to link a compassionate nature to the wonders of healing technology" (Turow, 12).

The prose in the Kildare novels is often crisp and clipped in the style of the hard-boiled detective school, especially the dialogue. For instance, near the end of *The Secret of Dr. Kildare* (a 1939 film and a 1940 book) the underlying romance between Jimmy Kildare and Mary Lamont is couched in the language of affectionate sarcasm:

> "I was going to tell you [Kildare says] that if you were a few years older and I were making some money, I'd probably ask you to marry me."
>
> She stepped in close to him. Under her coat he could see the white of her uniform at the throat and there was a dim high light on her cheek and in her eyes.
>
> "You're damned nice," said Kildare. "You're going to be gentle and cherishing and all that before you smack me down."[6]

This novel, the first Kildare story published as a Dodd, Mead book (even though it was the fourth to be released as a motion picture), contains a number of particularly effective passages. It also blends together all of the previous Kildare elements plus a social-class concern in the character of the wealthy Paul Messenger, who figures in later plots as well. Messenger, Kildare realizes, "considered the rest of the world an infinite step beneath him and his peers. To Kildare a man was what he seemed to be, and a good fellow until he was proved otherwise by the course of events" (107). As a result, the novel's plot not only must resolve disease, romantic problems of the human heart, and an ethical dilemma for Kildare, but it must also reform the rich man's undemocratic attitudes. Given the sheer wealth of material in the story, it was a good choice by Dodd, Mead as the first Dr. Kildare book.

Not all matters are always resolved in a Max Brand story, of course. In *Dr. Kildare's Crisis* (a 1940 film and a 1942 book) one of the reappearing characters is killed off in an ambulance wreck. Even the great Dr. Gillespie's skill cannot save him, nor can the doctor offer the man's survivors any real condolence. Medicine and surgery are all panaceas, he tells Mary Lamont. "If I were a boy again," he says, "I'd make a new start all over again, and do you know what I'd do, my dear girl? I'd learn how to pray. I'd learn one damned good prayer and have it ready when the time comes that nothing else can help."[7] Kildare, too, has his moments of despair: "Sometimes the whole profession of medicine was abhorrent to him" (98).

Such statements illustrate the central contribution of Max Brand to the popular culture of medicine: the sense of dedicated professionals in tune both with scientific knowledge and their own humanity. Even Jimmy Kildare's frequent trips to McGuire's bar are part of the picture, showing clearly that despite the special, almost romantic calling that raises the moral stature of Kildare and Gillespie high above others, the doctor is even more of a hero because he can identify with common humanity.

Faust quit writing Kildare stories in 1941 after MGM released *The People vs. Dr. Kildare* in May. Although his work was lucrative and Faust once had felt that stories about the intern could be generated indefinitely, he was discouraged by a studio decision to elevate the character of Gillespie over Kildare. As he told Brandt later, "The movies, because . . . they laid the emphasis on Gillespie and turned Kildare into any young doctor, do not understand that the opposition between the old man and the young one is at the heart of the business."[8] At the time of this statement, in May 1942, Faust suggested that he re-enter the Kildare business, perhaps even by sending the intern to war in the medical corps, but nothing came of the idea.

By 1941 Faust had lived with Dr. Kildare for five years as a constant fictional creation and, as it was, constant re-creation. While the literary value of this production may be negligible in ordinary terms, Dr. Kildare was no small matter in other ways, including its impact on the general image of the medical profession. It is no wonder that the American Medical Association found it easy to praise the Kildare movies – and no doubt that Max Brand increased the post–World War II earning power of American physicians.

Conclusion

But the best ending of life seems to be a question mark.
                    – Letter to Grace Flandrau, 1942

The ending of Frederick Faust's life could have been written by Max Brand. Like many pulp stories, it was an awakening to heroic action and the facing of mortal danger beyond the call of necessity. That his death took place in the Italy he loved seems almost a poetic touch to the event, perhaps even the way that Hollywood would have chosen to portray it.

"I have been trying to wangle ways of getting at least within the sound of gunfire, but people in authority monotonously insist that I am fifty and have a silly ticker," Faust told a friend in early 1943.[1] The "ticker," his heart, was indeed part of the difficulty he faced in getting overseas. A year later, however, he received an ambivalent clearance from his doctor and an assignment from *Harper's* as a correspondent. He wanted to write the story of the war as it was lived by infantry soldiers. Although Dorothy and other members of his family felt that he was simply desperate to escape his personal problems at home and his Hollywood routine, no one could stop him. By late April of 1944 he was in Italy, assigned to the 88th Infantry Division of the U.S. Fifth Army north of Naples, where the Allied command was preparing an offensive to flush out the firmly entrenched German forces in central Italy. To Dorothy and others he mailed back long, almost daily accounts of his experiences and impressions.

On the eleventh of May he finally had the chance to see combat – something that he had desired since 1915. The battalion he had joined was assigned to clear German troops from the nearby town of Santa Maria Infante as part of the big Allied push to Rome. At 11 P.M. the men moved forward, with the unarmed Faust refusing to stay behind as he had been advised to do. The battalion suddenly found itself engaged in a 60-hour battle against unexpectedly strong opposition. Shortly after the fighting began Faust was wounded by mortar fire. Urging others to continue fighting, he waited for

161

stretcher bearers to reach him. When they did, he was dead, from either a shell fragment or the final failure of his "silly ticker." In his death, said one of the soldiers in his battalion, he showed "coolness under fire and his gallant disregard of personal safety." He was "an inspiration to all who saw him on the battlefield that night."[2]

In his final days – out of place, overaged, and burdened with a weak heart – Faust rose above his limitations and did, indeed, achieve a form of heroism. In a similar manner, his work as Max Brand frequently rose above the limitations of its intent and its commercial content. At its ordinary level, Max Brand was popular entertainment, for its own times, presented in an engaging style and offering its readers a view of human life inspired, as Harry Destry says, "by love and high aspiration." At its best, Max Brand was a means of tapping into rich veins of human fantasy.

The limitations of Max Brand are obvious, and Frederick Faust knew them well. "Now and then in short stories, I've barely rubbed elbows with painful truth," he told the writer Grace Flandrau in 1942, "but I've never liked that truth; it's always seemed horrible to me."[3] Although Max Brand stories are often filled with violence and death – obsessively so in some cases – they almost always lack a sense of "painful truth." Faust could not write a good Civil War novel in his closing years, no doubt, because the horrible tragedy of that war was beyond his sensibility. To some extent the same problem appears, in different form, in his poetry, where experience itself seems distant, lurking somewhere behind a screen of unnecessarily abstract and dated language.

But if the limitations are easy to describe, the central meaning of Max Brand is not. It is tempting and somewhat expected to seek a unitary explanation for a writer's literary achievement. The sheer quantity of Max Brand fiction is a large part of the problem; it begs for concepts capable of handling the whole. Some scholars, therefore, have tended to take a reductive view of Max Brand, sorting through the fiction to locate traits that illustrate particular hypotheses. For Christine Bold, the central fact of Max Brand is a divided allegiance to money and art as illustrated by his roles as commercial writer and classical poet: in Bold's view, the struggle "between classicist and hack" is also the basic struggle within Max Brand novels (Bold, 92). For Cynthia Hamilton, Max Brand novels are "intensely personal myths" that show psychological origins in Faust's child-hood (Hamilton, 115). For Jon Tuska, taking a more expansive view, Max Brand stories are Jungian "psycho-dramas" clothed "in suppos-edly realistic fiction"; Max Brand Indians are thus "archetypal embodiments projected from the unconscious," and Frederick Faust was a writer uniquely capable of embedding universal themes in his work.[4]

Such views are intellectually compelling and offer useful insight into much of Max Brand; but the sheer diversity of Faust's fiction raises questions about any unitary explanation. It is difficult even with Max Brand westerns to reconcile the instinctual animalism of a hero like Dan Barry with the growing self-awareness of a Harry Destry. Moreover, knowledge of the entire range of Max Brand sto-ries makes it difficult even to single out one genre as most significant. While westerns are the best known and most discussed, the histori-cal novels have compelling themes and the crime stories are often written in a distinctive prose style. The Kildare work shows extraor-dinary facility in the manipulation of plots and character types. Then there are the sometimes brilliant short stories published in pulp, slick, and highbrow magazines – and some work so bad that it deserves the term "brainless drip" that Faust occasionally applied to all of his prose. Hardly anything is unitary about Max Brand.

Perhaps Faust himself should have the last word on Max Brand. In 1942 he proposed to his old friend Walter Morris Hart at Berkeley a Hawthorne-like distinction between "tales" and fiction. "The tale seems the better thing to me. It is a purer form," he said. "Would you not say that the tale, like poetry, freely abandons all attempts to give an exact replica of life, of reality, and writes the reader out the door . . . into the world of open conceiving, so that in spite of its apparent simplicity it is a truer art form?"[5] If not instances of a truer art form, the tales of Max Brand certainly deserve the light of "open conceiving." And the most obvious trait on exhibit in Max Brand, the unifying element in millions of words, is simply Faust's talent for cre-ating stories.

Notes and References

Chapter One

1. The known pseudonyms under which Faust's professional work was published during his life are Frank Austin, George Owen Baxter, Lee Bolt, Max Brand, M.B., Walter C. Butler, George Challis, Martin Dexter, Peter Dawson, Evan Evans, Evin Evan, John Frederick, Frederick Frost, Dennis Lawton, David Manning, Peter Henry Morland, Hugh Owen, and Nicholas Silver. In college he published a newspaper column under the byline "Little Bobbie"; he later submitted (but apparently did not publish) poetry under the alias of Henry Uriel, and he was the ghostwriter of a historical novel published with Robert Simpson listed as author. He also published many works under his real name.

2. William F. Nolan, *Max Brand: Western Giant* (Bowling Green, Ohio: Bowling Green State University Popular Press, 1986), 2; hereafter cited in text.

3. William F. Nolan, Introduction to *Max Brand's Best Western Stories* (New York: Dodd, Mead, 1981), 21.

4. Letters to Carl Brandt, 21 November 1936, and to Dorothy Faust, 13 October 1932, Faust Papers (hereafter cited as FP), Bancroft Library, University of California at Berkeley.

5. Martha Bacon, "Destry and Dionysus," *Atlantic*, July 1955, 73-74; hereafter cited in text.

6. Letter to Jane Faust, 25 November 1939, FP.

7. Steve Fisher, "A Farewell to Max Brand," in Nolan, *Western Giant*, 43.

8. This and the other writings about Faust mentioned in the remainder of the chapter are listed in the Bibliography.

Chapter Two

1. Unless otherwise noted, general information about Faust's life comes from two sources: Robert Easton's biography, *Max Brand: The Big "Westerner"* (Norman: University of Oklahoma Press, 1970), and John Schoolcraft's long unpublished manuscript, "The Fabulous Faust," a copy of which is among Faust's papers at the Bancroft Library and from which

Easton drew heavily. Both works are hereafter cited in text. Some additional details come from correspondence with Faust family members.

2. Letter to Jane Faust, 25 November 1939, FP.

3. Letter to Dorothy Schillig, 21 December 1915, FP.

4. Letter to Jane Faust, 25 November 1939, FP.

5. Much of the information about Dr. Cooper and Modesto comes from an interview with the author in August 1985.

6. Published in his high school literary magazine, the *Sycamore*, June 1911.

7. Verne A. Stadtman, *The University of California, 1868-1968* (New York: McGraw-Hill, 1970), 277.

8. Henry Morse Stephens in the university yearbook, *Blue and Gold: 1913* (Berkeley: University of California, 1913), 23.

9. Dorothy Rieber Joralemon, "Growing Up in Berkeley, 1900-1917," *American West*, July-August 1983, 43-44.

10. Letter to Jane Faust, 25 November 1939, FP.

11. John Cooper, December 1984 telephone interview with Robert Easton, reported in a letter to the author, 31 December 1984.

12. "Guenevere," *Occident* 63, no. 3 (November 1912): 31.

13. "Oscar Wilde," *Occident* 63, no. 2 (October 1912): 28-36.

14. W. Lewis Jones, "The Arthurian Legend," *The Cambridge History of English Literature*, vol. 1, ed. A. W. Ward and A. R. Waller (New York and London: G. P. Putnam's Sons, 1907), 303-4.

15. "Palomides," *Occident*, 65, no. 1 (September 1913): 42.

16. "College Sonnets" (untitled), *Occident*, 67, no. 1 (September 1914): 17-27.

17. *Pelican* (publication of the University of California) 21, no. 1 (September 1916): 19.

18. Editor's comments, *Pelican* 17, no. 1 (September 1914): 15.

19. Editor's comments, *Pelican* 17, no. 4 (December 1914): 63.

20. Editor's comments, *Pelican* 18, no. 1 (January 1915): 17.

21. "Pelican Interview," *Pelican* 18, no. 3 (March 1915): 10.

22. "Faust Revealed as Little Bobbie," *Daily Californian*, 27 April 1915.

23. Harvey Roney, "Seven Years with Heinie Faust," *Faust Collector*, no. 7 (August 1970): 2; hereafter cited in text.

24. Letter to Thomas Downey, 2 August 1915, FP.

25. Benjamin Ide Wheeler, "Commencement Address," *University of California Chronicle* 17 (July 1915): 258-59.

26. Letter to Harvey Roney, 29 October 1918, FP.

Chapter Three

1. As one of Faust's classmates later said, it was a time of "war in Europe, revolution in Mexico, revolution in China, . . . strikes up and down the coast, and the professions too full, with room only at the top" (Irma Riley, "California 1915," in *25th Reunion: Class of 1915* [Berkeley, 1940], a publication prepared by the class of 1915, p. 5). Faust's intentions to travel to India are explained in Easton's biography and also in correspondence in his papers at the Bancroft Library. Unless otherwise noted, the source of the basic biographical information presented here and later in the chapter is Easton's biography.

2. Letter to D. Schillig, 15 September 1915, FP.

3. Letter to J. Schoolcraft, 20 October 1915, quoted in Schoolcraft.

4. Letter to D. Schillig, 21 December 1915, FP.

5. Ronald G. Haycock ("The American Legion in the Canadian Expeditionary Force, 1914-1917: A Study in Failure," *Military Affairs* 43 [October 1979]: 112-20) documents the unit that Faust joined.

6. Letter to J. Schoolcraft, early 1916, quoted in Schoolcraft.

7. Letter to J. Schoolcraft, 1916, quoted in Schoolcraft.

8. Letter to J. Schoolcraft, 28 September 1916, quoted in Schoolcraft.

9. See also Robert Easton to W. Bloodworth, 19 January 1993.

10. Howard V. Bloomfield (ex-Munsey editor), interview with author, 22 November 1986; Edward H. Dodd, Jr., "Twenty-Five Million Words," in *Max Brand: The Man and His Work*, ed. Darrell C. Richardson (Los Angeles: Fantasy Publishing Co., 1952), 60.

11. Letter to R. H. Davis, 8 April 1917, Davis Papers (hereafter cited as DP), New York Public Library.

12. Letter to R. H. Davis. 16 April 1917, DP.

13. *All-Story Weekly* 52, no. 3 (23 June 1917), 441.

14. Max Brand, *Fate's Honeymoon* (London: Hodder & Stoughton, 1926), 64. Originally published as a serial in *All-Story Weekly*, beginning 14 July 1917.

15. Easton provides this information, pp. 50-51.

16. Letter to R. H. Davis, 23 May 1917, DP.

17. John Frederick, *The Sword Lover* (New York: Henry Waterson Co., 1927), 10; hereafter cited in text. Originally published as a Max Brand serial in *Argosy*, beginning 10 November 1917. The use of a different pen name – John Frederick in this case – for the hardcover version of a novel was common practice in Faust's career.

Chapter Four

1. Letter to R. H. Davis, 18 October 1918, DP.

2. Dorothy Rieber Joralemon, unpublished diary, quoted in a letter to W. Bloodworth, 6 October 1985.

3. *Harrigan* was republished in 1971 by Dodd, Mead.

4. Max Brand, "Above the Law," *All-Story Weekly*, 31 August 1918, 55. Faust's use of rape fears is obvious after the heroine, Ruth, is captured by Black Jim's gang and one member of the gang says, "She don't savy yet, boys, that she's in a real democracy where everything's common property" (48).

5. Max Brand, "Bad-Eye, His Life and Letters," *All-Story Weekly*, 19 October 1918, 603.

6. Max Brand, "No Partners," *All-Story Weekly*, 26 October 1918, 53.

7. Max Brand, *The Untamed* (New York: Pocket Books, 1955), 9; hereafter cited in text. This paperback is a reprint of the 1919 Putnam hardcover.

8. "Above the Law," 55.

Chapter Five

1. Letter to R. H. Davis, 17 February 1918, DP.

2. Letter to R. H. Davis, 18 April 1918, DP.

3. Letter from R. H. Davis, 13 October 1918, DP.

4. Letter to R. H. Davis, 1 April 1919, DP.

5. Letter from R. H. Davis, 27 February 1919, DP.

6. Letter from R. H. Davis, 17 April 1919, DP.

7. Letter from R. H. Davis, 17 April 1919. DP.

8. Letter to R. H. Davis, 21 April 1919, DP.

9. Letter to R. H. Davis, 17 May 1919, DP.

10. Letter to R. H. Davis, 30 August 1919, DP.

11. John Frederick, *Riders of the Silences* (New York: A. L. Burt, 1920), 16. Originally published as "Luck," by John Frederick, an *Argosy* serial, beginning 9 August 1919.

12. Max Brand, *The Night Horseman* (New York: Pocket Books, 1954), 205. Originally published as a book by Putnam in 1920.

13. Max Brand, *The Seventh Man* (New York: Warner Books, 1974), 70. Originally published as a book by Putnam in 1921), 70.

14. See Richard Slotkin, *Regeneration through Violence: The Mythology of the American Frontier, 1600-1860* (Middletown, Conn.: Wesleyan University Press, 1973).

15. Letter to D. Faust, 18 February 1919, FP.

16. Max Brand, *Trailin'* (New York: Warner Books, 1975), 186. Originally published as a book by Putnam in 1920.

17. John Frederick, "Pride of Tyson," *Argosy-All Story Weekly*, 7 August 1920, 179. This serial appeared in the first issue of a magazine that combined *Argosy* and *All-Story Weekly*. The use of the John Frederick pseudonym suggests that Faust intended it for *Argosy* and the magazine's editor, Robert Simpson. The serial was published as a hardcover book in 1926 by Hodder & Stoughton in London; it has never been published in book form in the United States.

18. Max Brand, *The Garden of Eden* (New York: Warner Books, 1976), 160. Originally published as a book by Hodder & Stoughton in London, 1926.

Chapter Six

1. Tom Mix played Dan Barry in both *The Untamed* (1920) and *The Night Horseman* (1921), both produced by Fox. He also starred in the Fox version of *Trailin'* (1921) and in four other movies based on Max Brand westerns. Dustin Farnum, Buck Jones, and Ken Maynard also starred in film versions of Max Brand westerns during the 1920s.

2. Letter from R. H. Davis, 27 February 1919, DP.

3. Quentin J. Reynolds, *The Fiction Factory* (New York: Random House, 1955), 176; hereafter cited in text.

4. Frank E. Blackwell to John Schoolcraft, 29 May 1950, FP.

5. Letter to J. Schoolcraft, 29 April 1921, quoted in Schoolcraft.

6. Publication figures are from the list of Faust's fiction in Nolan, *Western Giant*, 114-39.

7. Cynthia S. Hamilton, *Western and Hard-Boiled Detective Fiction in America* (Iowa City: University of Iowa Press, 1987), 42-43; hereafter cited in text.

8. Christine Bold, *Selling the Wild West: Popular Western Fiction, 1860 to 1960* (Bloomington and Indianapolis: Indiana University Press, 1987), 91-104; hereafter cited in text.

9. Max Brand, *Wild Freedom* (New York: Warner Books, 1983), 74. Faust's western heroes often read Malory. For Lee Garrison of *Galloping Danger* (1923), *Morte d'Arthur* "was his first love among books and would remain his last."

10. Max Brand, *The Smiling Desperado* (New York: Warner Books, 1974), 19.

11. Max Brand, *Trouble Trail* (New York: Warner Books, 1972), 7-8.

12. Max Brand, *Border Guns* (New York: Warner Books, 1975), 17.

Chapter Seven

1. Letter to D. Faust, 18 February 1919, FP.

2. Memorandum from Dr. Robert Halsey, n.d., FP.

3. The meeting with Jung came after Faust met one of Jung's protégés, with whom Leonard Bacon had been in contact. Faust used the opportunity to discuss literature and art more than health. In a letter to Bacon, Faust said, "I have seen Jung. He told me, in short, that the only way to be honest in writing was to search my own mind, because no outsider could put his finger on what was bunk in me and what was real." Referring to psychoanalysis in general, Faust said, "I gathered an impression that there is a great deal of mist and mystery in Switzerland" (Letter to L. Bacon, 14 October 1925, Bacon Papers, Beinecke Library, Yale University; hereafter cited as BP).

4. Letter to J. Schoolcraft, 22 July 1918, quoted in Schoolcraft.

5. Frederick Faust, "Balin," in *The Village Street* (New York: G. P. Putnam's Sons, 1922), 97.

6. Letter to J. Schoolcraft, 21 March and 20 May 1921, quoted in Schoolcraft.

7. Letter to Harvey Roney, n.d., quoted in Schoolcraft.

8. Letter to L. Bacon, 30 August and 30 September 1925, BP.

9. Letter to J. Schoolcraft, 13 August 1921, quoted in Schoolcraft.

10. Letter to G. W. Fish, 4 July 1931, FP.

11. Letter to Carl Brandt, 4 August 1931, FP.

12. Easton cites one review, by a Berkeley professor, a friend of Leonard Bacon, in the *University of California Chronicle* (Easton, 152).

13. Frederick Faust, *Dionysus in Hades* (Oxford: Basil Blackwell, 1931), 89.

Chapter Eight

1. Letter to J. Schoolcraft, 25 March 1921, quoted in Schoolcraft.

2. Letter to J. Schoolcraft, 19 August 1921, quoted in Schoolcraft.

3. Letter to Chandler Barton, 30 July 1925, FP.

4. Letter to R. Easton, 1942, quoted in Schoolcraft, who gives only the year as the date.

5. Caradoc is the only knight of the Round Table whose wife remains faithful to him. While Faust's novel does nothing with this motif, faithfulness itself plays a role in the relationship between the two male characters, Rhiannon and Caradac.

6. Max Brand, *Singing Guns* (New York: Dodd, Mead, 1938), 138; hereafter cited in text. The novel was first published as a *Western Story* serial under the pseudonym of George Owen Baxter, beginning 15 December 1928; it was not published as a book until 1938.

7. In discussing *Singing Guns*, Hamilton says that Rhiannon's values (loyalty and a sense of responsibility) conflict with the "social Darwinist" values of Caradac (105-6).

8. From 1919 to 1928, beginning with *The Untamed*, Putnam published 10 Faust serials as hardback novels. Around 1927 Faust severed his long-standing arrangement with Robert H. Davis, his old Munsey editor, who had been placing his pulp fiction with Putnam and with Hollywood. Thereafter, Faust's agent was Carl Brandt, who placed dozens of serials with Dodd, Mead. Dodd, Mead continued to publish Max Brand books until the late 1980s.

9. Details regarding publication and screen versions of *Destry Rides Again* come from David L. Fox's unpublished M.A. thesis, "The History of a Hero: A Study of Max Brand's *Destry Rides Again*" (Western Carolina University, 1984); hereafter cited in text.

10. Max Brand, *Destry Rides Again* (Boston: Gregg Press, 1979; originally published by Dodd, Mead in 1930), 267-78.

11. Jane Tompkins, *West of Everything: The Inner Life of Westerns* (New York and Oxford: Oxford University Press, 1992), 13-15.

Chapter Nine

1. Letter to G. W. Fish, 22 March 1926, FP.

2. Letter to D. Faust, 13 February 1929, FP.

3. Letter to D. Faust, 13 February 1929, FP.

4. Letter to G. W. Fish, 5 August 1931, FP.

5. Letter from Carl Brandt, 5 August 1931, FP.

6. Letter to C. Brandt, 6 April 1932, FP.

7. Letter from R. H. Davis, 7 September 1927, DP.

8. Letter to R. H. Davis, 12 March 1930, DP.

9. Letter to D. Faust, 10 May 1932, FP.

10. Letter to D. Faust, 10 May 1932, FP. The reference to his writing as a joint project had some basis in fact because he discussed many of his stories with Dorothy, and she read his manuscripts for errors before sending them to his agent.

11. Letter to Walter Morris Hart, 9 June 1932, FP.

12. Letter to C. Brandt, 30 July 1932, FP.

13. Letter to G. W. Fish, 1 August 1932, FP.

14. Letter to C. Brandt, 30 July 1932, FP.

15. Letter to D. Faust, 13 September 1932, FP.

16. Letter to D. Faust, 10 September 1932, FP.

17. Letter to D. Faust, 30 September 1932, FP.

18. Frank E. Blackwell to C. Brandt, 28 November 1932, FP.

19. Letter to L. Bacon, 31 July 1933, BP.

20. Letter to D. Faust, 30 September 1932.

21. Letter to C. Brandt, 15 December 1932, FP.

22. Letter to D. Faust, 13 October 1932, FP.

23. Letter to R. H. Davis, 15 July 1934, DP.

Chapter Ten

1. Edgar L. Chapman, "The Image of the Indian in Max Brand's Pulp Western Novels," *Heritage of Kansas* 2 (Spring 1978): 26-27; hereafter cited in text. In this essay about many Faust novels, Chapman points out that *Tamer of the Wild* appeared sixteen years before Elliott Arnold's *Blood Brother* (1947), a sympathetic story about the Apache leader Cochise, which was the basis for *Broken Arrow*, the 1950 Hollywood film.

2. Max Brand, *Lucky Larribee* (New York: Dodd, Mead, 1957), 135. Originally published as a George Owen Baxter serial in *Western Story*, beginning 2 April 1932.

3. Max Brand, *The White Cheyenne* (New York: Warner Books, 1974), 78. Originally published as a Peter Henry Morland serial in *Western Story*, beginning 12 December 1925.

4. Easton (169) points out the influence of Grinnell and Schultz.

5. Davis told Faust how well the book had been received by an army officer Davis had encountered. "I brought to the attention of an army officer Schultz's *My Life as an Indian*," Davis wrote Faust. "I enclose his pencil observations about that book. He came in yesterday and talked about it for two hours. Never saw a guy so het up" (Letter fom R. H. Davis, 22 November 1926, DP).

6. Letter to Dan Moore, 16 December 1932, FP.

7. Letter to Dan Moore, 16 December 1932, FP.

8. Letter from Dan Moore, 31 December 1932, FP.

9. Max Brand, *War Party* (New York: Warner Books, 1973), 186; hereafter cited in text. Originally published as Max Brand's "The White Indian," an *Argosy* serial, beginning 9 September 1933.

10. Max Brand, *Frontier Feud* (New York: Warner Books, 1973), 141. Originally published as an *Argosy* serial, "Brother of the Cheyennes," beginning 17 March 1934.

11. Max Brand, *Cheyenne Gold* (New York: Warner Books, 1972), 7; hereafter cited in text. Originally published as Max Brand's "The Sacred Valley," an *Argosy* serial beginning 10 August 1935.

Chapter Eleven

1. Letter to D. Faust, September 1932, quoted in Schoolcraft.

2. According to Easton, Canfield wanted to know whether any publisher had ever put up "real money" to promote one of Faust's books (160-61). Also, he apparently felt that use of the Max Brand pseudonym would not appeal to booksellers.

3. During Faust's lifetime Harper published only the Montana Kid series (1934-36). After Faust's death, however, the firm revived the Evan Evans byline and published under it eight other novels between 1947 and 1954. All were pulp serials that had appeared earlier in magazines but not as books.

4. Evan Evans, *Montana Rides Again* (New York: American Reprint Co., 1976), 35. The cover of this paperback edition refers to its author as "Max Brand writing as Evan Evans." Originally published as a six-part serial in *Argosy* beginning on 28 April 1934, then as a book by Harper in 1934.

5. Evan Evans, *The Song of the Whip* (New York: American Reprint Co., 1976), 191. Originally published as a six-part serial in *Argosy* beginning 28 March 1936, then as book by Harper in 1936.

6. Max Brand, *Smugglers' Trail* (New York: Paperback Library, 1967), 73. Originally published by *Argosy* as a Max Brand serial in six parts, "The Scourge of the Rio Grande," beginning 20 October 1934. It has been reprinted several times, first as a Harper book in 1950 under the Evan Evans byline. The use of Chinese characters in the story was not Faust's first effort in that direction, such characters having played important roles in a 1920 western, *Clung*.

7. Max Brand, *The Streak* (New York: Pocket Books, 1953), 43. Originally published as a six-part serial in *Argosy*, beginning 25 January 1936, then as a book in 1937.

8. Max Brand, "Dust across the Range," in *Max Brand's Best Western Stories*, 108-109. Originally published as a four-part serial in the *American Magazine*, beginning in November 1937.

Chapter Twelve

1. Letter to D. Faust, 7 October, 3 October, and 4 November 1932, FP.

2. Max Brand, *Children of Night* (New York: L. Harper Allen, 1928), 67. Originally published as a Max Brand serial in *All-Story Weekly*, beginning 22 March 1919.

3. Nicholas Silver, "Sealed for Fifty Years," *Detective Story Magazine*, 9 December 1922, 41-76, and "Stolen Clothes," *Detective Story Magazine*, 30 December 1932, 3-35.

4. Quoted in Russel B. Nye, *The Unembarrassed Muse* (New York: Dial Press, 1970), 256.

5. Letter to D. Faust, 29 October 1932, FP.

6. Editorial procedures required quick decisions. According to Bloomfield, there were two associate editors and a secretary on the staff of *Detective Fiction Weekly*. The secretary divided incoming manuscripts into two piles, one from known writers, the other from unknown. The second pile was called "slush." "All writers emerged originally from slush, of course. Our aim was to make decisions within two weeks. Slush was the big pile. It got a scanning by associate editors. Finding a good new writer in the slush was like discovering America. So, a good opening assured further reading. Poor opening, rejection slip. The shorter the ms., usually the more amateurish" (Howard V. Bloomfield to W. Bloodworth, 11 December 1986). Faust habitually wrote good openings and seldom submitted a short manuscript.

7. In April 1933 Davis read a synopsis of the story three times, he said, "each with added bewilderment" (Letter from R. H. Davis, 27 April 1933, FP).

8. Max Brand, *The Night Flower* (New York: International Polygonics, 1987), 62; hereafter cited in text. Originally published as *The Dark Peril*, by Max Brand, in *Detective Fiction Weekly*, beginning 16 December 1933.

9. Max Brand, " *–Murder Me!*," *Detective Fiction Weekly*, 21 September 1935, 6.

10. *Detective Fiction Weekly*, 26 October 1935, 112.

11. *Detective Fiction Weekly*, 2 November 1935, 116.

12. Frederick Frost, *Secret Agent Number One* (New York: Macrae-Smith, 1936), 40. Originally published as a series of four novelettes in *Detective Fiction Weekly*, between 5 January and 9 February 1935.

13. Frederick Frost, *The Bamboo Whistle* (New York: Macrae-Smith, 1937), 251.

14. Max Brand, *War for Sale*, originally published as an *Argosy* serial, beginning 24 April 1937. "Blind Bluff" (*All-American Fiction*, January 1938) is another Max Brand espionage story; it involves the stealing of a French inventor's plans for a deadly new machine gun.

15. Max Brand, *Flower of Hell*, originally published as a *This Week* serial, beginning 24 April 1938.

16. Max Brand, *Dead Man's Passport*, originally published as an *American Weekly* serial, beginning 12 January 1941.

17. The best of the betrayal stories are "The Hound of the Hunter," *McCall's*, July 1936; "Five Minutes to Twelve," *Cosmopolitan*, November 1936; and "A Silence in Tappan Valley," *This Week*, 9 January 1938.

18. "A Silence in Tappan Valley," 14, 15.

Chapter Thirteen

1. George Challis, *The Splendid Rascal* (Indianapolis: Bobbs-Merrill, 1926), 315. Faust had first used the George Challis byline in January 1926 in a *Western Story* serial, "The Tyrant" (later published by Bobbs-Merrill as a novel, *Monsieur*), with a Frenchman as the protagonist. Thereafter Faust reserved the byline for historical adventures. It never appeared again in *Western Story*.

2. Frederick Faust, *The Naked Blade* (New York: Lancer Books, 1967), 5; hereafter cited in text. Originally published as a George Challis serial in *Argosy*, beginning 10 February 1934.

3. Most likely for this reason the second novel was never republished after its appearance as an *Argosy* serial, by George Challis, beginning 7 September 1936.

4. One chapter of the novel is titled "How Madelin Played Guerilla."

5. *The Firebrand* (New York: Harpers, 1950) combined three short *Argosy* serials: "The Firebrand" (beginning 24 November 1934), "The Great Betrayal" (beginning 2 February 1935), and "The Storm" (beginning 6 April 1935). *The Bait and the Trap* (New York: Harpers, 1951) combined three novelettes: "Claws of the Tigress" (13 July 1935), "The Bait and the Trap" (3 August 1935), and "The Pearls of Bonfadini" (24 August 1935). All of the *Argosy* material appeared under the George Challis byline, as did the novels, even though they were published posthumously. All works (Harper novel editions) hereafter cited in text.

6. George Challis, *The Golden Knight* (New York: Greystone Press, 1937), 123. (Further page references are cited in parenthesis.) To Blondel's description, Richard replies, perhaps more knowingly than he realizes, "Witch! There's a word that puts a thought in my mind."

7. George Challis, "The American," *Argosy*, 27 February 1937 (1st installment), 16.

8. *Argosy*, 6 March 1937 (2nd installment), 64.

9. *Argosy*, 3 April 1937 (6th installment), 110.

10. *Argosy*, 3 April 1937 (6th installment), 114, 116.

Chapter Fourteen

1. Letter from Carl Brandt, 19 August 1936, FP.

2. Letter to C. Brandt, 7 July 1936, FP.

3. Letter to C. Brandt, 20 August 1936, FP.

4. Letter to C. Brandt, 12 June 1937, FP.

5. Letter to C. Brandt, 27 November 1936, FP.

6. Letter to D. Faust, 20 April 1937, FP.

7. Letter to C. Brandt, 4 January 1938, FP.

8. Otto Friedrich, *City of Nets: A Portrait of Hollywood in the 1940s* (New York: Harper & Row, 1986), 110.

9. Letter to G. W. Fish, 26 March 1938, FP.

10. Letter to D. Faust, 4 May 1938, FP.

11. Even as he was first settling into Hollywood, Faust began to complain about the studios' commercial tone, referring irritatedly in a letter to Dorothy even to "the poisonous Jewishness of this atmosphere," a slur quite at odds with the pride he took in the Jewish connotation of "Max Brand" and the positive treatment of Jews in his stories (Letter to D. Faust, 21 April 1938, FP).

12. Collier Young to C. Brandt, 5 May 1938, FP.

13. Letter to C. Brandt, 27 May 1938, FP.

14. Letter to Dan Norton, 3 September 1938, FP.

15. Judith Faust to W. Bloodworth, 21 September 1984.

16. Leonard Bacon to J. Schoolcraft, 5 April 1951, BP; Letter from Walter Morris Hart, 8 October 1939, FP.

17. Collier Young to C. Brand, 5 May 1938, FP.

18. Letter to C. Brandt, 24 May 1938, FP.

19. Collier Young to C. Brand, 27 May 1938, FP.

20. Jane Faust Easton, *Memories of the '20s and '30s: Growing Up in Florence, New York, and Los Angeles* (Santa Barbara, Calif.: privately printed, 1979), 136.

21. Judith Faust to W. Bloodworth, 21 September 1984. Information about Mary Churchill comes from a 1984 interview with Carol Brandt, Carl's wife.

22. Max Brand, *The Secret of Dr. Kildare* (New York: Dodd, Mead, 1940), 65.

23. Collier Young to C. Brand, 3 November 1938.

24. Joseph Blotner, *Faulkner: A Biography* (New York: Random House, 1974), 1122-24.

25. Letter to Pinckney McLean, February 1944, FP.

26. Frederick Faust, "Distance," *Harper's*, January 1942, 38.

27. Letter to D. Faust, 8 October 1941, FP.

28. Letter from C. Brandt, 17 June 1940, FP.

29. Letter to Grace Flandrau, ca. 1942, FP. Faust had met Flandrau, who spent considerable time in New York, through Carl Brandt.

30. Letter to John F. Faust (his son), 18 March 1944, FP.

31. Frederick Faust, *Max Brand's Best Stories* (New York: Dodd, Mead, 1967), 5-6. "The King" was originally published in *This Week*, 21 November 1948.

Chapter Fifteen

1. Easton claims that the title for the first Kildare story arose out of a conversation between Faust and Carl Brandt. According to Easton, as Faust was telling Brandt about some of Fish's experiences, including contacts with the New York underworld, he said "internes can't take money," at which point Brandt said, "There's your title and there's your story" (Easton, 183).

2. Quoted in Sidney De Boer, "Call-ing Doctor Kil-Dare," *P & S Quarterly* (a publication of the Alumni Association of the Columbia University College of Physicians and Surgeons), March 1966, 20.

3. Max Brand, "Internes Can't Take Money" in *Wine on the Desert* (New York: Dodd, Mead, 1940), 130-31; hereafter cited in text.

4. Joseph Turow, *Playing Doctor: Television, Storytelling, and Medical Power* (New York and Oxford: Oxford University Press, 1989), 14; hereafter cited in text.

5. Max Brand, *Calling Dr. Kildare* (New York: Dodd, Mead, 1940), 29; hereafter cited in text.

6. Max Brand, *The Secret of Dr. Kildare* (New York: Dodd, Mead, 1940), 175; hereafter cited in text.

7. Max Brand, *Dr. Kildare's Crisis* (New York: Dodd, Mead, 1942), 206; hereafter cited in text.

8. Letter to C. Brandt, 25 May 1942, FP.

Conclusion

1. Letter to Dino Spranger, 18 February 1943, FP.

2. S/Sgt. Richard W. Courtney to "Whom It May Concern," 18 May 1944, FP. Faust's final months are described in detail in Easton's biography.

3. Letter to G. Flandrau, ca. 1942, FP.

4. Jon Tuska, unpublished manuscript for the Faust entry in the forthcoming second edition of the *Encyclopedia of Frontier and Western Fiction* (University of Nebraska Press).

5. Letter to W. M. Hart, 20 June 1942, FP.

Selected Bibliography

There are three especially problematic features of any Max Brand bibliography: the variety of pseudonyms; changes in pseudonyms when a magazine story was published as a hardcover and sometimes again when published later as a paperback; and changes in titles when a work was reissued as a hardcover or paperback. Fortunately, William F. Nolan's *Max Brand: Western Giant* presents an accurate and complete listing by both byline and title of all of Faust's books. It also presents a chronological listing of all other publications – including films and adaptations for radio, television, and stage – up to 1985 and is an indispensable resource for the study of Max Brand and Frederick Faust.

Faust's papers are in the Bancroft Library at the University of California at Berkeley. The American Heritage Center at the University of Wyoming also has substantial holdings of Faust material.

The following list of primary works is selective, presenting a reasonable and representative sample, including most of the works discussed in this study. For novels, the most recent edition and title is cited; in the case of some important Faust novels, other editions that readers may be able to locate without great difficulty are also listed. The list is arranged chronologically with the date of first publication – either magazine or book – noted in parentheses after the title except in those cases where the item listed represents its first appearance in print. A phrase identifying the genre of the work follows the bibliographical data.

PRIMARY WORKS

Max Brand. *Fate's Honeymoon* (1917). London: Hodder & Stoughton, 1926. Romantic adventure.

John Frederick. *The Sword Lover* (1917). New York: Henry Watterson, 1927. Historical adventure.

Max Brand. *Harrigan* (1918). New York: Dodd, Mead, 1971. Adventure at sea.

Max Brand. *The Untamed* (1918). Boston: Gregg Press, 1978. Introduction by Jack Nachbar. (New York: Pocket Books, 1955. New York: Dodd, Mead, 1949. New York: G. P. Putnam, 1919.) Western.

Max Brand. *Children of Night* (1919). New York: L. Harper Allen, 1928. Urban suspense.

John Frederick. *Riders of the Silences* (1919). New York: H. K. Fly, 1920.
(New York: Dodd, Mead, 1986.) Western.

Max Brand. *Trailin'* (1919). New York: Warner Books, 1975. (New York:
Dodd, Mead, 1961.) Western.

Max Brand. *Clung* (1920). New York: Dodd, Mead, 1969. Western.

Max Brand. *Pride of Tyson* (1920). London: Hodder & Stoughton, 1927.
Contemporary western.

Max Brand. *The Night Horseman* (1920). New York: Pocket Books, 1954.
(New York: Dodd, Mead, 1952.) Western.

Max Brand. *Way of the Lawless* (1921). New York: Dodd, Mead, 1978.
(Originally published as *Free-Range Lanning*.) Western.

Max Brand. *Gunman's Reckoning* (1921). New York: Dodd, Mead, 1976.
Western.

Max Brand. *The Seventh Man* (1921). New York: Warner Books, 1974. (New
York: Dodd, Mead, 1958.) Western.

Max Brand. *The Garden of Eden* (1922). New York: Dodd, Mead, 1963. Contemporary western.

Max Brand. *Devil Horse* (1922). New York: Warner Books, 1974. (Also *Alca-
traz, the Wild Stallion.* New York: Dodd, Mead, 1959.) Western.

Frederick Faust. *The Village Street.* New York: G. P. Putnam, 1922. Poetry.

Max Brand. *Wild Freedom* (1922). New York: Dodd, Mead, 1981. Western.

Max Brand. *Hired Guns* (1923). New York: Dodd, Mead, 1948. Western.

Max Brand. *Dan Barry's Daughter* (1923). New York: Dodd, Mead, 1959.
Western.

Max Brand. *The Trail to San Triste* (1924). New York: Dodd, Mead, 1983.
Western.

Max Brand. *Smiling Desperado* (1924). New York: Dodd, Mead, 1953.
Western.

John Frederick. *The Bronze Collar* (1924). New York: G. P. Putnam, 1925.
Historical adventure.

Max Brand. *The White Cheyenne* (1925). New York: Dodd, Mead, 1960. Historical adventure.

George Challis. *Monsieur* (1926). Indianapolis: Bobbs-Merrill, 1926. Historical adventure.

Max Brand. *Outlaw Breed* (1926). New York: Dodd, Mead, 1955. Western.

Max Brand. *Trouble Trail* (1926). New York: Dodd, Mead, 1937. Western.

George Challis. *The Splendid Rascal.* Indianapolis: Bobbs-Merrill, 1926.
Historical adventure.

Max Brand. *The Iron Trail* (1926). New York: Dodd, Mead, 1938. Western.

Max Brand. *The Gentle Desperado* (1927). New York: Dodd, Mead, 1985.
Western.

Max Brand. *Border Guns* (1928). New York: Dodd, Mead, 1952. Western.

Max Brand. *The Border Kid* (1928). New York: Dodd, Mead, 1941. Western.

Max Brand. *Singing Guns* (1928). New York: Dodd, Mead, 1938. Western.

Max Brand. *Destry Rides Again* (1930). New York: Dodd, Mead, 1930. Western.

Max Brand. *The Stingaree* (1930). New York: Dodd, Mead, 1968. Western.

Max Brand. *Vengeance Trail* (1931). New York: Dodd, Mead, 1941. Western.

Frederick Faust. *Dionysus in Hades*. Oxford: Basil Blackwell, 1931. Poem.

Max Brand. *Lucky Larribee* (1932). New York: Dodd, Mead, 1957. Western.

Max Brand. *The Longhorn Feud* (1932). New York: Dodd, Mead, 1933. Western.

Evan Evans. *Montana Rides!* (1933). New York: Harper, 1933. Western.

Max Brand. *Silvertip* (1933). New York: Dodd, Mead, 1942. Western.

Max Brand. *The Man from Mustang* (1933). New York: Dodd, Mead, 1942. Western.

Max Brand. *Brothers on the Trail* (1933). New York: Dodd, Mead, 1934. Western.

Max Brand. *Silvertip's Strike* (1933). New York: Dodd, Mead, 1942. Western.

Max Brand. *Silvertip's Roundup* (1933). New York: Dodd, Mead, 1942. Western.

Max Brand. *Silvertip's Trap* (1933). New York: Dodd, Mead, 1943. Western.

Max Brand. *Silvertip's Chase* (1933). New York: Dodd, Mead, 1944. Western.

Max Brand. *The Fighting Four* (1933). New York: Dodd, Mead, 1944. Western.

Max Brand. *War Party* (1933). New York: Dodd, Mead, 1973. Western.

Max Brand. *Silvertip's Search* (1933). New York: Dodd, Mead, 1945. Western.

Walter C. Butler. *The Night Flower* (1933). New York: Macauley, 1936. Crime novel.

George Challis. *The Naked Blade* (1934). New York: Greystone Press, 1938. Historical adventure.

Max Brand. *Frontier Feud* (1934). New York: Dodd, Mead, 1973. Western.

Max Brand. *X, the Murderer* (1934). *Detective Fiction Weekly*, 17 March 1934ff. Detective serial.

Evan Evans. *Montana Rides Again* (1934). New York: Harper, 1934. Western.

Walter C. Butler. *Cross over Nine* (1934). New York: Macauley, 1935. Detective novel.

Evan Evans. *Smuggler's Trail* (1934). New York: Harper, 1950. Western.

George Challis. *The Firebrand* (1934). New York: Harper, 1950. Historical adventure.

Frederick Frost. *Secret Agent Number One* (1935). New York: Macrae-Smith, 1936. Spy novel.

Frederick Frost. *Spy Meets Spy* (1935). New York: Macrae-Smith, 1937. Spy novel.

George Challis. *The Bait and the Trap* (1935). New York: Harper, 1951. Historical adventure.

Max Brand. *Cheyenne Gold* (1935). New York: Dodd, Mead, 1972. Western.

Max Brand. " *– Murder Me!" Detective Fiction Weekly*, 7 December 1935ff. Detective serial.

Frederick Frost. *The Bamboo Whistle* (1935). New York: Macrae-Smith, 1937. Spy novel.

Max Brand. *The Streak* (1936). New York: Dodd, Mead, 1937. Western.

Evan Evans. *The Song of the Whip* (1936). New York: Harper, 1936. Western.

George Challis. *The Golden Knight* (1936). New York: Greystone Press, 1937. Historical adventure.

Max Brand. *The American. Argosy*, 27 February 1937ff. Historical adventure.

Max Brand. *Six Golden Angels* (1937). New York: Dodd, Mead, 1937. Crime novel.

Max Brand. *The Phantom Spy* (1937). New York: Dodd, Mead, 1973. Spy novel.

Max Brand. "A Silence in Tappan Valley." *This Week*, 9 January 1938. Short crime story.

Max Brand. "Whiskey Sour." *Cosmopolitan*, April 1938. Short medical adventure story.

Max Brand. *Young Dr. Kildare* (1938). New York: Dodd, Mead, 1941. Medical adventure.

Max Brand. *Calling Dr. Kildare* (1939). New York: Dodd, Mead, 1940. Medical adventure.

Max Brand. *The Secret of Dr. Kildare* (1939). New York: Dodd, Mead, 1940. Medical adventure.

Max Brand. *Dr. Kildare's Search* (1940). New York: Dodd, Mead, 1943. Medical adventure.

Max Brand. *Dr. Kildare Takes Charge* (1940). New York: Dodd, Mead, 1941. Medical adventure.

Max Brand. *Dr. Kildare's Crisis* (1940). New York: Dodd, Mead, 1942. Medical adventure.

Max Brand. *Dead Man's Passport. American Weekly*, 12 January 1941ff. Adventure serial.

Max Brand. *Luck of the Spindrift*. New York: Dodd, Mead, 1942. Adventure serial.

Max Brand. *Dr. Kildare's Trial* (1941). New York: Dodd, Mead, 1942. Medical adventure.

Max Brand. *Mister Christmas. Brooklyn Eagle*, 22 January 1944ff. Crime serial.

Frederick Faust. *After April. Saturday Evening Post*, 10 June 1944ff. Romantic adventure serial.

Collections

Max Brand. *Wine on the Desert*. New York: Dodd, Mead, 1940. Stories.

Frederick Faust. *The Notebooks and Poems of "Max Brand."* Edited by John Schoolcraft. New York: Dodd, Mead, 1957.

Max Brand. *Max Brand's Best Stories*. Edited by Robert Easton. New York: Dodd, Mead, 1967.

Max Brand. *Max Brand's Best Western Stories*. Edited by William F. Nolan. New York: Dodd, Mead, 1981.

Max Brand. *Max Brand's Best Western Stories Volume II*. Edited by William F. Nolan. New York: Dodd, Mead, 1985.

Max Brand. *Max Brand's Best Western Stories Volume III*. Edited by William F. Nolan. New York: Dodd, Mead, 1987.

Max Brand. *Max Brand's Best Poems*. Edited by Robert and Jane Easton. Santa Barbara, Calif.: Fithian Press, 1992.

SECONDARY WORKS

Bacon, Leonard. "Frederick Faust." *Saturday Review of Literature*, 27 May 1944, 28-29. A tribute to Faust, paying some attention to the character of the author and to his poetry.

Bacon, Martha. "Destry and Dionysus." *Atlantic Monthly*, July 1955, 73-74. An impressionistic portrait of Faust in Italy.

Bloodworth, William. "Max Brand's West." *Western American Literature* 16 (Fall 1981): 177-91. Discusses Max Brand's departure from the traditional mythology of the American frontier.

———. "Max Brand." In *Fifty Western Writers*, edited by Fred Erisman and Richard W. Eutlain, 32-41. Westport, Conn.: Greenwood Press, 1982. Provides a general survey of Max Brand's western fiction.

Bold, Christine. *Selling the Wild West: Popular Western Fiction, 1860-1960*. Bloomington and Indianapolis: Indiana University Press, 1987. Discusses Max Brand as part of the "selling" of the West; sees Max Brand novels as largely a result of commercial forces.

Cawelti, John G. *Adventure, Mystery, Romance: Formula Fiction as Art and Popular Culture*. Chicago: University of Chicago Press, 1976. Discusses Max Brand as an example of formulaic popular literature.

Chapman, Edgar L. "The Image of the Indian in Max Brand's Pulp Western Novels." *Heritage of Kansas* 11 (Spring 1978): 16-45. A lengthy and detailed study of Faust's treatment of American Indians in his westerns.

_____. "Max Brand/Frederick Faust." In *Popular World Fiction*, vol. 1, edited by Walton Beacham and Suzanne Niemeyers, 176-96. Washington, D.C.: Beacham Publishing, 1987. A general essay with sections on *Singing Guns, Destry Rides Again*, and the *Montana Rides!* trilogy.

Easton, Jane Faust. *Memories of the '20s and '30s: Growing Up in Florence, New York, and Los Angeles.* Santa Barbara, Calif., 1979. A private printing of the memoirs of Faust's elder daughter.

Easton, Robert. *Max Brand: The Big "Westerner."* Norman: University of Oklahoma Press, 1970. A well-written comprehensive biography.

Fox, David L. "The History of a Hero: A Study of Max Brand's *Destry Rides Again*." M.A. thesis, Western Carolina University, 1984. Discusses the novel and its film adaptations.

Hamilton, Cynthia S. *Western and Hard-Boiled Detective Fiction in America.* Iowa City: University of Iowa Press, 1987. Discusses Max Brand westerns as reflective of Faust's psychological development as presentations of "underdog heroes."

Nolan, William F. *Max Brand: Western Giant.* Bowling Green, Ohio: Bowling Green State University Popular Press, 1985. A complete bibliography, conveniently arranged, with several essays about Faust drawn from previously published material and letters.

Nye, Russel B. *The Unembarrassed Muse: The Popular Arts in America.* New York: Dial Press, 1970. Contains a section on Max Brand.

Richardson, Darrell C., ed. *Max Brand: The Man and His Work.* Los Angeles: Fantasy Publishing Co., 1952. A collection of articles about Faust by fans and fellow writers. Includes Edward H. Dodd's 1938 *Publishers Weekly* article, "Twenty-Five Million Words."

Sampson, Robert. *Yesterday's Faces: A Study of Series Characters in the Early Pulp Magazines.* Bowling Green, Ohio: Bowling Green University Popular Press, 1983. Contains a section on Max Brand, paying particular attention to the Dan Barry series.

Singing Guns: A Journal of Comment and Analysis. Published since the fall of 1990 by David L. Fox in Cullowhee, N.C. Contains bibliographical, biographical, and interpretive items on Faust.

Turow, Joseph. *Playing Doctor: Television, Storytelling, and Medical Power.* New York and Oxford: Oxford University Press, 1989. Presents a compelling discussion of Faust's role in shaping the public image of the practice of medicine.

Index

The Author

William A. Bloodworth, Jr., is president of Augusta College, Augusta, Georgia. Earlier he served as professor of English and in several administrative positions at East Carolina University and Central Missouri State University. He is the author of *Upton Sinclair* (1977) and of articles on Sinclair, Native American literature, and the literature of the American West in *Western American Literature*, *Great Plains Quarterly*, *MELUS* (the journal of the Society for the Study of the Multi-Ethnic Literature of the United States), *South Dakota Review*, and other journals. A native of San Antonio, Texas, Bloodworth holds degrees in English from Texas Lutheran College and Lamar University; he received his Ph.D degree in American civilization from the University of Texas at Austin.

The Editor

Joseph M. Flora earned his B.A. (1956), M.A. (1957), and Ph.D. (1962) in English at the University of Michigan. In 1962 he joined the faculty of the University of North Carolina, where he is now professor of English. His study *Hemingway's Nick Adams* (1984) won the Mayflower Award. He is also author of *Vardis Fisher* (1962), *William Ernest Henley* (1970), *Frederick Manfred* (1974), and *Ernest Hemingway: A Study of the Short Fiction* (1989). He is editor of *The English Short Story* (1985) and coeditor of *Southern Writers: A Biographical Dictionary* (1970), *Fifty Southern Writers before 1900* (1987), and *Fifty Southern Writers after 1900* (1987). He serves on the editorial boards of *Studies in Short Fiction* and *Southern Literary Journal*.